Seymour B. Sarason

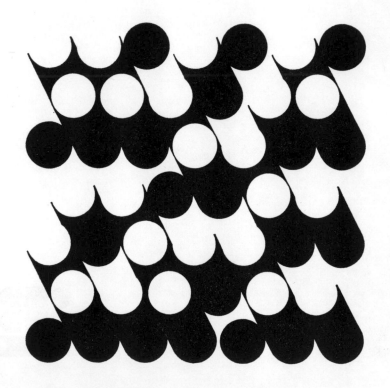

THE PSYCHOLOGICAL SENSE OF COMMUNITY

Prospects for a
Community Psychology

Jossey-Bass Publishers
San Francisco · Washington · London · 1974

THE PSYCHOLOGICAL SENSE OF COMMUNITY
Prospects for a Community Psychology
by Seymour B. Sarason

Copyright © 1974 by: Jossey-Bass, Inc., Publishers
615 Montgomery Street
San Francisco, California 94111
&
Jossey-Bass Limited
3 Henrietta Street
London WC2E 8LU

Library of Congress Catalogue Card Number LC 73-20962

International Standard Book Number ISBN 0-87589-216-7

Manufactured in the United States of America

JACKET DESIGN BY WILLI BAUM

FIRST EDITION

Code 7411

The Jossey-Bass
Behavioral Science Series

For my mother
and sister
with thanks

Preface

Initially it was my intention to write a book about community psychology in which I would try to make sense out of my experiences and those of others who, directly or indirectly, have contributed to this relatively new academic field. This meant that I would present, discuss, and evaluate the different stances people have taken about theory, action, and evaluation. Although it was not my intention to write a textbook, I did expect that the book would contain the substance of what a number of people have thought and done. But my intentions ran into several obstacles or dilemmas. The first was rather personal, in that I had come to believe that community psychology, as a field, had largely failed in realizing its exciting potentials as an intellectual and social force, and that this relative failure was in large part rooted in the traditions of American psychology. But inasmuch as these traditions inevitably reflect the larger American society, an explanation cannot be limited to the traditions and characteristics of a single academic field. The scope of the problem was thus widened considerably, and to an intimidating degree.

The second obstacle was thornier and, ultimately, decisive for the scope and thrust of this book. Could *I* write a book about community psychology without putting into center stage my belief that the dilution or absence of the psychological sense of community is the most destructive dynamic in the lives of people in our society? That I hold this belief is less persuasive than the fact that it has been for several hundred years a theme noted and discussed with ever-increasing frequency and urgency in Western society. Beginning in 1972 I began to keep a tally of the number of books reviewed in several national book review periodicals that clearly dealt with themes of loneliness, alienation, rootlessness, and not belonging. After three months I stopped tallying because I saw no point in confirming the obvious. The important point is that regardless of the political, religious, and philosophical persuasion of the authors, they agreed that the destruction of the psychological sense of community (and they differed considerably in how this has come about or what needs to be done) was the central problem in social living. I have been influenced by this literature because it helped me order my own thinking and experiences, at the same time that it gave me a sense of historical continuity. Specifically, it meant that a field which purported to be concerned with community had to be concerned with and based on the development and maintenance of the psychological sense of community.

No field is value free; its existence in an institutional sense is always justified by faith in certain values, however implicit or unrecognized they might be. It is my belief that community psychology can be justified on several bases, but that the keystone value in its foundation is the development and maintenance of the psychological sense of community. Therefore, the major thrust of this book became the psychological sense of community as a basis for building a community psychology. In one sense, then, this is a narrower book than I intended even though it is concerned with the ever-important question of what social life might or should be. I say this not by way of apology, but in explanation. I wrote the book I felt I had to write. It is narrower, more focused, and (I would like to believe) more valuable than the book I initially intended to write.

In a very direct way the major theme of this book is an outgrowth of the years I was director of the Yale Psycho-Educational Clinic. The founding of that clinic reflected several major considerations and motivations, not the least of which was the hope that a group of very diverse persons could develop and maintain a psychological sense of community without sacrificing individuality at the altar of a suffocating togetherness. Could a sense of mutuality be achieved—could priority of group survival be maintained—in the face of inevitable external pressures and internal tensions and controversy? Could we become and stay a network of dependable relationships that would have overarching significance in our lives because we would know that without it we would be unhappily and individually alone, mired in a privacy that whatever its virtues (and it does have some) founders ultimately on the fact that people need people? Anyone familiar with my book *The Creation of Settings and the Future Societies* (1972) will perceive the continuity between it and this volume.

Once I decided what the central thrust of this book would be, I was faced with the problem of how best to emphasize the nature and significance of the psychological sense of community. As I said earlier, there is a vast literature on this concept, and I had neither the desire nor the knowledge to review it. Besides, others had done it well from different perspectives, depending on their times and special interests. What I wanted to do was to discuss it in terms that would illuminate our culture at the same time that it would have obvious relevance for community psychology. The problem was easy for me to resolve because thirty years of experience in schools and institutions led me (finally!) to understand that segregation (in special classes, mental hospitals, "reform" schools, institutions for the retarded), justified as it always is by "humane" considerations, was cause and symptom of the dilution or absence of the psychological sense of community. Why this is so occupies several chapters of this book.

Two very dear friends were of inestimable help to me in

thinking about and writing this book. Burton Blatt and N. Dickon Reppucci listened to, argued with, and stimulated me. Their work and achievements, as later chapters will show, provided confirmation of my belief in the significance of the psychological sense of community, of the conclusion that our "humane" institutions are manufacturers of social disease, and of one of the central points in this book: social action can be for the university researcher a potent vehicle for contributing to general knowledge (see Chapter 10). Anita Miller, my secretary and friend for ten years, typed the first draft of this book before leaving New Haven. Had she left before that draft was done I doubt that this book would have seen the light of published day in this decade. Miss Eleanor Smith typed and proofed the final draft in superb fashion, and I am indeed grateful to her. I am also grateful to Yale's Institution for Social and Policy Studies for providing me with facilities and support which made writing less of a torture than it usually is.

Writing, like any other form of behavior, has diverse motivations. One of my motivations has been, as it always will be, to be able to say to my family: this is what I have thought and done and this book is a token of thanks for your unconditional love and support.

New Haven, Connecticut   Seymour B. Sarason
January 1974

Contents

xi

The Psychological Sense of Community

Prospects for a Community Psychology

I

Overview

I have never met anyone—young or old, rich or poor, black or white, male or female, educated or not—to whom I have had any great difficulty explaining what I meant by the psychological sense of community. My explanation or language varied, of course, depending on whom I was talking with, but it never took long for them to comprehend that what I was getting at was the sense that one was part of a readily available, mutually supportive network of relationships upon which one could depend and as a result of which one did not experience sustained feelings of loneliness that impel one to actions or to adopting a style of living masking anxiety and setting the stage for later and more destructive anguish. It is not merely a matter of how many people one knows, or how many close friends one has, or even the number of loved ones—if they are scattered all over the country or world, if they are not part of the structure of one's everyday living, and if they are not available to one in a "give and get" way, they can have little affect on one's immediate or daily sense of community. Indeed, for many people these treasured but only occasionally available relationships accentuate the lack of a feeling of community. At a social gathering a colleague of mine once remarked: "If in the community you live you have more than two close friends, you have one more than par." Nobody disagreed. Immersed as we all are in a sea of human interaction it is the rare person who does not feel adrift, without a secure compass, and perceiving the signs of impending storm. Alienation, anomie, isolation, and words of similar meaning have flooded our language and literature. And paralleling this flood has been an outpouring of social and group techniques to give people at least a transient experience of "authenticity" and "togetherness." The group dynamics and encounter movements (a bewildering array of ideas and techniques), communes, the different youth countercultures, the increasing frequency of formation of new fundamentalist religious groups which give meaning and direction to every hour of a member's day—these are only some of the indications of how earnestly people strive to be and feel part of a network of intimate relationships that gives one the sense of willing identification with some overarching values.

The community in which we live is a geo-political entity with which we feel little kinship. We may work in the community, pay taxes, and vote, but in no other respect feel a part of it. In fact, we may feel repelled by it because of the violence, crime, and conflict within it. We wish things were otherwise, but we feel impotent to do anything. We are aware that much money is being spent to repair our community, socially and physically, but the feeling persists that the seams of the community are not being tightened. We do not feel *needed* in our community and we rarely if ever seriously think about how we can contribute to the solution of its problems. We are busy during the day, tired at night, and seek recreation and entertainment on the weekends. And if we are parents, there are children who need our attention every day. Where is there time to engage in a community activity? What community activity? What do I have to contribute? Where am I *needed*? Our lives are circumscribed spatially and psychologically, and it all seems so natural except for those poignant moments, quite frequent for many people, when we yearn to be part of a larger network of relationships that would give greater expression to our needs for intimacy, diversity, usefulness, and belongingness. The concept of the psychological sense of community is like that of hunger: neither is easy to define, but there is no mistaking it when an individual experiences the lack of a psychological sense of community, just as there is no mistaking what we think an individual experiences as a result of starvation.

If I thought that the frequency with which many people experience the absence of the psychological sense of community was a projection of my own experiences and observations, I would be most reluctant to write about it, let alone put it in the title of a book. One has to be inordinately dense or illiterate (or both) to remain unaware of the centrality of this theme in various literary forms (fiction, nonfiction, poetry, plays), films, journals, newspapers, Sunday sermons, and political campaign speeches about binding up the wounds in the community. And if one's work involves him with the personal problems of troubled people, the themes of unwanted destructive loneliness and social isolation are unmistakable (and monotonously repetitive), as is the fact that they are reflections of the nature and structure of living in our communities; it is the recognition of the latter fact that has introduced a strong note of pessimism about the potentialities of the therapeutic endeavor. To view the absence of the psychological sense of community as a peculiarity of an individual requires the assumption that society does not exist, and even the most diehard advocates of "intrapsychic supremacy" (a felicitous phrase coined by Dr. Murray Levine) would be cautious about accepting that assumption.

What I have described is not a modern phenomenon. Our society was not born yesterday, or a hundred years ago. It may be true that more people today than ever before experience the destructive aspects of the absence of the psychological sense of community, but the social-historical complex of factors giving rise to such aspects and their increase in frequency goes back several centuries. The reader who believes that social and intellectual history of Western society is interesting because it illuminates the past, and only the past, and not because it is contained in our living present should read Nisbet's *The Quest for Community* (1970), and Mumford's *The Culture of Cities* (1966). Phenotypically our society has changed enormously. Genotypically the change has been far less striking.

But what is the link between the psychological sense of community and the new field of community psychology? The answer lies in the events of the sixties out of which the need for a community psychology emerged, because that decade, like the decade of the thirties (the Great Depression), exacerbated in people the already existing feeling that our society in general and our communities in particular were becoming increasingly inimical to personal stability and safety. Assassinations, race conflicts and riots, the cancer of poverty, war, drugs, crime, student unrest—was it any wonder that there developed a flood of efforts, legislated or otherwise, to repair our communities, to try to stop or at least slow down the socially centrifugal forces, to instill and strengthen a greater sense of community, of mutual responsibility and help, of purpose that transcended irresponsible individualism and selfish group interest? Of course there was no consensus about what things should be done and how. There was agreement only about the fact that our communities were geo-political entities inhospitable to the psychological sense of community. Those were days of nervous excitement and hope, and the basis for the hope was the knowledge that there was action, and frequently by people who had never before engaged in social action.

In order to understand why I regard the psychological sense of community as the overarching criterion by which to judge any community effort—a value on which a community psychology can be developed—it is necessary first to focus on how the events of the feverish sixties impinged upon the university in general and psychology in particular (Chapter Two). The confrontation between the social realities and university traditions, a confrontation not yet ended, was not only philosophical and conceptual, it was frequently destructively physical. This confrontation not only facilitated the birth of community psychology but also underlined that its future would be shaped as much by the dominant traditions of American psychology as by social needs of the present. Indeed, as I suggest in Chapter Three, American psychology was ill-suited in its theories, practices, and values to develop a *community* psychology. How could it be otherwise when so much of American psychology was about the *individual* organism. Social psychology, a field one would have expected to be the basis for a community psychology, worshipped experimental methodology as the sure if not the only road to truth; it obtained its data in departmental laboratories, simulated social reality to the point of caricature, and concentrated on the nature and measurement of attitudes—sometimes enlarging its horizons by including personality variables which invariably reflected theories about the individual organism. The fact is that community psychology bore the imprint of clinical psychology, itself a struggling newcomer to an American psychology which had never looked kindly on psychologists who rendered practical services. As a result, the possibility of developing a community psychology rooted in the social sciences vanished, and community psychology became primarily an appendage to the community mental heath movement which was dominated by an American psychiatry that had long strived for respectability in schools of medicine. Since community psychology was so influenced by and related to the psychiatric setting and psychiatric theorizing, I devote Chapter Four to a discussion of how psychiatry was affected by and responded to the social eruption of the sixties. Unlike community psychology, which was a small, struggling, new field, community psychiatry, and its "basic" discipline, social psychiatry, was powered by federal legislation and funds. As I have pointed out elsewhere (Sarason, 1972, Chapter Five), the community mental health act of 1963 reads like the psychological equivalent of the economic goal of a chicken in every pot and a car in every garage. Rarely has so much been promised to so many with so little recognition of tradition and resources.

One of the major points of these early chapters is that these new community fields, by virtue of their past intellectual roots and institutional values and characteristics, could not ask such questions as: How do we conceptualize the complexity of a community? What are the dimensions along which it is organized, how have they interacted to produce change, and how do they vary in impact and influenceability? Why is it that our fields were unprepared for the social eruptions and what does this suggest about reexamining our theories, practices, values and styles of being in a community? Are we translating the troublesome problems of the present into the familiar conceptual molds of the past not because these molds are adequate but because we are most comfortable with them? Since efforts at community change always reflect a judgment about what *should* be, what value or values should give justification and direction to our efforts as well as providing criteria by which we judge results? Neither community psychology, community psychiatry, nor social psychiatry were disposed to a searching self-examination. Flight into action (like the therapeutic flight into health), spurred as it was by societal pressures, prevented self-examination.

Such a reexamination could have pointed to a social science literature quite different from that with which these new fields were cognizant. To illustrate this point I discuss in Chapter Five some neglected writings of John Dollard (sociologist, social psychologist, psychoanalyst), James Plant (psychiatrist), and J. F. Brown (psychologist). Their books which should have been seminal in their effect appeared in the thirties and have had no lasting impact; they did not fit in with the dominant theories in psychology and psychiatry. Indeed, each of these books is a sophisticated indictment of the asocial or acultural character of psychological and psychiatric thinking, and each in its own way provides a way of looking at the community which would have prevented the new community fields from becoming unduly parochial and clinical. I also briefly discuss the Chicago school of sociology, dutifully referred to in the new community literature as, I presume, a token gesture to scholarliness and not as an acknowledgement of kinship. If the values which informed the work of the Chicago school were truly comprehended, it would be obvious that the root problem they addressed was how contemporary communities were destructive of the psychological sense of community; and their basic insight was that it was the task of social science to acquire that kind of knowledge and understanding which could be used to strengthen people's psychological sense of community. Ernest Becker, in his *The Lost Science of Man* (1971), discusses this theme most poignantly as he describes the tragedy of the professional life of Albion Small who founded the first department of sociology at the University of Chicago.

In Chapter Six I take up the kinds of obstacles we encounter when we try to conceptualize a community. A major obstacle is culture itself, because one of the consequences of absorbing and bearing the imprint of a culture is that we confuse the way things are with the way they could be. We take so much for granted about why and how things are organized as they are—indeed culture insures that we have to do little thinking about how our social world is organized—that it takes a major social disruption or a series of disturbing events to force into our awareness the fact that things were not even the way we thought they were, let alone what we expected them to be. I endeavor in that chapter to use examples (such as transportation, the elderly) that have several characteristics: they have in no way been central to the new community fields; their current status as major social problems cannot be understood except in social-historical-cultural terms; they have been major problems (for other fields) for a long time; and non-psychological factors have contributed to their nature and severity. This last characteristic is hard for psychologists to grasp and yet it is indisputable that a community cannot be comprehended only in psychological terms; and if we do not take this into account in our efforts at community planning and change we will continue to confront consequences rather than antecedents. It may appear to some readers that I am asking the community psychologist to be knowledgeable about economics, taxation, resources, geography, political science, religion, and so on. I am, but let us not confuse knowledgeability with expertise. The community psychologist must know more than psychology and for two reasons: the "more" is essential for understanding what a community is and the dynamics of its change, and it sooner or later affects the behavior and relationships of those in the community. I assume that most people look upon our highway system as a good thing, taking pride in its width, length, appearance, and efficiency. I also assume that most people are unaware of the consequences the system has had on the development of suburbia, on the reduction and deterioration of other forms of public transportation, and on the acceleration of the decay of and disorganization in the central city. That is to say, most people who take pride in our modern highway system cannot see a relationship betwen it and their complaints about the absence of a psychological sense of community.

It is not until Chapter Seven that I begin to deal directly with the concept of the psychological sense of a community. To convey what I mean by that concept, and to demonstrate what happens when it is ignored, I focus on the practice, legally and culturally sanctioned, of segregating atypical or deviant individuals. Nothing is as destructive of the psychological sense of community as segregation. The special class in the school, the residential institution for the retarded, or the "mentally ill," or the juvenile offender —in each of these instances we drastically alter the lives of people (the cared for and the caretakers, as well as other community individuals and groups) on the basis of the idea that we are providing humane treatment for the atypical individual at the same time that we are protecting the needs and interests of the rest of the community. I have chosen these examples for two reasons: first, they concern practices and values which seem "natural and right" to professional and layman alike; second, I have had a good deal of experience which, over the years, has forced me to the realization that what seemed "natural and right" about these instances was insidious and wrong because it was so destructive of the psychological sense of community. Is it not humane—is it not obviously progressive—to have a variety of types of special classes in our schools, enabling youngsters with special characteristics to get special attention? Chapter Seven explains why I answer this question in the negative, just as that chapter argues against the existence of many of our "humane" residential institutions. Chapter Eight describes a study which had two aims: to attempt to humanize an institution (for juvenile offenders) which had descended to the depths of disorganization, brutality, and public infamy and, at the same time, to demonstrate that the institution was not necessary. Although the second aim was not achieved, the partial success of the first illustrates well what can happen when the psychological sense of community is a value which informs action. In Chapter Nine I look at the residential institution from a purely financial point of view because one of its justifications has been economic feasibility—that is, it is less costly than alternative ways of dealing with the problems it purports to resolve. What emerges from this analysis is that these institutions are far more costly in economic terms than their conventional budgets suggest, and that the more we put into them the less we are likely to get from them. It also becomes clear that these institutions are embedded in a state apparatus which has a vested interest in maintaining them despite their self-defeating nature.

Many readers have had little first-hand contact with some of the specific settings (special classes, institutions for the mentally retarded or juvenile offender) I use to raise and discuss the significance of the psychological sense of community. Community psychology has shown little interest in these settings, although this degree of interest is far greater than that found within community psychiatry. This situation reflects interrelated historical-traditional roots in psychology and the larger society, but at the very least it is a consequence of the failure to confront the question What is a community? After all, when we talk about these settings we are not talking about small numbers of people or small amounts of money. Far from it, for when we think, as we must, in terms of families, resources, services, and personnel, we are faced with a sizeable portion of a community. And yet, the social sciences (with the exception of sociology in regard to criminology) have shown little interest in these settings. Race, poverty, the "normal" school populations, alternative school settings, the nature and structure of the delivery of health services, the training of paraprofessionals—these are some of the fashionable problems to which community-oriented psychologists have gravitated. At the same time that they are fashionable they are also important problems, and if they do not occupy center stage in subsequent chapters, it is not because I wish to downgrade their significance to the community. I chose the settings I did because they permitted me—more than my experiences in other community settings would have—to state and discuss the reasons I consider the psychological sense of community to be the overarching value by which to judge efforts to change any aspect of community functioning. I hope the reader will have no difficulty comprehending the major thrust of these chapters and relating it to the settings with which he is more familiar. Although some of the settings I discuss may be unfamiliar to many readers, I urge them to bear in mind that phenotypic differences among settings (and people) in our society are, unfortunately, effective barriers to the perception of genotypic communalities. Nowhere is this more true than when one deals with a concept and value like the psychological sense of community.

Before Chapter Ten I discuss only briefly the dilemmas and problems of action aimed at effecting community change, a "slighting" that was intentional because clarity about the nature and origins of the values justifying action is a task prior to that of action itself. I restrict the discussion to social scientists in the university, not because university people have been in the vanguard of social action or because their illuminations of social process and reality have been especially clear, but rather because I have come to see that university traditions and attitudes toward social action effectively rob the social scientist of new and more productive knowledge. Lest the reader conclude that I advocate that all social scientists (upon whom the community psychologist must depend for conceptual direction) become do-gooders, I explain that by social action as a vehicle for learning and for contributing to knowledge, I refer to any instance in which an academic person takes on a socially responsible role—in government, politics, business, schools, poverty agencies—which will allow him to experience the natural functioning of that particular aspect of society. The role must be an operational one with responsibility and some decision-making powers. He becomes an insider. He is not a consultant with the luxury of giving advice without responsibility for implementation. He is at bat. He is not sitting in the stands passively observing the game and passing judgment on the players. He is in the game and he is a player. Finally, he assumes the new role not only to learn but to change and move things. He is there to "win," and winning is defined in terms of ideas and theories about the game that he or others developed prior to assuming the new role. He assumes the new role to test the adequacy of ideas and theories, to see how they fit with social realities. His motivations have both an intellectually selfish and a selfless quality. The period of time he spends in this role will vary, but there is no doubt in his mind that at the end of the period he must discharge the obligation to determine and communicate the general significance of his experience.

Part of winning is in contributing to new and general knowledge about man and society.

The central thrust of Chapter Ten is that university people have to be prepared to use any and all ethical means to obtain new knowledge, and if that means engaging "in the real world" that is what one *has* to do. That part of the university tradition that says that we should not become fulltime participants in society because we will be contaminated by it, and that instead we should stay within the university except for quick excursions or forays now and then, rests on a most superficial and distorted conception of culture, society, and the university. If I challenge these traditional attitudes it is not to demean the quest for conceptual clarity and intellectual vigor, but to expand and exalt it.

In the final chapter I caution against naivete about the relation of values and actions. The psychological sense of community has a virtuous sound, stimulating as it does visions of togetherness and cooperation uncluttered by conflict, controversy, and divisiveness. Such visions are hard to resist, but they must be resisted because they are illusory. The psychological sense of community is at best a transient experience preceded and at some point followed by some kind of tension or threat to the sense of community. The consequences of such tension will be determined by the strengths with which people hold the psychological sense of community to be the overarching value by which they wish their relationships to be judged. It is easier to get agreement about values than about actions deriving from these values, a fact which should be a potent caution against the tendency to oversimplify the complexities and dangers in the relation between values and actions.

It will become apparent to the reader that I regard the new field of community psychology as not fulfilling its original promise of the turbulent sixties when our communities appeared to be coming apart at the seams. This does not mean that much has not been done and learned, but rather that community psychology very quickly became an appendage of the community mental health movement, a restriction in scope that directed attention away from *community* in its geo-political, social, and psychological interrelationships. Community psychology was not intended to be restricted to psychopathology, but rather it was to be a field that tried to see the community in its complexity (see, as examples, Anderson, Cooper, and others, 1966). Interestingly enough, what was at stake was not only the autonomy, scope, and viability of community psychology but the question whether those seeking to pioneer in the more narrow mental health fields could withstand being "pathologized" by the tradition behind "major mental illness." Let us listen to Cowen and Zax in their introductory chapter to *Emergent Approaches To Mental Health Problems* (Cowen, Gardner, and Zax, 1967). They are discussing the report of the Joint Commission on Mental Illness and Health (1961) set up by Congress in 1955 "to survey the resources and make recommendations for combating mental illness in the United States."

It is well to underscore the values that are reflected in this pivotal recommendation: (1) that psychosis is the central problem of the mental health fields, (2) that intensive treatment is the method of choice, (3) that our hopes lie in massive augmentation of hospitals, clinics, and the supply of helping professionals, and (4) that the community is significant to the extent that it is instrumental in approaching the problems of "mental breakdown." These values are hammered home time and time again in the course of the final report, and admissible alternatives are, to a considerable extent, eschewed." . . . the bias of this report [gives] a little discomfort to some . . . who have a strong commitment toward practices and programs aimed at the promotion of positive mental health in children and adults. . . . We have assumed that the mental hygiene movement has diverted attention from the core problem of major mental illness. It is our purpose to redirect attention to the possibilities of improving the mental health of the mentally ill." Quite explicitly, the report goes on to say that its central concern is with ". . . various levels of service, beginning with secondary prevention . . . and continuing through intensive and protracted treatment of the acute and chronically ill."

Serious question must be raised about the fundamental substance of the Joint Commission recommendations. Through its emphasis on secondary and tertiary prevention, it reinforces utilization of a model that has not met with distinguished success in the mental health areas and which may not be well suited for dealing with such problems. Its call for a multiplicative thrust in expansion of facilities and relevant personnel may, therefore, be based on shaky premises. The overriding salience attributed by the report to the problems of major mental breakdown (i.e., psychosis) suggests a point of application in time for our mental health efforts, which may be much too late. Moreover, largely because of the primacy attributed to problems of the psychotic, there is a disconcerting "tunnel vision" for many pathways that demand consideration as part of a comprehensive analysis of our mental health situation: prevention of disorder, the young, the unreached, and positive building for mental health.

It is not that the values reflected in the Joint Commission Report are "bad" ones in the absolute sense. Certainly the problems to which the report speaks are real and pressing. However, the critical issue facing the mental health fields today, given the reality of limited resources, is that of the *relative ordering of many values, each of which may be "good" in the absolute sense.* Critics of the Joint Commission Report have been quick to seize on this point and have made a compelling case for the consideration of approaches which seek to prevent the occurrence of disorder. The present authors believe that were we to be guided by the spirit and force of the Joint Commission recommendations, it would leave unexplored some of the most promising pathways toward resolution of mental health problems. We must, therefore, question its sufficiency as a blueprint for our mental health operations in the coming decades [pp. 21–22].

Cowen and Zax were apprehensive, and their fears have certainly been borne out. Similar apprehensions had been voiced in 1966 by Smith and Hobbs in an American Psychological Association position paper on comprehensive mental health centers:

The objective of the center staff should be to help the various social systems of which the community is composed to function in ways that develop and sustain the effectiveness of the individuals who take part in them, and to help these community systems regroup their forces to support the person who runs into trouble. The community is not just a "catchment area" from which patients are drawn; the task of a community mental health center goes far beyond that of purveying professional services to disordered people on a local basis.

The more closely the proposed centers become integrated with the life and institutions of their communities, the less the community can afford to turn over to mental health professionals its responsibility for guiding the center's policies. Professional standards need to be established for the centers by Federal and state authorities, but goals and basic policies are a matter for local control. A broadly based responsible board of informed leaders should help to ensure that the center serves in deed, not just in name, as a focus of the community's varied efforts on behalf of the greater effectiveness and fulfillment of all its residents [pp. 500–501].

But, as Iscoe and Spielberger (1970) comment in their introductory chapter to the book they edited, *Community Psychology: Perspectives in Training and Research,* psychologists seeking a broad involvement in and conception of a community, were faced with some weakness stemming from the narrowness of psychology:

For psychologists the prospect of community involvement poses both a threat and a challenge. With but a few exceptions, notably some of the programs described in this volume, the graduate training of psychologists contains little that will prepare them to understand community problems and work effectively in community settings. Consequently, if psychologists are to be involved in community affairs, as indeed they must be if the recommendations of the APA position paper are taken seriously, then training programs in psychology must provide students with opportunities to learn about social systems and the sociopolitical realities that must be confronted by those who work in community settings [p. 10].

Why none of these new community fields realized their promise is one of the central questions I address in this book. And when Cowen and Zax emphasize that the critical issue is that of the "relative ordering of many values, each of which may be 'good' in the absolute sense," they are pointing to still another central theme of this book: the problem of deciding by what value or values one justifies action. It is the basic problem, and I hope it will become clear to the reader why I chose the psychological sense of community as the overarching value giving justification and direction to a community psychology.

II

The Societal
Origins of
Community Psychology

═══════════════════════════════════════

Community psychology is a relatively new field within academic psychology. It is somewhat more than a decade old. Prior to that time, as will be evident in later pages, there were psychologists with a community orientation, but it was not until the early sixties that community psychology began to be viewed as a distinctive field requiring new ways of thinking, training, and practicing. As is the case with any "infant" field, its entry into the academic world was marked by proclamations of its necessity and distinctiveness as well as the recognition that its development would require changes in

16

the established order of things. There were many people who were disposed to welcome this presumably new field into the academic family; there were many more who were skeptical and resistant. The welcomers tended to see it as an opportunity for psychology to become more relevant to the needs of society; the resisters tended to view it as another example of the unfortunate tendency within psychology to become, prematurely, a service profession founded more on a desire to help than on the needs to know, understand, and investigate. These are long standing tensions within American psychology, and it should have surprised no one that the claims of community psychology met with a very mixed reaction.[1] It would be a mistake to view this in terms of the usual oversimplified polarities: traditional versus new, scientist versus practitioner, helper versus researcher, applied versus basic. These polarities had been explicitly crystallized and heightened in intensity when, immediately after World War II, clinical psychology became a substantial part of academic psychology. The fact that the proponents of community psychology primarily came from clinical psychology (and it was clear that they were critical of some of the emphases and conceptions of clinical psychology) meant that this new field would have "in house" problems. From one standpoint, therefore, the emerging conflict was between different ways of "doing good." From another standpoint, community psychology encountered obstacles from two traditions: the "new" traditions of clinical psychology and the much older traditions of "scientific" psychology. The strength of these and other ideological obstacles was heightened by a simple fact ordinarily obscured in such situations: because the resources of any academic department are limited, any new field almost always requires for its entry and maintenance a (perceived or real) dilution in the resources potentially available to existing fields. Altruism is no more

---

[1] These tensions have not been peculiar to psychology. They have long characterized many academic fields, and the resolution of these tensions has led to the creation of new university departments and schools to serve the so-called practical needs of society. The private universities have resisted such developments far more than the state universities, a fact which is the basis for the snobbish view of the former towards the latter. It is worth noting that in the case of clinical psychology it has been only in the private universities that this field was never accepted or, if accepted, was subsequently dropped.

an operating principle in university departments than it is in community settings.

Writing a book about a fledgling field is always a dangerous task because one runs the risk of either unduly confining it to the immediate problems on the basis of which it claims distinctiveness, or of viewing it so broadly as to hinder productive conceptualization or focused inquiry. As we shall see, community psychology already suffers from both tendencies, for example, on the one hand restricting the field to the problems of race, poverty, and "mental illness" or, on the other, viewing an entire community as a "patient" whom we have to understand and change. No less a danger is the difficulty one has in recognizing the shaky foundations of the time perspective from which one is viewing the new field. This is particularly true for community psychology, the substance of which is so highly correlated with events and forces in our society. The very fact that community psychology is not comprehensible apart from the history of our own society should sensitize us to the necessity of an historical stance. Is community psychology a new field because there are new problems in our society? If they are old social problems, how do we understand why community psychology took so long to emerge? If community psychology is a relatively new field (trying to define itself, to describe its methods and theoretical foundations, and to formulate a program of personnel selection and training), should we not endeavor to determine if it is, so to speak, reinventing the wheel? What is community psychology's usable past? What is the past of which it seems to be conscious and of what past should it be aware? In our individual lives, time perspective is always an implicit (and less frequently an explicit) force in our thinking and actions. It is no less a force when we don our professional caps. There are those who view the present and recent past in psychology and in our society as if we were dealing with a distinctively qualitative change rather than one of degree or emphasis—a view which requires the assumption that the social world, or at least our society, was, so to speak, born yesterday. The awareness that change has taken place or is taking place too often obscures continuities and emphasizes discontinuities. There are, of course, those who are so impressed with the continuities that they are rendered insensitive to emerging patterns of social change—in part because they tend to project upon society their belief in the unchanging character of man.

To understand in depth the emergence of community psychology would require a separate volume demonstrating the interrelationships between social history, the history of ideas, and individual personalities. In part this has been done for the earlier decades of this century by the Levines in *The Social History of Helping Services* (1970), in which they discuss the changing interrelationships between theories, practices, and the social-political climate. For my present purposes, I shall endeavor only to sketch briefly some of the recent forces which have converged to give birth to a new field.

The Immediate Context

Certain events are significant for our purposes because they brought into focus, and compellingly directed attention and resources to, problems that could no longer be tolerated. There was nothing obscure about the presence or the nature of these problems, but they seemed to require a "happening" to arouse a concerted resolve to do something about them. The significant events occurred at different times, and they varied in their immediate consequences. The first such event was the Supreme Court's desegregation decision in 1954, influenced to an undetermined extent by briefs containing data from psychological research indicating the baleful effects of racial discrimination.[2] That decision brought to the surface and coalesced a variety of groups and forces, and it gave

[2] In its decision the Supreme Court refers to eight publications, half of which were by psychologists (Fellman, 1960, p. 138). The earliest of them was from 1944 and the latest from 1952. The use by the Court of formal psychological research and social science analysis was a door-opening step, not only because such publications were given the sanction of relevance to legal issues but also because it put social science on notice, if it was disposed to notice, that society would no longer be indifferent to the research and the scholarly findings of the university social scientist. This trend was confirmed in subsequent years as the courts increasingly were confronted with such issues as the effects of institutionalization, the civil rights of patients, the criteria for adequate treatment, the criteria for expert witnesses, the right to education, the effects of bussing, and so on. Social science *is* in the public arena, and like atomic science has to deal with this fact whether it likes it or not.

momentum to the emerging civil rights movement. But it also brought in its wake and spotlighted bitter antagonisms in our society on the issue. The spectacle of armed troops watching over the desegregation process in Little Rock, frenzied parents in towns and cities screaming vile epithets, and civil authorities impotent or unwilling to act demonstrated to everyone that our society was in trouble. Initially it appeared that the major battles would take place in Southern communities, but it was not long before it was obvious that all of our urban communities would have a similar experience.

University faculty members and students were, of course, far from indifferent to what was happening, and many sensed at the time that these events were the prologue to even more serious divisions and problems. As citizens they participated in a variety of ways, some as militant activists, others as soothers or peacemakers. Inevitably, many professional people in the social sciences and mental health fields began to ask themselves some uncomfortable questions: why was their knowledge, and the problems they studied, seemingly irrelevant to the needs of a troubled society? Was it not socially irresponsible, and should it not be a source of guilt, that the university had isolated itself from the problems of the "real world?" These questions were somewhat more acute for persons in the mental health fields (clinical psychology, psychiatry, psychiatric social work) because they were practitioners or they trained practitioners, and it was obvious that the kind of help they were trained to give, and the kinds of research problems with which they concerned themselves (such as psychotherapy, diagnostic tests, personality factors and organization, psychopathology) were nowhere near where the trouble was. In short, what began for many as the problem and the responsibility of an individual citizen became transformed into a problem of the university and the profession. The community rather than the individual became the patient.

A second event was in its own way quite spectacular and intrinsically unrelated to the recent development of community psychology. This was the successful orbiting of the Russian Sputnik in 1957. To understand why this astronautical feat becomes part of our story it is necessary to recognize what a massive wound it was to American pride that Russia won the race to outer space. This required not only that the United States should catch up with and surpass the Russians but that an explanation for our secondary status be found. Of all the explanations offered, few seemed to heal the wound to the national ego as well as the charge that our public educational system was inadequate. Justification for this explanation was not hard to find. For some years different parts of our universities had been very critical of our schools, particularly in regard to the teaching of mathematics and science. Various universities had become centers for the development of new curricula. Some leading scientists had spearheaded these efforts. The traditional core of the American university (the colleges of arts and sciences) had always viewed the quality of public schools and teachers, let alone the teacher of teachers, with some disdain.[3] The first Russian Sputnik provided many university faculty members with more justification for their efforts to improve the quality of public education. But now it was not only in the context of education *qua* education but in the context of national pride, international supremacy, and (for some) even national survival. At the same time that these efforts were picking up steam (and governmental support), the public schools increasingly were front page material because of the bitterness surrounding efforts at desegregation, as well as the recognition that there was an urban crisis of which the ghetto school was a compelling symptom. University faculty members were learning that when they took on the burden of reforming the schools they inevitably became involved in the nature and dynamics of a community. If they did not become involved, at least they were learning that the problems of public education were vastly more complex than they had imagined, and that a broader view of their mission was inescapable. How much good could one expect from changing curricula when conditions of poverty and racial discrimination and conflict remained unimproved? After all, if schools were inadequate was that not a reflection of the community in which they were embedded?

Again it was the mental health professions for whom the problems in the schools presented the most acute dilemmas. It was

---

[3] Is it not ironic that the traditional core of the university, which would have nothing to do with the field of education and forced it to go its own way, was now criticizing the field of education because its traditions and values were seen as antithetical to those of the core?

obvious, particularly to the clinical psychologists, that whereas they felt they should have a role in relation to the schools they had little or nothing to do with them. They worked in clinics and hospitals, and if they did research, the problems they investigated were not related to school or community problems. Later in this chapter I shall have more to say about the factors that directed clinical psychologists to work in schools and in community settings that were new to them. Two of these factors deserve mention at this point. First, as a separate area in American psychology, clinical psychology was still relatively new in the university and its traditions by no means rigidified. Second, clinical psychology had been under the domination of psychiatry, and its desire for independence, in the realms of both theory and practice, was very strong. For many clinical psychologists community problems began to have a fascination as strong as the complexities of the individual personality once had. They were as much pulled by the events in the larger society as they felt pushed by the professional controversies of the clinic and the hospital.

The third event that stimulated the growth of community psychology was President Kennedy's much-heralded message to Congress in 1963. The *community* mental health movement was "officially" recognized and money became available to develop *community* mental health centers, each of which was to serve thousands of people, and each of which would reflect the needs and plans of the local community and the appropriate state agencies. The message and the implementing legislation made clear that the mental health professions could no longer continue to serve very narrow segments of a community but instead had to develop views and services that would deal with the direct and indirect consequences of racial discrimination, poverty, ghetto schools, alcoholism, and so forth. Some of the services would be direct while others would be indirect, that is, offered through consultative services to various community agencies. Since most of these new community mental health centers would be affiliated with or under the aegis of departments of psychiatry in medical schools, and because of the ties between departments of psychology and departments of psychiatry, the university's relationship to the community took on a somewhat new cast. There was no problem in attracting staff members for the community mental health centers, first because there was government funding (with the prospect of much more money in the future!), and second because it provided a vehicle through which many mental health professionals (as well as a number of sociologists and anthropologists) could lessen or eliminate the gap between their responsibilities as citizens and professionals.

The fourth event, announced with no less fanfare than the third, was President Johnson's War On Poverty program. Clothed as it was in the rhetoric of utopianism and powered by a moral indignation that could seemingly shatter all the obstacles of evil, the official pronouncements had the clear effect of directing critical attention toward the social-economic fabric of the American community. The basic problem was not mental health, or education, or violence, or racial discrimination, but a combination of factors, values, and traditions that, whatever their positive virtues had been, was no longer tolerable. The level of national guilt was high and matched in intensity only by the resolve to change the quality of American life. In addition to guilt there was fear that if appropriate changes were not made, whatever was good in American society would disappear in the deterioration and strife within American communities. As many were quick to say, our communities were "sick." Although it was not clear who the physician for such a sickness should be, many candidates offered themselves or were chosen.

Whatever traditional reluctance the university community had felt about immersion in the practical affairs of the everyday world could not withstand the demands for healing from society. For an increasing number within the university, the distinction between their responsibilities as citizens and as scientists or professionals became increasingly fuzzy, and for some this represented a desirable change. In the case of some universities, particularly those in urban settings, this kind of change was also in the interests of their own survival because they were surrounded by all the social evils named in the War On Poverty pronouncements. Their relationship to the social problems of their communities was not new; for example, their medical schools and hospitals had long been "in contact" with the local community, more perhaps because it suited their research and training needs than because of feelings of social obligation. What was new was the increase in the number of individuals in all parts of the university who began to direct their professional and scientific interests to the problems of their communities. (If one has any doubt on this score he should peruse the contents of the proceedings of national professional and scientific societies for the years 1955–1965.) Nowhere is the change in thinking and roles of university people more marked than in the mental health fields and the social sciences. The beginning of the War On Poverty was also the beginning of the introduction into the university of community psychology training programs. Golann's (1964) survey of university curricula turned up only one graduate program in 1962 devoted explicitly to community mental health, although the seeds of other programs were already planted. Today there are scores of such programs, small and large.

In or near the center of all of these events and the interrelated forces they represented was the country's youth. The steady increase in juvenile delinquency was already noted in the fifties and was one of the potent arguments for urban renewal. But it soon became apparent that all segments of the younger generation were behaving in ways that were disquieting, to say the least, to the older ones. New ways of dress, drug use, social withdrawal, militancy, and opposition to institutional authority—all these seemed to be ways of rejecting long-standing traditions of the society. Younger people plunged into the civil rights movement, and the practice of civil disobedience became a routine affair. Some became radicalized; few remained indifferent. And, of course, as our involvement in Vietnam mounted so did the massive resentment and opposition of young people. The morality of government was called into question, and so was the morality of the university, which was viewed as a witting or unwitting ally of national agencies and policies.

The university became a battleground, and although it was not always clear who it was that the students considered to be the enemy, it was clear that they had strong and numerous allies in the faculty. If there was agreement on anything it was that the university could no longer justify aloofness from immediate social problems and injustice. Relevance and justice had to replace, or at least had to be regarded as no less important than, intellectual curiosity and freedom of inquiry as criteria for entry into the academic community. Community psychology was in its infancy and the force of events robbed it of a childhood. It was but an instance of what was happening throughout the academic community. The research interests of many faculty members changed, and some established individuals ceased to engage in traditional scholarly and research activities because of their presumed irrelevance to the serious problems of the society (for example, Duberman, 1969). Absorption in the past, be it in such fields as history and the humanities, was viewed by some as a mixture of futility, irresponsibility, and escapism. How, some asked, could one justify writing and teaching about Chaucer or Alexander Pope when the foundations of society were no longer adequate? Who wanted to fiddle while Rome burns? There were too many fires to be put out. One cannot say how many faculty members felt this way, but whatever their numbers they were vocal and persuasive, particularly to students for whom the lecture hall and seminar had long been a cure for any form of sleep problem. Students became involved in all kinds of community settings, created new instrumentalities for service and social action, and pulled many faculty members with them. And since by its very nature community psychology was seen as requiring some kind of involvement with and intervention in community problems, it was a "natural" for the times.

Aspects of what I have outlined have been described and discussed by Robert Nisbet in his book *The Degradation of the Academic Dogma* (1971). It is a book which everyone should read and ponder, and I shall have more to say about it in later pages. Aside from looking at events of the last twenty-five years from a historical perspective, and demonstrating the utility and validity of viewing social forces as continuous and incapable of being pigeonholed in the categories of past and present except at the expense of attaining a balanced picture of social dynamics and change, Professor Nisbet forces us to confront the dilemmas and dialectical consequences of institutional change. He is no reactionary or uncritical defender of academic traditions. The central point in his argument is that when one sets out to change the university, to forge new traditions and new alignments of forces, particularly when all of this is in the cause of social justice and in the context of strife, it is all too likely that much of what should be preserved will be destroyed. With the best of social intentions, he points out, we can destroy the best of academic tradition. The pressure to act and to solve immediate problems can produce the opposite of what we intend, and is not conducive to consideration of alternative actions which can produce something new without destroying what is productive in the old.

These are precisely the problems and dilemmas of the psychologist when he ventures forth into the community to change other types of settings. As we shall see, the community psychologist views himself as an agent of community change, selected or self-appointed. Explicitly or implicitly he is critical of existing traditions in the communty settings in which he works, and there can be no doubt (at least in my mind) that each of these settings will be found wanting in numerous respects. But it does not necessarily follow that these settings should be essentially destroyed or that what will take their place will be any better. Indeed, we have no reason to be at all enthusiastic about the consequences of the community psychologist's efforts. I do not maintain that we preserve what exists because it exists. I would not deny that some of our community institutions are appallingly self-defeating of their own goals. But it simply does not follow that all that they stand for is without merit, and that we therefore know how to replace them with something better. It is also too frequently the case that when we "blame" a setting for its inadequacies we are so caught up in the present that we fail to understand the complex of social forces that produced the situation. As a consequence of this ahistorical stance, our efforts to promote change only tend to confirm that the more things change the more they remain the same.

Much of this book will be devoted to examining and illustrating these issues. I have brought them up at this early point because one cannot understand community psychology independent of the social context from which it emerged in the university. The concatenation of social events and forces which helped change the university climate from which community psychology emerged, and the conflicting traditions which heralded its "birth" (it is really an old field!)', raise issues no different from those which arise when the community psychologist focuses on another community setting.

The fact that members of the academic community have come to direct their efforts to social change is a secure basis for expecting that they will be faced with several obstacles which will defeat them if they are not recognized. The first is that they do not possess the kind of knowledge or experience that is adequate to solve the problems with which they have newly chosen to deal. In fact, the obstacle is more complicated for them because they have much to unlearn at the same time they have much to learn. The second obstacle is all that is involved whenever one changes roles— when one perceives one's self as taking on new and difficult responsibilities involving new types of relationships and expectations. There is always a conflict between what one is and was, between an uncertain future and a rejected past, between the security of the old role and insecurities of the new one.

A third obstacle, and in some ways the most subtle and insidious one, is the tendency unwittingly to transform new problems into familiar terms—which is the way in which the rejected past most often comes back to haunt the present. When we adopt radically new roles in order to tackle what are for us radically new problems, our ways of thinking and conceptualizing, our deeply ingrained categories of thought, are not dissolved and quickly replaced. What is so highly overlearned is highly resistant to change. More than that, the unverbalized character of our basic assumptions insures that our thinking in the present will bear the stamp of our past. The fourth obstacle is that when new roles and fields emerge as a result of social conflict and disorder, it is inordinately difficult to recognize the first three obstacles; they are ignored or oversimplified, or derogated as a form of resistance to action in general and to justice in particular.

Nisbet's book should dissuade any reasonable person from holding the notion that what happened in our universities was "caused" by a particular generation coping with new ideas and forces. Such a notion simply is not supported by the facts of social history. If one wished to pursue the mischievous game of labeling decades, as if the beginning of a decade (or century) has the power to influence events, one could argue that the "turbulent" sixties came after the "conceptual" late forties and fifties. In psychology and sociology, at least, there were some notable individuals whose writings not only foreshadowed the issues around which the university turmoil of the sixties would revolve, but whose ideas implicitly or explicitly raised the issue of the relationship between the academic and the social world, that is, between knowledge and the *responsibility* to act.

Kurt Lewin, who died in 1947, was a major influence in American psychology, and this influence burgeoned as he became increasingly involved in the problems of the everyday world. Although he always basically remained a scientist and theory-builder, he came to believe that academic psychology could not remain aloof from society's problems—at least not without running the risk of becoming sterile, trivial, and irrelevant. The theories and methodologies of psychology should be applicable to the "real world," and the process of application would be mutually enriching. The concept of action research was developed by Lewin. What propelled him to this view of the relation of psychology to society is no mystery. He fled from Nazi Germany, he anticipated the coming of World War II, and he was alarmed (to put it mildly) by the strength of the forces that made for group and national conflicts. For Kurt Lewin, as citizen and psychologist, the problems of society had to be understood and dealt with; they were not reasons for escaping to the conventional academic setting. As Marrow (1969) states in his biography of Lewin: "Lewin became skeptical about remaining in a conventional academic setting as his concept of the organization of action research developed. It could be best developed, he felt, if he presided over an autonomous institute affiliated with a university, but not subject to its routines. Of course, group dynamics and action research were debatable projects among his academic peers. Most preferred the nonactivist tradition of academic psychologists and yearned to return to teaching, writing, and research in the security of Academe. So Lewin went his way on his own work" (p. 158). Academic psychology in general, and community psychology in particular, now take a very different view of group dynamics and action research, and in large measure this is because of the writings and work of Kurt Lewin. There were many psychologists immersed in the turbulence of the sixties who did not know that a solid part of their thinking, actions, and techniques bore the stamp of Lewin's work of two decades earlier.

Strange though it may seem to some, B. F. Skinner must also be considered as a major influence on the developments of the sixties. In *Walden Two,* published in 1948, Skinner makes a number of points similar to those made by Lewin. He is highly critical of the irrelevance of much of psychology to the problems of society. He is equally critical of the deliberate aloofness of the university from the self-destructive forces in society. He emphasizes the need to test theory by social action, and to apply scientific knowledge to solving social problems. *Walden Two* is not only an indictment of our society (which includes the university!) but a clear call to action. Indeed, the book was a major stimulus to the intellectual and activist tendencies of that and subsequent generations. In universities around the country the book was read, started heated controversies, and inspired plans to start communes. Group conflict, destructive competition, wasted potential, boredom, discrimination against women and other minorities, pollution—these were some of the insidious and urgent problems that Skinner confronted and for which he presented his own solutions. However much one may disagree with his solutions, the fact remains that Skinner called for a changed relationship between psychology and society, between theory and action, and between science and social responsibility. It is no wonder that in the following decades the applications of Skinnerian principles and technology to different social problems mushroomed. Kurt Lewin and B. F. Skinner were radically different kinds of individuals and psychologists, and yet each in his own way advocated that psychology had to be concerned with social problems and in the vanguard of forces acting, if not to make the world better, at least to slow down the rate at which the social fabric was deteriorating.[4] One was a native American, the other a political

[4] It is interesting to note that both Lewin and Skinner adopted the same view toward historical explanations of behavior, that is, both were exquisitely sensitive to the "here and the now" dynamics of social behavior and looked to historical factors only to the extent that they were operative in the present. The group dynamics movement fathered by Lewin and the behavior modification movement deriving from Skinner start with analyses of the "here and the now."

and religious refugee, and these differences were clearly reflected in the substance and scope of their theorizing as well as in their methodologies. And yet, strangely enough, both were similarly appalled at the state of society, were critical of the university's aloofness from society, advocated activism both as a way of gaining new knowledge and as a way of ameliorating social problems, and stimulated their students to a new view of the relationship between their science and their society.

C. Wright Mills was another influential academic who was scathingly critical of the irrelevance of sociological theorizing and the trivial quality of most empirical studies. In his 1959 book, *The Sociological Imagination,* he states:

> Of late the conception of social science I hold has not been ascendant. My conception stands opposed to social science as a set of bureaucratic techniques which inhibit social inquiry by "methodological" pretensions, which congest such work by obscurantist conceptions, or which trivialize it by concern with minor problems unconnected with publicly relevant issues. These inhibitions, obscurities, and trivialities have created a crisis in the social studies today without suggesting, in the least, a way out of that crisis . . .
>
> Many practitioners of social science, especially in America, seem to me curiously reluctant to take up the challenge that now confronts them. Many in fact abdicate the intellectual and the political tasks of social analysis; others no doubt are simply not up to the role for which they are nevertheless being cast. At times they seem almost deliberately to have brought forth old ruses and developed new timidities. Yet despite this reluctance, intellectual as well as public attention is now so obviously upon the social worlds which they presumably study that it must be agreed that they are uniquely confronted with an opportunity. In this opportunity there is revealed the intellectual promise of the social sciences, the cultural uses of the sociological imagination, and the political meaning of studies of man and society [pp. 20–22].

To a far greater extent than either Lewin or Skinner, Mills explicitly and caustically dissects some of the work of leading sociologists and social psychologists whom he regards at best as unnecessarily obscure and at worst self-serving empire builders who substitute methodology for intellectual substance. For example, Mills maintains that Talcott Parsons' 555 page book, *The Social System,* can be "translated" into four paragraphs without doing violence to any of his few ideas! Mills then comments on such "grand" theorizing:

> The basic cause of grand theory is the initial choice of a level of thinking so general that its practitioners cannot logically get down to observation. They never, as grand theorists, get down from the higher generalities to problems in their historical and structural context. This absence of a firm sense of genuine problems, in turn, makes for the unreality so noticeable in their pages. One resulting characteristic is a seemingly arbitrary and certainly endless elaboration of distinctions, which neither enlarge our understanding nor make our experience more sensible. This in turn is revealed as a partially organized abdication of the efforts to describe and explain human conduct and society plainly.
>
> When we consider what a word stands for, we are dealing with its semantic aspects; when we consider it in relation to other words, we are dealing with its syntactic features. I introduce these shorthand terms because they provide an economical and precise way to make this point: Grand theory is drunk on syntax, blind to semantics. Its practitioners do not truly understand that when we define a word we are merely inviting others to use it as we would like it to be used; that the purpose of definition is to focus argument upon fact, and that the proper result of good definition is to transform arguments over terms into disagreements about fact, and thus open arguments to further inquiry.
>
> The grand theorists are so preoccupied by syntax meanings and so unimaginative about semantic references, they are so rigidly confined to such high levels of abstraction that the "typologies" they make up—and the work they do to make them up—seem more often an arid game of Concepts than an effort to define systematically—which is to say, in a clear and orderly way—the problems at hand, and to guide our efforts to solve them [pp. 33–34].

From World War II until the turbulent sixties there were

people in the university community who believed that American
social science, worshipping as it did at the altar of methodological
rigor, and absorbed as it was in building temples of theory, was
distracted from any real understanding of the nature of the society
to which it was presumably relevant. This criticism took any or all
of the following forms. First, the dominant sociological and social
psychological theories simply did not realistically mirror or take
into account the bases on which society was organized, its values,
dynamics, and modes of change. Second, precisely because social
science adopted a "value free" orientation, it could not recognize
wherein it was itself a reflection of the values of its society, that is,
it was an instrument of that society and in ways which prevented it
from being a critic of those values. Third, the time was past (as it
was for the atomic scientist) when the social scientist could remain
indifferent to how the knowledge he acquired was being applied.
Fourth, as never before, the social scientist was required to adopt
a new perspective on *his* social action, and for two reasons: the
first his recognition of the depth, severity, and universality of social
conflict and disease, and the second his need of a corrective against
irrelevant theorizing.

It would be a mistake to consider these critics as activists
intent on downgrading theory and research, and recommending that
the social scientist, Don Quixote style, begin to solve the ills of the
world. On the contrary, they were men of ideas who saw themselves
and their fields as inevitably part of a society which did not ignore
them and which they in turn could not ignore. By no means did they
agree either on the substance of their social analysis or social
criticism or on a course of action. Indeed, if some of them (for
example, Lewin, Skinner, and Mills) had been forced to live together on a desert island until they agreed on a social diagnosis
and courses of action, they never would have returned to civiliza-
tion. They were in agreement on three points: the destructive forces
in society were in the ascendant, there was the possibility that
society as we know it would disappear, and the social scientist
could not be indifferent to what was happening or could happen.
These critics were a minority in the university, but their influence
was disproportionate to their numbers, particularly among students. The majority took a more conventional view of the role of

the social scientist, although many of them changed their views quite remarkably as the turbulent sixties roared on. Strangely, there was little recognition that what the critics of the fifties had been saying had already been confirmed in the early forties. World War II involved the university, and willingly, in the most comprehensive "community psychology" program ever.

World War II, The University, and Community Involvement

Unlike the Vietnam war, World War II engendered in our society an amazing degree of societal cohesion. German and Italian fascism, Japanese militarism and imperialism, the overrunning of France, the bombing of England, the German invasion of Russia, and the bombing of Pearl Harbor made our own declaration of war inevitable and rallied almost all citizens to the country's defense. For at least a decade before, an increasing number of citizens looked anxiously at the string of fascist "successes." The threat was external and it was viewed as a truly serious challenge to American society. By the time of Pearl Harbor it is likely that a majority of the people were resigned to war against the evils of fascism. Those who felt or wished otherwise changed their minds when Pearl Harbor was bombed.

For a brief time there was a real question as to how many colleges and universities would survive, not only because a sizeable segment of the college population was to be drafted but also because many faculty members were either being drafted or trying to locate positions which would allow them to help in the war effort. The colleges did not go out of existence. The initiation of a variety of armed services training programs insured their continuation. In fact, many young people received a college education who ordinarily could not have afforded one, and a good number went to universities they could not have entered in peace time. The university was quite responsive to societal needs and pressures, and willingly so. Ethnic, religious, and racial entrance "quotas" received one of their strongest setbacks. After all, how could one justify discrimination when our society was in danger? How could higher education remain preciously selective when the very existence of our society was in question? When the emotions of patriotism are triggered by the perception of a national emergency or catastrophe, values and practices change rather quickly—which is another way of saying that the substance of the sense of community changes.[5]

A sizeable segment of university faculties entered the armed services, in many instances not for the purpose of doing basic research (or research at all), or because they could *directly* apply their knowledge and skills to the war effort, but rather with the hope that they would be able to make some meaningful contribution. Many of those who remained in the university were either traveling back and forth to one or another governmental agency or armed services' facility, or redirecting their teaching to fit in with the needs of special training programs. There was hardly an academic department that was not involved to a degree in the total effort. For example, linguistics and anthropology, small and "pure" fields, became much in demand as the armed services recognized that they would be dealing with peoples whose language and cultures they did not comprehend. It is fair to say that the university became quite "applied" in its desire to play a role in the problems of the society. This was not done with any intention permanently to alter the traditional values and role of the university. But neither was it done reluctantly. It seemed natural enough that those were times when the needs of the larger society should take precedence over those of the university. In short, as the critics of the fifties pointed out, the university could not in any permanent way remain aloof from what was happening in the larger society, regardless of whether the threats to the society's viability were external or internal. Indeed, the social analysis and predictions of these critics in regard to the internal threats to social harmony, overlooked or ignored by most, later came to (and continues to) haunt the university community, which was as unprepared for dealing with these kinds of threats as the country was unprepared on December 7, 1941, for dealing with an external one—perhaps less prepared.

---

[5] The role of women changed drastically during World War II. They suddenly became a valuable part of the labor market and opportunities within and without the armed services opened for them that hitherto had not existed. Still another group ordinarily discriminated against, the aged, enjoyed a new status during the war. They were not only "invited" into the job market but they were made to feel needed.

The significance of World War II for the university was not only in the obvious fact that there are times when the university feels it cannot or should not be aloof from the problems of society, or that society requires that the university change its traditional stance and role, albeit temporarily. (To ignore this historical fact is possible only for those who do not possess the conceptual knowledge and tools to understand that the university is part and parcel of the social fabric and that whenever that fabric changes there are reverberations in all parts of the university. Such individuals cannot comprehend that the question is not whether the university should be involved in society's problems but rather how it is involved and how such choices come about or are justified.) An additional significance of World War II for the university was more subtle and revolutionary. *The involvement of university disciplines in immediate and practical problems in the field and natural settings; the necessity to act, to influence, to change, and to improvise; and the opportunity to experience the fit between theory and practice radically changed these disciplines' substantive scope, basic theorizing, and long-term directions.*[6] It is unfortunate

[6] Garner (1972) has recently written a short but illuminating paper describing how the substance of basic research and theorizing in experimental psychology was changed by its contact with "real" problems, and some of the examples he gives took place in World War II. He could have given many more examples from his own war experiences. His concluding remarks are worth quoting: "I think that by now my message is clear. We have all, to a greater or lesser extent, accepted the premise that basic research should at least ultimately help solve real problems which exist in the society which supports the research. My point, however, is that the quality of the basic research is improved by communication between the basic research scientist and the people who have problems to solve. Thus for scientists to engage in goal-oriented research, research aimed at solving problems already known to exist, is both to perform a service to society and to improve the quality of the basic research itself.

"I am not arguing that these real-life problems should be attacked as emergencies, since such research frequently leads to very specific information, of little use in solving later problems. The doing of good basic research requires a reasonably long time perspective, and this requirement should not be forgotten as the scientist undertakes to talk to people with real problems, and just as important, if those people will talk to those of us who are scientists, then both those who acquire knowledge and those who apply it will benefit. The relation is truly symbiotic.

"One last brief comment concerns the role of serendipity in basic research. I have often heard, as argument for pure research done by scientists

that it took a war to produce the conditions that would be so productive of new knowledge.

"Modern" Clinical Psychology

Before World War II clinical psychology was not part of academic psychology. It became a sizeable part after World War II, in direct response to the experiences of the war years. For one thing it was glaringly obvious that there was a desperate shortage of psychological diagnosticians and therapists, and the shortage would become even more pronounced after the war in regard to millions of returning veterans. But unconscionable shortages and a large supply of federal funds were not by themselves sufficient to introduce and sustain clinical psychology as a part of academic psychology. What was necessary was that the university be willing to meet this need of society and, just as important, that it perceive this new field as compatible with its traditions of research and scholarly contributions to knowledge. And these conditions existed. First, a number of academic psychologists had become involved in the war in some aspect of the clinical endeavor, exposing them not only to the extent of the need but also to new observations of human behavior as well as new problems in theory and practice. Second, it was inescapable to many that academic psychology, whose existence could only be justified by its illumination of human behavior, was surprisingly wanting in its relevance to understanding and changing nonlaboratory behavior. Psychology, as well as the psychologists who participated in the war, was forever changed in outlook and activity.

There were some, albeit a minority, who opposed the introduction of clinical psychology into the academic community.

---

isolated from the real world, that many great discoveries have occurred serendipitously. What rarely gets said, but is a logical implication of the argument, is that serendipity can only occur if the scientist somehow doesn't know where he's going. How absurd an argument that is! Serendipity can occur just as well with goal-directed research as with non-goal directed research, and in my personal experience has been even more apt to happen then. So the fact that we scientists sometimes learn something valuable that we weren't looking for is no argument against looking for something fairly definite in the meantime."

There were those, of course, who felt that the commitment of academic psychology to "basic" research would be diluted by its concern with "practical" problems—that in dealing with the problems of people and society, psychology would be engaging in some form of prostitution. Perhaps a better metaphor would be that the purity of psychology would be contaminated by contact with the impurities of everyday life. The academic ghetto had been a rather pleasant place, and opponents of this type knew well that if the ghetto walls broke down the quality of academic life would be altered. Dimly they knew that when institutions change, however willingly, one cannot always control the pace and direction of change. What they could not comprehend was that as a result of *their* enthusiastic willingness to commit American psychology to the war effort, they had helped start a revolutionary dynamic in their own field. But to have understood this would have meant that they had a psychological orientation relevant to institutional and social change, an orientation not characteristic of academic psychology before World War II.

There was another group of critics who, far from being opposed to a different relationship between the university and societal problems, warned against the narrow view that psychology was taking of these problems (Sarason, Levine, and others, 1966). Their argument consisted of several major points. First, it was unduly constricting of the potentialities of psychology in general and clinical psychology in particular to tie the new field to clinics and hospitals. These were not the only community settings in which human misery flourished. Second, by allying clinical psychology to psychiatry and the medical tradition, it restricted the populations that could be served and studied (populations that were primarily white, male, adult veterans), as well as the diagnostic and therapeutic techniques to which its students would be exposed. Third, the preventive or public health orientation essentially was being rejected, and in the long run this would prove to have been a major mistake. It is not surprising that these cautions were ignored. Those who were planning for the new field were still under the influence of their war experiences; the needs of the returning veterans were compelling and staggering; and there was a lot of federal money to help universities set up training programs.

The thrust of these cautions was amply confirmed over the next twenty-five years. This is not to say that these were unproductive years for clinical psychology, or that people were not helped, or that new problems and knowledge were not uncovered. These were far from sterile years. But they were also years of fast learning and disillusionment. The discrepancy between the number of those who needed help and those who could give it was obviously unsolvable by existing training programs, and the level of therapeutic knowledge and efficacy were not causes for enthusiasm. Personality theories and the clinical tactics derived from them dealt very inadequately with the different kinds of social contexts in which personal problems arose and were treated; the nature and severity of these problems as well as their amenability to therapy were very much determined by social factors and contexts of which the nuclear family was but one. "Mental illness" or "mental health" was not simply a peculiarity of an individual, but in ways not yet well-understood also reflected characteristics of American life. Within the clinic and the hospital the clinician became increasingly aware that outside forces were powerful obstacles to his therapeutic efforts.

This period of learning and disillusionment was taking place internally at the same time that the events and forces I described earlier in this chapter were changing American society. The interaction between the internal and external forces provided the soil from which community psychology emerged in the university. In a relatively short period of time clinical psychologists who had spent their working days in their offices dealing with the intricacies and mysteries of the *individual* personality, and social psychologists who had collected the attitudes of anonymous *individuals* toward myriads of issues, and child psychologists who had spent most of their time studying *individual* children and their parents began to look at and become involved in their communities in heretofore undreamed ways. It seemed as if adopting the label of community psychologist was a symbol of relevance, if not honor.

The purpose of my brief account of the recent social context out of which community psychology emerged has been to indicate that it was a *reaction* to what was happening in the larger society, that this reaction brought to the surface long-standing characteristics and conflicts within the university, and that the attempt to forge a new field in response to society's problems would encounter serious obstacles, obstacles stemming from the nature of the university, unfamiliarity with the world of action, and social science theorizing that was inappropriate for understanding either the university or society. I shall have more to say about these problems in subsequent chapters, but I wish to note here that my sketch suffers from at least one major limitation: in dealing only with recent times, and in viewing them from the standpoint of the American university, I may have given the impression that we are dealing with fairly modern social phenomena and problems. This is hardly the case, however much we like to believe otherwise. The relationship of science to society, of man to his work, of technology to family and social relationships, of science to the values which justify and guide our thinking and actions, of man to his regions and sense of community, of man to the state—these relationships have been in the center of thought and controversy for several hundreds of years. There were those who viewed the use of science and technology as the guarantors of human progress and liberation from ignorance and superstition, as the providers of a durable foundation for human happiness, as the destroyers of greed, poverty, and injustice. Science and technology would and should change society, and those who thought otherwise were regarded as worse than opponents of progress—they were enslavers seeking to keep man in chains. To all this the opponents replied that man was possessed of more than reason, that he needed more than knowledge and material things, and that science was a false god which could never provide man with a basis for finding satisfying human relationships and could never answer his questions about the meanings and purposes of human life. To overevaluate reason, to deemphasize man's need to belong and to feel continuous with past and future would have the disastrous consequence of increasing his sense of loneliness and casting him adrift in a sea of meaninglessness.

When life today is described by such adjectives as lonely, alienated, absurd, splintered, and anxious; when in our own times we witness wars and holocausts; when we look with awe and pride at explorations of outer space at the same time that we are gripped with the feeling that our society is coming apart at the seams; when the traditional religions continue to lose their power to attract and soothe at the same time that so many people, particularly the young, view science as irresponsible and insensitive; when we are witness to the cynicism and disillusionment experienced by those who had high hopes for a bold new world being created in other countries—when we look at all of this we are looking at some old problems and issues. What is modern about them is their particular shape and patterning, not their central content. When the Voltaires and the Diderots inveighed against religion there was much truth in what they said. But there was also much truth to the argument of equally brilliant divines and statesmen that science *qua* science could not solve human problems, and that between the findings of a value-free science and their application to the general welfare was the realm of values: the shoulds and the oughts that are inevitably in all of us. If the question of what to do with the fruits of science could not be satisfactorily answered by traditional religions, neither could it be answered by a science that prided itself on its neutrality and objectivity. The argument has changed somewhat in our day as critics, within and without science, see science as increasingly co-opted by the state for purposes that are counterproductive to the general welfare. The development and use of the atomic bomb destroyed two illusions: that science could be indifferent to how its discoveries would be used by society, and that it was a scientific issue to decide upon the process by which these discoveries could be used by society. If it destroyed these illusions it at least had the virtue of underlining the clarification of values as the first order of the day— not that clarification of values insures appropriate actions but simply that it is a process that cannot be bypassed.

Community psychology is "modern" in the sense that it developed as a reaction to contemporary events, but these events took place in a society whose intellectual, social, and economic foundations were built a long time ago, and embedded in those foundations were conflicts and controversies that have not been resolved. The label *community* psychology was not fortuitously chosen, although few people bothered to justify its use. Perhaps it was obvious to all that the label pinpointed the major problem as well as the overarching criterion by which it should be approached. That is to say, the major problem was how to prevent further social disintegration or deterioration in our communities—not in individuals, or in this or that famliy, or this or that social setting, or in one or another age or racial or ethnic group, but in terms of their actual or potential interrelatedness. The overarching criterion by which this was to be judged was the degree to which citizens could experience a psychological sense of community: the sense that one belongs in and is meaningfully a part of a larger collectivity; the sense that although there may be conflict between the needs of the individual and the collectivity, or among different groups in the collectivity, these conflicts must be resolved in a way that does not destroy the psychological sense of community; the sense that there is a network of and structure to relationships that strengthens rather than dilutes feelings of loneliness. If community psychology did not have these objectives, it had no way of justifying its birth; it would be old wine in new bottles. The contextual origins of community psychology required a label which would differentiate its subject matter from that of older fields. It also required an equally distinctive value or criterion by which to judge or guide its practices. Neither the problem nor the criterion was really new. But why was this important to know? For one thing it should prevent us from indulging the hope or fantasy that we can quickly alter ways of thinking and patterns of social and community living, an indulgence which time and again has ended in pervasive cynicism and indifference. If our society was not born yesterday, neither will it be reborn tomorrow. Far from being an excuse for inaction and passivity, a realistic time perspective is one of the most secure bases for personal integrity (if not sanity) for anyone engaging in community change. More substantively, a knowledge of this social history will disabuse us of our tendency to psychologize: to see the sweep of events primarily in terms of the characteristics of individuals or, worse yet, to apply these characteristic to groups, institutions, or nations. Rather we will be impressed with the "impersonal" factors like economics, geography, natural resources, architecture, health and disease, transportation, political organization, invention—an amalgam of factors that helps explain similarities and differences among communities, regions, and countries. In fact, one might seriously question the advisability of the label "community psychology" because its emphasis on psychology is likely to result in the neglect of nonpsychological concepts essential to comprehending the complexity of a community. Certainly the study of the human mind and behavior can illuminate aspects of the nature of a community, but it is equally true that what one learns about human behavior will in part be determined by how one conceptualizes the dimensions which explain the hows and whys of community organization and functioning. Finally, when we take the long view of our past we can deepen our understanding of the force of culture: the way it stimulates and accommodates to change at the same time that it keeps us tied to tradition; how it inevitably provides us with a definition of reality that excludes awareness or sensitivity to its relativity; how so much of culture is implicit or unverbalized and why relatively few people are able to discern and state its contents; and how culture can be such an organizing and conserving force that it blinds us to forces in the present that are shaping a future full of evil foreboding. When one truly comes to grips with the nature of culture (its mixed blessings and dialectical consequences)—exemplified in Nisbet's *The Quest for Community* (1970), Lewis Mumford's *The Culture of Cities* (1966) or any of his other books, Charles Becker's *The Heavenly City of the Eighteenth Century Philosophers* (1932), and Peter Gay's two-volume *Study of The Enlightenment* (1966, 1969)—one's view of the present and one's attitude toward the future will not be subject to the criticisms of narrowness and superficiality. It is not that we have "lessons" to learn from this social history, but that we have kinship with it; it is not a guide to predicting or determining the future, but it may prevent us from reinventing various types of wheels. We are living and will continue to live that history, and if we know that, we have added to our knowledge of ourselves and our society.

Community psychology is a recent, miniscule, and uncertain field seeking a place in the university and the world of ideas. Precisely because it was a reaction to a society in turmoil, and a self-conscious challenge to certain professional and institutional traditions, its significances are broader than one might think at first glance, if only because it brought to the surface the problems and process of institutional change in our society. Although the next two chapters are restricted in time and scope, devoted as they are to aspects of American psychology in recent decades, they deal with issues that have a long history and a problematic future in our society.

III

Some Unfortunate Aspects of American Psychology

In this chapter we shall restrict our focus to one part of the university, psychology, and the way in which its traditions interacted with the swirl of events and forces that marked the sixties to give rise to the field of community psychology. In taking this tack we are raising a question that lies at the heart of the process of institutional change: what is the role of tradition and the existing pattern of practices in facilitating or retarding institutional change? Bringing clarity to an existing pattern of practices is not easy, but it is easier by far than clarifying a tradition, in which the implicit and the explicit, the stated value and the un-stated belief, are woven into a view of the past that is no less selective and imprisoning than its perception of the future, and which inevitably defines the boundaries between the permissible and the impermissible. It is precisely because community psychology arose in the context of societal conflicts and the clamor for institutional change that we must resist the temptation to focus immediately on those community settings toward which the new field directed its energies; if we were to do that, we might fail to recognize that *community psychology was faced, inside the university, with the same issues that it was pressuring other community settings to confront and resolve.* The "know thyself" approach is, I believe, a potent, if imperfect, corrective against personal and institutional egocentricism.[1] More than that, it can have important consequences for theory and practice, a point well demonstrated by Freud in his development of personality theory and therapeutic practice. Before we change the world, should we not examine our own response to change? Before we criticize other community settings for their inadequacies and resistance to change, should not our criticisms be tempered, at the very least, by our own understanding of the same characteristics in our own setting? Do we need two theories of action and institutional change: one for "us" and one for "them?" If not, we must begin by examining psychology in the university and discover how traditions and practices influenced the emergence of community psychology.

Attitudes Toward Action

As the sixties came to a close, pressure arose from students and faculty members for the university to engage in internal change

---

[1] Coser (1970, p. 247) has said this well in regard to the sociologist: "the sociologist would be untrue to his calling were he not to attempt to delineate, to the limits of his ability and with the highest possible degree of objectivity, the main role and position of the intellectual in his own time and society. It is indeed easier to study social roles and status positions ranked lower than one's own, which is one reason why sociologists have typically been drawn to the study of prostitutes and hoboes, mental patients and juvenile delinquents. To turn the spotlight upon roles and people whose ranks are more nearly equal to one's own is a much more complicated and demanding task, making more stringent demands on one's ability to remain detached and objective. To study congeries of roles that one plays oneself is, finally, the most exacting and difficult. Nevertheless, it cannot be avoided if the sociologist is to live up to the ancient injunction to 'know thyself,' "

and external action. Increased admission of minority group members, introduction of new curricula, greater participation of students in decision making, elimination of contracted relationships with agencies of the armed services, dilution if not elimination of the "publish or perish" criterion for faculty promotion, more hiring and greater support for faculty members with special skills and interests in community action, the explicit adoption by the university of the obligation to help alleviate the problems of the community which surrounded it—these pressures on the university were, as often as not, framed as demands. Someone remarked, with great satisfaction, that the university, far from being aloof from the real world, had become the eye of the social hurricane. He was wrong, of course. The eye of the hurricane is an area of calm. The university was in the hurricane, all right, but this hurricane seemed to have no oasis of calm at its center.

The pressures for change were not all of a piece, in the sense of challenging the same traditions to the same degree. The most serious challenge by far was to the idea that faculty members, at least some of them, should be actively engaged in some form of community repair and that some of them should even be permanently retrained if they had special skills relating to community action. This was a direct and two-pronged challenge to the tradition that a faculty member autonomously determines what he will study and how he will go about it. For a faculty member to bend his pursuits to respond to practical problems and pressing social issues, many felt, would be to kill the goose that laid the golden eggs—it would be to dilute the significance of basic theory and research, without which human knowledge and progress were not possible. Furthermore, to accept into the academic community individuals who were not committed to the pursuit and examination of ideas would be to place the same value on action as on research and scholarship, which would fly in the face of precisely the way in which the university had contributed to the improvement of life. Besides, the defenders of tradition said, engaging in social action was what academics did least well.

No university department exceeded psychology in the zeal with which it accepted these traditions. Since the turn of the century, when psychology seceded from departments of philosophy, it took pride in seeing itself as one of the basic sciences dedicated to the untrammeled study of the nature of man. And in line with the traditions of the natural sciences with which it identified, every self-respecting department had its own laboratories. And if a stranger wondered why so much of what went on in these laboratories did not involve the human animal, why so much of it centered on the Norway rat, two explanations were ready at hand.[2] First, psychology was basically a biological rather than a social science, and second, the basic principles of animal behavior could be discerned more clearly in lower animals. To study man in his natural settings was to confront a clutter that obscured "basic" processes. And let us not forget that in these early decades there was one other source of clutter for many psychologists, and that was consciousness and the human mind. (Far from being seen as a pariah, John Watson, the behaviorist, was viewed by much of American psychology as a prophet.)[3]

The fate of John Dewey in American psychology illustrates its parochial and super-scientific characteristics. It is recognized, of course, that in his early years Dewey made substantial contributions to the emerging discipline of psychology. (If only because of his

[2] Frank A. Beach's (1950) presidential address to the Division of Experimental Psychology of the American Psychological Association, entitled "The Snark was a Boojum," was a plea by a comparative psychologist that psychology's dependence on the Norway rat was a good way of learning about blind alleys. Developments in subsequent decades confirmed Beach's cautions. Whereas the rat and the (male) college student were the most frequently studied subjects, the college student is now indisputably in first place.

[3] One of the consequences of Watsonian behaviorism, indeed one of its intended effects, was to do away with concern for a study of values and purposes, so much the "stuff" of consciousness. How could you have a science of psychology if its subject matter dealt with non-observables? How could psychology ever be on a par with the older sciences if it did not define its subject matter and employ methodologies which were quintessentially objective and value-free? After all, psychology had long been smothered and retarded by its origins in philosophy, and the greatest care had to be exercised that in becoming a "true" science psychology got rid of philosophical ruminations about the nature and purposes of man. Psychology was psychology and philosophy was philosophy and let us not get them mixed up with each other! And if some people thought this was a strange way of viewing man, it reflected their lack of understanding of science and their imprisonment in the morass of philosophical speculation which had long characterized Western thinking, and adversely so.

critical and still relevant paper on the "reflex arc" type of explanation, Dewey's place in psychology is an assured one.) But in
historical accounts of American psychology Dewey is seen primarily
as an educator and philosopher. The label educator was afixed
because he was an articulate critic of educational practices, and
he created and developed his own school. From a superficial standpoint Dewey was seen as interested in societal reform, concerned
with practical affairs, willing to devote his time and energies to
organizing a new kind of school having novel relationships with
parents and the community, let alone a school with novel types of
teacher-child, teacher-teacher, teacher-principal, teacher-parent,
teacher-community relationships (Mayhew and Edwards, 1966;
Sarason, 1971). To call Dewey an outstanding educator is praise
enough, but not when it obscures the fact that creating the school
was a bold way by which he tested his basic conceptions about
human intelligence, curiosity, the nature of learning, social context
and atmosphere, and the manner in which school-community relationships can instill a sense of personal identity with present and
past social history. The intimate interrelatedness between the
individual and society was a Deweyan conception, no less than his
view of the mutual relationships between theory and practice.
(When Garner in 1972 pleads for a reexamination by psychology
of its accustomed pejorative distinction between the theoretical
and the practical, the basic and applied, he is in the tradition of
Dewey.) Part of the reason that Dewey was, so to speak, "read out
of" American psychology can be inferred from the following statement by Lynd (1939) in his incisive book, *Knowledge for What?*
The Place of Social Science in American Culture:

> Social science, as a part of culture, is carried in the
> habits of social scientists. Human beings seem to exhibit con-
> siderable resistance to making multiple radical changes at the
> same time. While subjecting themselves to the strain and risk
> of novelty in a given direction, they tend to hold everything
> else as fixed as possible. The status of the professional econo-
> mist, political scientist, or other social scientist is deeply
> committed, by training and by the need for security and ad-
> vancement, to the official concepts, problems, and theoretical
> structure of his science. Quantification and refined measure-

ment carry heavy prestige, in part related to the reliance upon them by the authoritative natural sciences. When, therefore, these human beings who are social scientists were confronted simultaneously by the invitations both to experiment in the manifestly safe enterprise of quantifying their familiar problems and to engage in the more hazardous venture of faring forth into unfamiliar problem areas, it is not surprising that they so predominantly elected the first of the two options. Admirable advances in quantitative techniques have resulted, but at a cost too little reckoned. In the case of social psychology, for instance, the ensuing situation has been penetratingly appraised by a leading social psychologist (Gardner Murphy) as follows: "undoubtedly a large part of our trouble has been an over-rapid development of research techniques which can be applied to the surface aspects of almost any social response and are reasonably sure to give a publishable numerical answer to almost any casual question. . . . Woe to that science whose methods are developed in advance of its problems, so that the experimenter can see only those phases of a problem for which a method is already at hand" [pp. 17–18].

Dewey was, of course, a philosopher, and proudly so, but one has only to sample the corpus of his later work to recognize how much of it is directly relevant to present-day psychology's problems as a *social* science—the nature of inquiry, the means and end of action, and the processes of social change. Dewey created his school at the University of Chicago in 1896, a time when psychology was winning its independence from philosophy and advancing into the laboratory to study the elements of human behavior, or that of some other animal, with the methodological trappings of science. The bold, freewheeling scientific spirit became a sacrifice to the worship of false gods. It is no wonder that for decades Dewey was viewed as an erstwhile psychologist who became an educator and philosopher.

A close friend and colleague of Dewey at the University of Chicago was George Herbert Mead, a social psychologist, who developed a theory about how the sense of self arises out of an interpersonal context (Strauss, 1959). Mead's influence has been much greater in sociology and psychiatry (via Harry Stack Sullivan) than in psychology, probably as much because his theories seemed speculative and nonquantitatively oriented as because he emphasized the phenomenological, which psychology was beginning to eschew. (The apex of the rejection of the "subjective" is revealed most clearly in the pronouncements of John Watson.) Today it is Skinner who wages the battle against anything resembling phenomenology. The battle is far from over.

To a lesser extent William James suffered a fate similar to that of Dewey, as his interests and activities took him from the psychological laboratory to such areas as pragmatism and religious phenomena. From the standpoint of academic psychology he too "became" a philosopher. What did pragmatism and religious phenomena have to do with psychological science? In his account of the Chicago school of sociology, R. E. L. Faris (1967) notes that the thinking in Dewey's paper "The Reflex Arc Concept in Psychology" influenced Mead's description of the emergence of the sense of self, and then goes on to point out the cybernetic character of Dewey's explanation. As Faris puts it:

> The cybernetic functioning of consciousness, as outlined by Dewey and employed by Mead, makes possible the substitution of a trial-and-error process in imagination for an overt trial-and-error process, with its costly requirements of time and energy in its possible penalties for error. One commences a gesture in a tentative, inhibited way, responds to it presumably as another would respond, and redirects the unfolding action according to the judgment of the imagined consequences, thereby gaining in efficiency. The same sort of response gives meaning to language. 'You ask somebody to bring a visitor a chair. You arouse the tendency to get the chair in the other, but if he is slow to act you get the chair yourself. The response to the vocal gesture is the doing of a certain thing, and you arouse that same tendency in yourself. You are always replying to yourself, just as other people reply [p. 97].

This kind of 'mentalism' did not sit well with the new science of psychology. James, Dewey (influenced by James), and Mead (a student of James) had a number of things in common, one of which was their lack of sustained influence on academic psychology. Today James and Dewey are "returning" to psychology because of developments in cognitive psychology, existentialism, and the increasing involvement of academic psychologists in school learning.

The depth of pride with which academic psychology viewed its commitment to basic theory and research was matched only by the strength of its derogation of any form of applied psychology. But even here there were exceptions that illuminated aspects of the dominant tradition. For example, before World War II clinical psychology was hardly represented in academic psychology, and in most universities it was represented not at all. It is fair to say that academic psychology was anticlinical rather than aclinical; it was more than content to let psychiatry deal with problems of human distress. It was assumed, of course, that the basic problems with which academic psychology was dealing would someday provide a truly sound scientific foundation for therapeutic applications, but the dominant tradition ruled out the study of the therapeutic process as either desirable or fruitful. Engaging in the therapeutic process simply did not fit in with psychology's conception of acceptable methodology. This previous view of aceeptable methodology explains in part why the applications of academic psychology to certain problems in education and industry were less frowned upon—the problems there were readily adaptable to the requirements of statistical analysis and "objective data." Standardizing intelligence and achievement tests, objectifying personnel selection techniques, and filming and measuring job performance were not "science," but at least, it was argued, they reflected the proper concern for methodological rigor.

Nevertheless, there were two classes of citizens: those who were in the scientific heaven because of their commitment to science for science's sake, and the "fallen" or less gifted or inappropriately inspired psychologists who tried to solve practical problems. This quasi-religious division of psychologists into the "saved" and the "fallen" is nowhere stated in the traditions of academic psychology, if only because of the tendency to state tradition, particularly scientific tradition, as the unfolding of logical and rational thinking unaffected by the human capacity to be prejudicial. This represents a kind of thinking which insures that a good part of tradition is mythology. (It is also the kind of thinking that permitted the university during this period to revere in public its tradition of being open to all, on the sole basis of excellence of performance or potential, regardless of religion, ethnic origin, race, and sex.)[4]

Pre-World War II academic psychology had no tradition that would have permitted or encouraged action in the everyday social world as a method for increased understanding of man and society. It goes without saying that action for the purpose of social or institutional reform, or even to help individuals with personal problems, was a transgression of the university's values and functions. What needs to be emphasized, because the stated academic tradition has tended to obscure it, is that action in the "real world" for the purpose of understanding better the nature of man and sociey was viewed as an aberration. Why this was (and remains) so will become clearer later in this chapter when we take up another fragment of academic psychology's mythology.

In this connection the relation of academic psychology to psychoanalysis, as theory and therapy, is interesting. Academic psychology never really came to grips with psychoanalysis until the late 1930s, and even then relatively few psychologists were involved. The Yale Institute of Human Relations and the Harvard groups

[4] A colleague of mine, a minority group member, showed me a two-page letter he received in 1939 upon being admitted to graduate work in a prestigious, private university. The letter was from the chairman of the department, and he was a most eminent individual. The thrust of the letter was quite clear: do not come here with any expectation of getting a job in a university after receiving your doctorate. We have had outstanding members (names given) of your religion but we have been unable to place them in academic positions (they were "placed" after World War II). If you view coming here as an intellectual adventure, and no more than that, come join us. The letter mirrored reality, but that is not the point—the letter was not newsworthy then. The point is that stated traditions are no more than that, and they never should be confused with the whole tradition and belief system. And the parts that do not get incorporated into the rhetoric probably explain more, or as much, about a setting as the parts that do. The letter also nicely illustrates the thesis that there is not a community problem, in the generic sense, that cannot be found in the university.

My words may sound as if I take an unusually dim view of the academic tradition, particularly in psychology. If such an interpretation is made it is not because I intend it. What I intend is to give a realistic picture of the stated and unstated tradition, if only because honesty should begin at home. What is splendid in the academic tradition needs no defense by me.

under Henry Murray's leadership (for example, Murray, 1938) were the two most important university centers with a major interest in psychoanalysis, and even there the emphasis was on psycho-analytic theory and not on therapy. It is not surprising, therefore, that neither center made a contribution to the clinical aspects of psychoanalysis. The distance that academic psychology was from psychoanalytic theory and therapy can be gauged by the fact that the *Journal of Abnormal and Social Psychology* provided space to several psychologists who had been analyzed so that they could tell their brethren how it felt.[5]

World War II, as I indicated in the previous chapter, changed much in American academic psychology, not the least of which was its attitude toward its relationship to society and its problems. But the degree of change can be overestimated, and in the flush of the war and its aftermath it was. I am not maintaining that there was no change, but rather that the degree of change on tradition was vastly overestimated. I stress this point because I am aware of no reason, stemming from theory or historical account, that would justify the expectation that deep and long-standing institutional traditions can undergo fundamental change quickly. This is a lesson that many social scientists have learned in recent years as they have tried to change different community settings. In the case of psychologist it was a lesson they could have learned from the history of their own field. Clinical psychology is a case in point.

The introduction of clinical psychology into academic psychology was indisputably an effort to respond to certain needs in society. But in academic psychology at that time there was never any question that the primary aim of the new graduate programs was to train research psychologists. In fact, few people disagreed with the often-heard statement that "first we train psychologists and *then* clinical psychologists." In practice this meant that the first two years of graduate education were not too different from what they were in the prewar years. In the modal program there was a two-year sequence in statistics, research design, and experi-

---

[5] These accounts were published as "Symposium: Psychoanalysis As Seen By Analyzed Psychologists" in the *Journal of Abnormal and Social Psychology,* 1940 (January and April issues).

mental psychology, at least one intensive course in physiological psychology, and one or two courses in learning (long considered in American psychology to contain the "core" issues of human behavior and development). There was a heavy dose of personality theory, and, of course, a theoretically oriented seminar in abnormal psychology. And at the end of the first two years, the student could count on a series of comprehensive examinations to test his knowledge of the "basic" fields in psychology.

The thrust of these two years was explicitly positive in one respect and implicitly negative in another. The positive aspect was to give the student a healthy respect for psychology as a basic science. The negative aspect was that this indoctrination had to precede the student's exposure to patients in clinics and hospitals; otherwise, it was felt, the academic innoculation might not "take" or, worse yet, the student might be seduced by the fascination of all that was involved in the practical task of helping others. The student saw patients only infrequently, and was almost never given any meaningful degree of clinical responsibility. Clinical activity was a kind of rich, non-nutritious dessert which could be digested only if the main course had been a really healthy one. Put in terms of a metaphor we shall employ later, making contact with or taking action in the real world exposed one to the risk of contamination— the everyday world was full of disease and the longer one stayed away from it the better.

The third year was for the internship, which was in a clinic or hospital staffed by psychiatrists, clinical psychologists, and psychiatric social workers. The primary responsibility for supervising the intern was given to the clinical psychologist, who rarely had an appointment in the academic department; he was a *practicing* psychologist, after all, and therefore lacked the appropriate values or credentials for appointment. The clinical faculty from the university saw the intern from time to time, but their visits, whatever other functions they may have served, were not supervisory in a clinical sense. In the course of this year the intern learned several things that would be crucial to his developing sense of professional identity. First, his two years at the university had ill-prepared him for the realities of the clinic and hospital. Second, just as in the university he had come to feel himself a second-class citizen because he was not studying in a "basic" area, in the clinic and hospital he found his status quite secondary to that of the psychiatrist. (This should have occasioned no surprise because it was clear that these facilities were not developed and maintained for the training of psychological personnel.) Third, there seemed to be an immense gulf between the research methodologies he had learned in the university and the substantive problems that he encountered daily. Fourth, there were two role models of the clinical psychologist with which he could identify, and these were not only different but frequently in conflict: the research-oriented, non-clinically involved faculty member, and the practicing clinical psychologist—the former viewing himself as more basic and therefore superior and more important, and the latter viewing himself as more relevant and practical.

The final hurdle for the doctorate is the dissertation, and it was the rare student who was able or permitted to attack a clinical problem, that is, a problem arising directly from the clinical endeavor, the study of which would bear directly on its nature and on the efficacy of solutions for it. For example, there were few dissertations on psychotherapy because of the student's sparse exposure to this relationship. The fact is that most dissertations were done (not always with humans) on problems that conformed to "acceptable" criteria of research. This is not to say that the problems were not important, or that they had no relevance for the clinical endeavor, but rather that the choice of problem was very much determined by the answer to the practical question of what would be an acceptable thesis problem to the academic department.

This brief account of the early years of modern clinical psychology illuminates the ways in which institutional traditions roll with punch, so to speak. The isolation of problems in the laboratory, a particular view of what constituted scientific respectability, the worship of methodological rigor almost as an end in itself, pride in the freedom to be irrelevant to the needs of society, a view of action (in regard to societal dynamics) as antithetical to objectivity and the attainment of true knowledge—this belief system, rarely made explicit, was a part of the traditions of academic psychology which insured that clinical psychology would in some ways be transformed to be compatible to these beliefs. It would have been amazing, if not unique, if it had happened otherwise. There had been too much overlearning. And, let us not forget, each aspect of the belief system could be buttressed by *some* specific historical account or example. What had happened, however, was the result of the familiar tendency to confuse what is sometimes true with what is always true, what has sometimes happened with what will always happen, and what has sometimes worked with what will always work. In its strenuous effort to be scientific, academic psychology had become religious. It possessed the "truth" and like the good zealot it sought to make sure that its adherents were protected from evil.[6] We must therefore seek to determine the characteristics of the evil that psychology feared, and where they came from.

The Myth of Contamination by Society

When one cuts through the rhetoric of tradition and disentangles the different strands of the belief system, one comes to a surprising conclusion. The world is divided into two parts. One part is the university, populated by impartial truth-seekers possessed of a unique social organization and a set of traditions which insulate them from all external sources of distraction and prejudice, and thereby permit them to see clearly and deeply into the nature of man and society. The other part is the rest of society, populated by myriads of types of people, organized and disorganized, passionate and materialistic, superficial and self-serving—a kind of diseased social organism that contaminates all who come in contact with it, a part of the world to be dealt with only out of sheer necessity, a territory to be scouted but not confronted. This is not unlike the romantic contrast between the peaceful little village and the teeming, corrupting big city ruled by the bitch goddess Success.

Myth is almost always a mixture of fantasy and truth, and I would not argue strongly against the position that the myth I have described has more than a single kind of truth to it. The

---

[6] Becker (1932) gives numerous examples from the past several centuries of how, in the process of fighting superstition, religion, and enslaving institutions, the militants of human reason (whatever the brand) end up with a version of heaven that bears some genotypical resemblance to the heaven of their opponents.

degree of truth is not at issue. The importance of the myth is that it has been part of the ideology of academic psychology and has served as an effective obstacle not only to action in society but also to the development of productive theorizing and research about man in his natural settings. It is a myth which helps explain why American social psychology is characteristically laboratory oriented, ingeniously experimental, and pathetically in search of social relevance. It also clarifies why so much of psychological theory is about the *individual* organism. I am in no way being facetious when I say that the course of American psychology would have been quite different if instead of studying one rat in a maze, there had been put two, or three, or four rats in the maze. Life for the theoretician and researcher would have been far more complicated, but at least they could not be accused of studying misleading issues.

To avoid any misunderstanding of my position, I will state what I am *not* suggesting or advocating. I do not maintain that action for the purpose of institutional or community change is inherently virtuous, or that the university has a primary responsibility to solve or ameliorate community problems, or that because an individual is particularly skilled in community intervention or organization he should therefore be a permanent member of the academic community.[7] I have instead attempted to make four assertions. First, those parts of academic psychology that purport to study man in society—which requires more than an understanding of individuals or of the characteristics of interpersonal phenomena—must be open to any methodology, or any form of intervention, or any relationship to the community that gives promise of contributing to knowledge. Second, to the extent that the preferred mode of attack is to simulate the "real world," to simplify problems in conformity with the requirements of the laboratory, there is the likelihood that what happens in the laboratory will unreflectively be equated with what occurs in natural settings. And the likelihood increases as the preferred mode of attack becomes the only mode of attack, that is, as laboratory findings remain only laboratory findings, and as the social origins of problems become lost or forgotten as fewer and fewer of their aspects are subjected to more and more

---

[7] The issues surrounding this point are taken up in Chapter Ten.

refinements. Third, there are countless ways in which an academic psychologist can be involved in community problems and settings for the purposes of learning how and why things work as they do, or discovering the responses to interventions and the processes of change, and it does not follow that these forms of action are inevitably corrupting or unproductive of new and important knowledge which can alter theory. Fourth, there has long been in the traditions of academic psychology an unreasoned view of action in society, a view that not only has resulted in a misperception of the historical relationships between basic theory and practical problems but also has drastically reduced the range of roles a psychologist can experience in his quest for understanding man in society. It says a good deal of academic psychology's belief system that in 1972, Wendell Garner had to point out that some of its cherished beliefs were on historically shaky grounds, and that far from fearing involvement with practical problems the basic scientist should welcome the opportunity, not in order to experience the passive delights of seduction but to satisfy his actual intellectual curiosity and the scientist's active need to be open to new experience and ideas. But this requires unlearning the fear of contamination from contact with society.

To some of the academic community, the financial crisis today in higher education will be regarded as a blessing in disguise because it may signal the end of the research entrepreneur who spends a good deal of time securing and administering funds for his research institutes or centers, traveling around promoting his work, offering consulting services to less enterprising academic and private settings—someone, as one wag put, bucking to become the Trans World Airlines Professor of Psychology. And if the financial squeeze means that a lot of "do-good" programs also go by the board, allowing the university to concentrate on its own business in the manner of the good old days, then so much the better. ("Do-good" programs almost always refer to activities involving problems and settings outside the university, pejoratively labeled as practical, applied, unimportant, or unproductive of any contribution to knowledge.)

Some who cherish the university as a retreat from the world use the argument that the good scholar and researcher is ill-

equipped to engage seriously in practical affairs, even if such
engagement is "scientifically" motivated. Neither by training nor
by temperament, the argument goes, is he able to cope with the
real world or to resist its intellectually and ethically debilitating
forces. It is not only that society is diseased but also that the
academic person is a frail, ignorant, country boy who will inevitably
be "taken."[8] As often as not, those who hold this view are the ones
who criticize colleagues who, despite a lack of entrepreneurial training, have managed to build booming research businesses on campus.
For some it is extraordinarily hard, and for others impossible, to see
the kinship between the university and the surrounding community.

The Uncertain Future of Community Psychology

Community psychology is too new a field for us to speak
of its future with a sense of assurance. The social forces which
sparked its emergence, the turmoil they caused in the university,
and the willing response to them by certain segments of the faculty
are bound to have some effect on the traditions of academic psychology. Nevertheless, it would not be pessimistic to warn against
underestimating the strength of these traditions, nor reactionary
to suggest that quick and dramatic change can be a mixed blessing.
To equate change with progress has long been a major source of
disillusionment.

The future of community psychology, like the past of the
university, will largely be determined by forces in the larger society.
At the very time this book is being written, a major economic
downturn is having serious repercussions in every center of higher
learning. It is apparent that without a massive influx of federal
funds the scope of university functions, dramatically increased in
previous decades by federal prodding and federal funds, will be
drastically curtailed.[9] In the face of this crisis it would be foolish

---

[8] The reverse argument is not infrequent, for the university is sometimes viewed by those within it as antithetical to the well-being of certain
groups—such as women, for example. What would happen to these poor,
frail, naive women when they got caught up in the not-always polite mascu-
linity of the university? For *their* sake we should keep them out!

[9] To most people today it is self-evident that the university *should*
receive a good deal of support from the federal government. They are un-

to expect that newer fields like community psychology would not be more adversely affected than older fields more congruent with long-standing traditions. If anything good comes of the current crisis, it is likely to be an awareness that the university's relationship with society, always intimate, has become blatant and problematic.

In writing a book about a field or discipline, one ordinarily first defines its characteristics and scope, then discusses its history, and relegates to a concluding chapter any attempts to read the future. This sequence did not seem desirable in this instance because of one overriding consideration: The most important theoretical and practical issues which confront the psychologist as he ventures forth into community settings are contained in his own field and academic setting. Whatever the depth of understanding he seeks or the scope of the intervention he undertakes, he confronts in these community settings problems which reflect in varying degrees the dilemmas of change as they are determined by implicit and explicit traditions, existing practices, and the relation of the setting to the wider community. In his effort to produce and study change, he heightens the conflict between the old and new, between the security of tradition and the ambiguity of innovation, between the pull of the past and the push of the present. What will be fateful for how he views his efforts and is affected by them—the time perspective he adopts, the commitments he makes, the turmoil he expects—will

---

aware that this view, at its root a judgment about what is "good" for the general welfare, is relatively recent in our society, and that in unreflectively accepting this view as the natural order of things, they have bypassed a set of issues that goes back a long way. What should be the relationship between the state and its citizens? What are the dangers of centralized authority and what does it do to institutions which become dependent on it? And what does an increasingly powerful state do to the sense of community? In the case of the university it took a drastic cutback in governmental support for it to realize that in becoming a willing dependent it may have jeopardized its autonomy and character (Nisbet, 1971). I do not raise these questions to suggest that we turn the clock back, but rather to warn that in looking to the future we must not be forgetful that there are some enduring issues and dilemmas which should restrain us from an unreflective acceptance of what seems right and good. It is interesting how many people in academia are willing to give more and more responsibility to the federal government at the same time they bemoan and fight against the tendency for centralized authority in our universities to become more powerful and insensitive to its "community of scholars."

be how well he sees and understands the same problems in his own field and setting. If he does not have such a conception (which would be like having one theory for the helium atom and another for hydrogen), he robs himself of an important source of understanding and increases the chances that he will experience the consequences of setting unrealistic goals.

Community psychology did not, of course, represent an isolated reaction in the university. It was but a very small aspect of what was happening in all the so-called mental health fields. Indeed, the shape and direction of community psychology were very much determined by these fields, because clinical psychology, from which community psychology was an institutional outgrowth, had been one of the mental health fields. Therefore, to understand why community psychology went in one direction rather than another requires some discussion of the dominant mental health field: psychiatry.

IV

Social Psychiatry, Community Psychiatry, and Community Psychology

◻▭▭▭◻▭▭▭◻▭▭▭◻▭▭▭◻▭▭▭◻▭▭▭◻▭▭▭◻▭▭▭◻

Students (and veteran professionals as well) often ask questions about the differences between community psychology, community psychiatry, and social psychiatry. Are these separate fields, and with some or a lot of overlap between them? Do they derive from similar social forces and from the same period of time? Do they differ in their theoretical foundations and methodology? These are the questions that will occupy us in this chapter. The reader should note that by their form, these questions require descriptive answers. Up to a point, as we shall see, the descriptive type of answer is illuminating, in the same way that a scorecard listing teams, players, and positions can add to one's understanding of a baseball game. But scorecards, like descriptions, are not very helpful for answering questions such as why are they playing the game, or why are they playing it in the particular way they do, or why do so many people come out to watch (and pay for it). And in the unlikely event that the scorecard addressed itself to these questions, the spectator still would not be in the position to raise and answer the question, What is the relation, in our society, between baseball as a game and baseball as a business? And it is not until one asks *that* kind of question that one realizes that "understanding" is a many splendored thing.

Social Psychiatry

The term social psychiatry gained currency after World War II and it rather deliberately reflected a reaction against what Dr. Murray Levine (1969) so aptly called the doctrine of "intrapsychic supremacy," the belief in the primacy of looking into the individual's mind to ferret out the mechanisms, events, motivations, and familial relationships that can "explain" his problems and symptoms. One had only to sample published case presentations, beginning with those by Freud, to realize the extent of the psychiatrist's absorption with what went on "inside" the human mind; it was as if the nature and structure of the outside social world, the nuclear family aside, were of minor significance. And if there were some who were aware of the social world outside, it was not clear what difference, if any, it made in theory or clinical work. To the social psychiatrist the near-exclusive emphasis on the workings of the individual's mind stood in the way of understanding how social factors and mental disorders were interrelated. Traditional psychiatric theories of personality and its disorders were not only incomplete, but also, to the extent that they ignored social and cultural factors, misleading and stultifying.

Social psychiatry directly challenged the belief that psychiatry was in a basic sense a medical discipline. There was no denying that biological and constitutional factors played roles in psychopathological phenomena, or that biological forms of treatment were productive and promising, but there were also no grounds for denying that an individual bore the stamp of his society and culture. More than that, it appeared that the expression of biological and constitutional symptoms depended on social and cultural considerations, and if this was hypothesis rather than fact it was one of the aims of social psychiatry to study and test the hypothesis.

The social sciences, their conceptions and methodologies, provided the new underpinnings for social psychiatry. The influx of social scientists into medical schools in general and departments of psychiatry in particular was a consequence of the growth of social psychiatry, as was the dramatic increase in publications jointly authored by psychiatrists and social scientists. As would be expected, social psychiatry focused on such variables as social class, ethnicity, mobility, religious affiliation, cross-cultural factors, and family organization. More recently the emphasis has shifted somewhat to issues of race, poverty, international tensions, youth culture and counterculture, and alienation.

S. R. Kaplan (1970) has defined social psychiatry as relating "to the study of, and the theoretical formulations about, the social and environmental determinants of mental health and mental illness." This is a fair statement of the goals of social psychiatry, but not necessarily an accurate description of what it has become. Although the definition includes "mental health," the social psychiatric literature is overwhelmingly concerned with psychopathology, and where it does not involve psychopathological populations the technical jargon is much more psychiatric than it is social-science. This should not be surprising, if only because most people who would be included in the field of social psychiatry (be they psychiatrists, psychologists, sociologists, or anthropologists) are members of a psychiatric setting. It requires no special social-science knowledge to know that institutional affiliation is a potent restricter and definer of how one thinks and what one studies.

To a large extent, what social psychiatry has borrowed from the social sciences are methodologies and classic variables that account for the existence of meaningful social groupings. But there seems to be little recognition that the overarching goal of the social sciences has been to conceptualize the relationships between man and society, and that this requires coming to grips with the nature of society: its structure (political and economic), diversity, dynamics, history, conflicts, and ideology. To understand and conceptualize society (or an aspect of it, such as a single community) requires more than a knowledge of concepts, such as those of social class, mobility, role, and status. Psychiatry never ceases to tell us how fantastically complicated the human personality is, and how devilishly difficult it is just to approximate an understanding of it. And when we look at the different schools of theoretical psychiatry, each of them claiming to possess a different version of the true understanding, we can only conclude that the task is both difficult and confusing.

I say this not in the spirit of criticism but as a way of pointing out that what light has been shed on the nature of the human personality has come from those relatively few people (Freud, Jung, Sullivan, Horner, Fromm, and Erikson, for example) who had "the psychiatric imagination"—the ability to think broadly, independently, and systematically. They were sensitive to details, but they did not start with details or get lost in them. They thought big because the problem as they saw it was big. The same, as Mills (1959) pointed out, has been true in the social sciences. Thinkers like Marx, Weber, and Veblen are among the few who looked at society broadly and analytically, and who provided us with potent new ways of understanding the nature of society and its differential effects on people. For these men "society" and "social" were not empty words or concepts; they referred to real institutions and forces, rooted in tradition and ideology, that are always changing and always influencing all major forms of human endeavor. And when they raised issues pertaining to human values and the quality of life, it was not because they were projecting them onto society but because the issues were both causes and consequences of society itself, because they were among the most important features of social reality, supplying much of its dynamism.

By defining its goal as the understanding of the social and environmental determinants of mental illness and mental health, social psychiatry has boldly arrogated to itself nothing less than the study of society. It is not unfair, I think, to say "arrogated" because neither by its traditions, theories, or practices is psychiatry schooled to deal with such a problem; yet I sympathize with this intellectual imperialism because I agree with Mills (1959) and Gouldner (1970) that much of American social science has managed to submerge the important societal questions in a sea of methodology. This is not to say that American social science has not contributed to our understanding of society; in later pages I shall attempt to demonstrate the absurdity of such a judgment. Suffice it to say here that those who have added to our understanding of our society have been (or are) in the tradition of what Mills called the sociological imagination. Many of them are not referred to in the social psychiatric literature, and when they are, one wonders whether it reflects a serious understanding or is simply a token gesture. For example, it is apparently fashionable to refer to the Lynds' studies of Middletown (1929, 1937), but I have yet to come across a reference to, let alone discussion of, Robert Lynd's *Knowledge for What?*, which offers reflections on American society and social science that are as passionate and yet as sober as one will find anywhere.[1]

Any field purporting to understand society must seek out and discover the nature of its own relationship to that society. After all, it is a part of that society, a reflection of it, and it interacts with it in ways that are mutually compatible. Ideologically and economically, society does not support fields that do not serve its purposes—an obvious enough fact of social life, but one that has serious implications when the purpose of the field is to understand the society itself. It says something positive about our society and our universities that this self-conscious questioning has not been

[1] This book was published before World War II and was in part a response to the significance of the Great Depression for social science. Its clarity and conceptual quality have not been matched or equaled by anyone responding to the events of the sixties. Lynd understood well that how social science related itself to society, and with what effects, would depend on its capacity to deal forthrightly with the problem of values. The very title of the book indicates that Lynd did not entertain the fantasy that knowledge could be neutral, in either its collection or its application. If Lynd did not give pat answers to certain questions or dilemmas, it was probably because he understood that the questions he was raising did not have single or simple answers. That is to say, values may be enduring, but how one implements them will vary depending on the times and events.

absent. There have always been a few with the insight and courage
to confront the implications of the issues involved. Psychiatry is not
unaware of the issues in regard to its own field, because one of
Freud's major contributions was to demonstrate two interrelated
facts: the helper and the helped are more alike than they are
different, and the process of helping can have unfortunate consequences for the helper. When Freud recommended that analysts be
reanalyzed every five years, it was not to insure that analysts would
always have patients, but to attack the self-corrupting tendencies
inherent in the helping process. To know thyself, he maintained,
was an easy victim of helping others. The principle is no less cogent
when the relationship is between a social science and the society it
aims to understand (or change).

Psychiatry has shown little tendency to examine its relationship to its society. It is only in the recent past that recognition was
given to the inequitable social class distribution of psychiatric
services, the scandalous state of public mental hospitals, the inability of the field to train discernibly more practitioners, the concentration of its members in a few large urban areas, and the social
class- and sex-bias of its theories, therapeutic practices, and goals.
Such recognition reflects the influence of social psychiatry on the
rest of psychiatry, and it is not a small accomplishment. But this
recognition has not led to a searching analysis of what all this
reveals about the traditions and history of psychiatry, its assumptions about the nature of man and society, the economic and institutional foundations of the field, the significance and consequence of
its being a part of American medicine, the ways in which the field
is related to certain aspects of the law, the factors that make for
high or low status in the field, how religious and ethnic factors
played a role in entrance to the field, and the struggle by psychiatry
to become a respected medical specialty. American psychiatry is
not Russian or French psychiatry, which is another way of saying
that American psychiatry bears the stamp of a distinctive society.
But social psychiatry is neither self-consciously analytical or comparative. It has been quick to pass judgment on society and how it
must change. If it has not been silent about its own house, neither
has it been profound. A wag once said of another person, deep
down he is shallow. The same might be said of social psychiatry.

Psychiatry's (and social psychiatry's) response to criticism and self-examination can be illustrated by the way it has responded to its most articulate critic, Thomas Szasz (1961, 1963, 1970). That he is a psychiatrist and a psychoanalyst—not a lay person whose criticisms could be attributed to ignorance—might lead one to expect that his criticisms would be dealt with forthrightly rather than ignored or dismissed. The discrepancy between the depth of antipathy which most psychiatrists privately express toward Szasz and the superficial attention they accord to him in their writings is marked indeed. It reminds one of psychiatry's response to Freud.

Szasz's criticisms are many, but in one or another way they deal with psychiatry's ideology, its relationship to medicine, its function in society, its place in the law, its political character, and the historical parallels between the functions of the psychiatrist and the priest. By any criterion he would have to be regarded as a social psychiatrist, though one who is primarily concerned with the relationship between psychiatry and society. And the range and depth of his scholarship are quite impressive; one cannot read his *Manufacture of Madness* without respecting his scholarship. Oversimplified, here are some of Szasz's major points:[2]

(1) The usual criteria by which medicine defines an illness (for example, cancer, tuberculosis, influenza) do not apply to the phenomena which psychiatry calls mental illness. Mental illness is a myth which has the function of obscuring the social character of disordered thinking and living.

(2) By propagating the myth that mental illness is like other forms of medical illnesses the psychiatrist acquires respect and other forms of reward that are a consequence of the medical role. That is to say, psychiatry has a vested interest in maintaining the myth of mental illness, even though many psychiatrists privately know better. Like the medieval guild or the priesthood, it views its knowledge and practices as unique, requiring long and arduous preparation every aspect of which is essential if it is to help those

---

[2] It is not my intention here to defend Szasz's positions, although I do agree with most of them. My intention is to emphasize that the psychiatric establishment's ignoring of him, except insofar as they argue that he is a contentious crackpot, cannot be attributed to his lack of clarity or of scholarship or of clinical acumen.

who seek its services. Those who lack this preparation but attempt to render similar services are viewed at best as irresponsible and at worst as charlatans, and so to protect *society* (not psychiatry) the legal foundations of and sanctions for the medical profession are called into play.

(3) Psychiatry has colluded with society's definition of behavioral deviancy and with society's prepotent tendency to segregate and isolate those so defined. In its role of willing instrument it has accepted conformity to society as an important value, and it has been agent by which scores of thousands of people have been institutionalized and deprived of their civil liberties. This was done, and is being done, despite the knowledge (exposed every few years in the mass media by "lay" people) that these institutions are dehumanizing. Psychiatry "manufactures madness" in at least three ways: by its conceptualization of "mental illness," by its relationship to the law, and by consigning people to the fate of institutional living.

(4) Psychiatry's theories and practices are value laden in ways that render it difficult for those it serves to be responsible for their own lives. Respect for the rights of the individual is a primary value that is increasingly ignored by psychiatry in particular and government in general. Szasz views the Small Brother or Big Brother role as inimical to the preservation of individual liberties. Just as Joan of Arc was burned to save *her* soul, so do the Big Brothers of modern society seem to be playing the same role and with a similar type of religious justification. That psychiatry has points of contact with the legal, political, and economic systems is not remarkable. That it has failed to scrutinize the nature, functions, and consequences of these contacts has made it an anti-libertarian force in society.[3] (Although Szasz takes the most direct

---

[3] A good example of what bothers Szasz is what happened during the 1964 presidential campaign when many psychiatrists went on record to state that Senator Goldwater was personally and mentally inadequate to be president. This revealed not only how many psychiatrists saw their role in protecting society against mental or temperamental disorders, but also an amazing and frightening confusion between personality and political theory. In more recent years we have witnessed similar but more blatant examples in the Soviet Union, where political dissidents are judged mentally incompetent and placed in psychiatric hospitals.

aim at psychiatry, he intends his criticisms to apply to all of the mental health professions.)

To expect that psychiatry would welcome these kinds of broadsides is as naive as if Freud had expected that the psychiatric fraternity of his day would welcome his discoveries and criticisms with delight, respect, and rapt attention. Freud struck at the roots of psychiatry's conception of man and its therapeutic ways of dealing with him. Szasz strikes at psychiatry's definition of its subject matter and its consequences for its role in society. Although this may explain psychiatry's affective reaction to his critique, it does not explain or justify the superficial intellectual response to him, when there has been a response at all. This is all the more strange in the case of social psychiatry, because it is in the social sciences that Szasz has engendered the most sympathetically critical response.

One can question whether social psychiatry is a distinctive discipline. Certainly its subject matter is not new. Long before the label became fashionable the substantive problems of social psychiatry were of research and theoretical significance among social scientists. And within psychiatry there have always been a few who attempted to put its theories and findings into a larger societal context. Adler, Reich, Roheim, Sullivan, Fromm, Erikson, Horney, and Kardiner, are a few who attempted either to expand the social-science base of psychiatry or to apply its findings and theories to societal problems. (In the next chapter I shall discuss in some detail a pioneer social psychiatrist who has yet to be rediscovered by social psychiatry, namely Dr. James Plant.) And let us not forget that Freud was mightily interested in anthropology, and that some of his most provocative theorizing was a response to the nature and consequences of World War I. According to Theodor Reik (Freeman, 1971) Freud was quite aware that as soon as psychoanalysis went beyond certain narrow limits in the attempt to see how the data of other fields would enrich understanding it was leaving its sphere of competence:

> Freud himself knew, of course, about the Horney group, who emphasize the sociological point of view. And Freud always said when he was talking about them: "I do not doubt that they are excellent sociologists. But the task of

psychoanalysis is a very restricted and modest one. Analysis has to deal with the unconscious—not only with the unconscious-repressed but with the unconscious in general—and its connection with the conscious thinking and conscious feelings. That is the narrow field of psychoanalysis." And about these sociologists he said: "It would be unfair to expect that we who are only psychologists should also deal with the sociological, economic, and other aspects of life, which no doubt have a great influence." He said we have to leave that to others. And he used another of his comparisons: "It would be as unfair as if in a concert orchestra, you expect that the man who plays the fiddle should at the same time play the trombone. The man is only a violinist, and only when all work together, play together, each his own instrument, can a symphony be performed. It is unfair to expect that an excellent fiddler must play the trombone" [pp. 107–108].

One appreciates the modesty and the acceptance in principle that "others" will have to assume the responsibility for the integration of knowledge, but this makes the musical analogy somewhat inappropriate because it is not a question of violinists becoming trombonists but whether a composer can write a new kind of music which properly orchestrated can make for a new and stirring musical experience, both for the members of the orchestra and for the audience. (It is also true that although violinists and trombonists use different instruments they have much more in common than separates them.) Social psychiatry would seem to have assumed the role of composing a new psychiatry/social-science music. We must await the composers who will provide the new music.

Social psychiatry is an unusually broad, ill-defined, hybrid, somewhat characterless field seeking a productive amalgam between the social-science and medical traditions. Thus far it has no independent status in the university in terms of programs (unlike community psychiatry). Its relevant literature ranges from informed journalism and social commentary, on one extreme, to focused research efforts on discrete problems, on the other. A "social-psychiatric imagination" is notable by its absence. It is unreflective about its relationship to the larger society at the same time that it is critical of that society, as if the field does not reflect the society. The tenor of its literature is anti-establishment, but against establishments that are "out there in society." It has helped break down some of the walls between disciplines without providing a clear view of what will be the overarching conceptions or intellectual keystones for a new theoretical structure.

Community Psychiatry

Kaplan (1970) has succinctly stated the relation between social and community psychiatry:

> Social psychiatry relates to the study of, and the theoretical formulations about, the social and environmental determinants of mental health and mental illness. Community psychiatry is the application of these studies and concepts to the development of programs for the prevention and treatment of mental illness. With some modifications I believe this definition reflects most of the existing opinions about the field of community psychiatry. The broadness of this definition is a result of the fact that the theories and practices in community psychiatry are still evolving, and little would be gained in attempting a more precise and specific definition [p. 61].

The development of community psychiatry is almost perfectly correlated with the serial emergence of different populations as objects of national concern: veterans, blacks, poor people, and certain ethnic groups. Daniels (1966) has noted that many features of community psychiatry had their origins in military experience: "The beginnings of many principles currently utilized in community psychiatry are to be found in these military experiences, e.g., early recognition, treatment close to the source of disability, crisis-oriented treatment promoting adaptation and return to duty, and consultation to command about issues of general concern." Planning vastly expanded programs for the care of unprecedented numbers of veterans began before the war ended, and with its end training programs were initiated that provided the mental health professions with challenging opportunities for research and service. Varieties of individual psychotherapies multiplied, group therapies came into their own, milieu therapies began to be developed, and new drug therapies were increasingly developed and tried.

Moving in these new clinical directions, however, did not in any direct way lead to a *community* psychiatry. One could argue, in fact, that these efforts represented a backward step from what was learned and done during World War II. "Early recognition, treatment close to the source of disability, crisis-oriented treatment promoting adaptation and return" to the natural community—these objectives were seldom achieved because the *hospital* was where the patients were sent and where the therapeutic action was. The role of the natural community was hardly conceptualized or dealt with. The hospital, of course, was seen as a community, although more often than not it was the ward that was *the* community. In either case, the rest of the world was a stage prop behind what was happening. (Matters were not very different in the outpatient clinics, where the weekly therapeutic or drug dispensing hour was the major vehicle for help.)

It could not have been otherwise, because the first decade after World War II was the era in which psychiatry promulgated the efficacy of psychotherapy as if it were the mental aspirin. Being a psychotherapist gave one status and, therefore, who could be a psychotherapist was a controversial issue, as was the question of *what* constituted psychotherapy. The absorption in the theory and practice of psychotherapy, with the hospital or clinic office being the arena in which "results" were gotten and evaluated, was obviously not conducive to a community psychiatry. It was antithetical to a community psychiatry. In fact, psychiatrists hardly left the hospital or clinic office. If a home needed visiting, or employment needed to be arranged, or if "something" needed to be done "out there," that was the responsibility of the psychiatric social worker, and it was a responsibility quite inferior to that of the therapeutic enterprise. It was the "natural" order of things, professionally speaking: the clinical psychologist was supposed to x-ray the mind, the psychiatrist was to repair it, and the social worker was to place it. Dealing with the community was a problem in foreign relations, not the concern of those dealing with domestic issues. This was a far cry from the flexibility and innovativeness that characterized psychiatry during World War II. It apparently takes a war or some other major social catastrophe to force professions to see that the "natural" order of things may be quite unnatural.

The influence of the VA experience on the development of a community psychiatry was indirect and subtle. One major influence was a consequence of the disillusionment with the efficacy of psychotherapy. This is not to say that psychotherapies came to be regarded as ineffective, but rather that for many persons their life situation outside the hospital and clinic subverted the therapy and rendered it either impotent or inappropriate or both. In many cases the use of psychotherapy was as foolish as attacking an elephant with a peashooter. Disordered family life, isolation within the family and from the community, job dissatisfaction or failure, inadequate supportive community resources, the cycle of personal misery, job instability, increased dependence, and increased misery —these conditions alone or in combination were often impervious to the effect of hospital or clinic therapeutic hours.

A second influence was a consequence of the VA system of disability benefits, in which the amount varied with the degree of war-incurred disability, and the benefits could continue as long as the disability was present. Not surprisingly, dependence on the benefits could work against "getting well"; there were real secondary gains to maintaining the psychological status quo, and so the hospital became a kind of refuge from one's self and the outside world. Some psychiatrists began to understand that they and the veteran were locked into a society-determined system of services, a system based on values and practices that were supported by highly organized pressure groups, in and out of legislatures, who did not look kindly on change. It was this and other factors (such as the shift from a younger to an older veteran population) that led to the conclusion that the rationale behind the VA planning for the post-war years had been in error, especially in its emphasis on building psychiatric hospitals and basing its programs primarily on various forms of psychotherapy. To an alarming degree, the hospital had become antitherapeutic.

A third influence was the most subtle of all, its nature hardly formulated or its consequences thought through: psychiatrists experienced what it was like to be part of a large, relatively impersonal, federal system in which it was far from clear who made what decisions and on what basis. (Not infrequently, when it *was* clear it seemed arbitrary and self-defeating.) Psychiatry, on an individual or departmental or hospital basis, began to comprehend how political and economic factors in the larger society directly and indirectly affected both the veteran and the psychiatrist. Kafka's castle began to dominate the professions in the valley below.

These influences did not directly lead to a community psychiatry. In fact, as we shall soon see, these "lessons" were to be experienced all over again when federal legislation establishing community mental health centers propelled psychiatry into the public arena. The direct effect of these influences was to disenchant psychiatry with its VA affiliation, so that it increasingly downgraded the VA setting for purposes of training and research. The affiliation had to be maintained, however, because it had become one of the economic pillars in the psychiatric edifice. (I presume there were some psychiatrists with the insight to see the generality of Marx's point about the relationship between an individual's "consciousness" and his working role. It was not only the "proletariat" whose constricted consciousness reflected a self-alienating connection to his work!)

The disenchantment reached a peak around the time of the publication of the reports of the Joint Commission on Mental Health (1961) and of the emergence of the constellation of problems around desegregation, civil rights, poverty, and urban crisis. The Joint Commission reports were no less than a polite indictment of mental hospitals, the maldistribution of services, and the parochialism of psychiatry, among other things (such as the lack of a relationship between psychiatry and schools). The constellation of social problems was in part a confirmation of the Joint Commission reports, and in part a magnet pulling psychiatry toward the community and its problems. As was the case with the Veterans Administration programs, the decisive push came from government policy and financing, in the form of the Community Mental Health Act of 1963.

Earlier in this chapter I described the prevailing view that social psychiatry was the discipline basic to community psychiatry— that social psychiatry provided the theoretical and research basis for the development of programs for preventing and treating psychiatric disorders. This view is, at best, only a partial explanation of the recent emergence of community psychiatry. Certainly the Joint Commission reports, a social-psychiatric endeavor by psychiatrists and psychologists, helped lead to the legislation establishing community mental health centers. These reports had a greater influence in Congress, which had set up the Commission, than it did in the mental health professions. However, from my reading of the literature and my professional experiences during the past three decades, I am forced to conclude that the emergence of community psychiatry was less a consequence of new theories and research data than a result of powerful social forces gaining momentum at the same time that psychiatry became disenchanted with its VA affiliation. And there was an additional force which for some time was unformed, inarticulate, and dissatisfied: the postwar generations of psychiatrists, who inevitably saw the world quite differently than their teachers did. A generation gap developed in psychiatry. For example, for a decade or so after World War II psychoanalysis became a major force in university departments of psychiatry, and it was a sign of distinction for the young psychiatrist to be admitted to psychoanalytic training, a sign of dedication that he was willing to devote years to gain advanced knowledge, a sign that he knew the difference between basic and superficial theory and practice. As time went on, fewer and fewer young psychiatrists could justify such training, not so much because of conceptual objections as because of the demands of social conscience. As one young psychiatrist put it to me: "I'm not knocking psychoanalysis. It's just that I can't ignore the atomic bomb, Senator Joseph McCarthy, racism, riots, and urban stink." The older generation of psychiatrists probably had no less of a social conscience, but they had been able to maintain, the society "permitted," a sharp distinction between the individual as professional and the individual as citizen. To many younger psychiatrists, such a distinction was a luxury that our changing society could not afford.

The shape of community psychiatry, then, was largely determined by the federal legislation which, in effect, promised all kinds of services to dramatically greater numbers of people than had ever been dreamed of before. As one colleague put it, "The mental health professions were catapulted into the supermarket era."

The services to be provided were not new. What was new was that
they were to be organized and made available in a community
mental health center serving all people in a geographical area.
The defining characteristics of community psychiatry are relatively
clear: an emphasis on non-dyadic treatment approaches (group
and family therapy, therapeutic ward communities, rehabilitation
programs); organization of service delivery by geographic areas;
formal ties with state and federal mental health agencies; consultation services to community agencies; planning and programs for
special populations (addicts, the aged, or suicidal, or disadvantaged); and the development and utilization of mental health manpower, professional and nonprofessional.

    Let us now turn to the problems encountered by community
psychiatry, not from the standpoint of its different programs or
services but from the light they shed on psychiatry as a discipline
and profession, on its conceptualization of and relation to "community," and on its possible futures. The first effect of federal
legislation was to widen the existing schism between the "old" and
the "new" psychiatry—between those who had long emphasized the
individual-centered, long-term, personality dynamics type of psychotherapy and those who were adapting a group-centered, ghetto-
oriented, social advocate role. There were, of course, some psychiatrists who viewed the new field as a potentially subverting force
in the quest for a true and deep understanding of the human mind
on the basis of which effective psychotherapies would be developed.
To them community psychiatry was more social work than psychiatry, more sociology than medicine. Although they were few in
number, they were sometimes in positions of power. A larger group
consisted of those who were tolerant or supportive of the new
development but were skeptical about psychiatry's ability to meet
its new goals, and were fearful that "basic" psychiatry would be
overwhelmed by its emphasis on mass applications. This was no idle
fear, because the infusion of federal funds had the effect of dramatically increasing the number of community oriented staff members
and attracting the young psychiatrists to the new centers. The
economic base of departments of psychiatry changed, and this of
course had direct effects on their internal political dynamics.

    One way of grasping what was at issue is to compare psychiatric training in the early sixties with training in the present. In 1965, Hassler published a study (presumably done a year or two before) surveying psychiatric residents in 22 approved training centers in Massachusetts, one of the major training areas in the United States. His procedure was as follows: "Each of the 22 approved training centers within the state was contacted, and a listing was obtained of all persons in formal psychiatric training who had at least one year of experience. The list included 158 possible respondents from all fields of training (general psychiatry, child psychiatry, research, and the like) and from all training settings (public or private hospitals or clinics as well as university programs). After one follow-up mailing 120 individuals had completed and returned the questionnaire; consequently the study had a return rate of 76 per cent" (Hassler, 1965).

Table 1 contains data on how the psychiatric residents reported the distribution of their training. Two things are noteworthy. First, there was very little exposure in such areas as "community organization or knowledge of community agencies," "public health principles or techniques," or "concepts of allied social sciences." Second, the school was not a "training area," although it was conceivable (but not likely) that some minimal exposure to schools was obtained in the training area of "consultation theory and techniques." Hassler reported other data that indicated a strong desire on the part of the psychiatric residents for more exposure to these neglected areas.

If one contrasts Hassler's study with the 1970 publication *Training Tomorrow's Psychiatrist: The Crisis in Curriculum* (Lidz and Edelson, eds.), one can see the degree of ferment and change which had occurred in psychiatry. Although it is far from clear in that book what the contributors regard as the nature of the crisis, it is hard to avoid gaining the overall impression that now and for some time to come psychiatry will be experiencing all the dynamics of an identity crisis. On the one hand there is a desire to adjust to the existence and implications of community psychiatry, while on the other hand the contributors leave no doubt that "basic" psychiatry should reflect "intrapsychic supremacy." At the same time that recognition is given to the basic significance of the social sciences for traditional and community psychiatry, the "more basic"

Table 1.
CURRENT TRAINING TIME AS REPORTED
BY PSYCHIATRIC RESIDENTS
(*percent distribution, one person = 0.8 percent*)

Training Areas	Much Time	Some Time	Little Time	No Time	No Response
1. Intensive depth psychotherapy	59.1	25.8	9.2	5.0	0.8
2. Consultation theory and techniques	13.3	39.2	32.5	15.0	–
3. Clinical diagnostic skills	34.2	52.5	11.7	0.8	0.8
4. Concepts of allied social science	1.7	19.2	55.8	22.5	0.8
5. Clinical research	6.7	16.7	29.2	45.8	1.7
6. Administration	22.5	16.7	32.5	28.3	–
7. Experience in training and teaching	5.0	31.7	35.8	25.8	1.7
8. Short-term or crisis therapy	12.5	31.7	35.0	20.8	–
9. Psychopharmacology or chemotherapy	10.0	24.2	43.3	20.8	1.7
10. Community organization or knowledge of community agencies	0.8	16.7	54.1	28.3	–
11. Clinical neurology	3.3	12.5	23.3	60.8	–
12. Epidemiology or ecology	–	–	25.0	74.1	0.8
13. Action research or program evaluation	1.7	5.8	12.5	79.1	0.8
14. Public-health principles or techniques	–	–	18.3	81.6	–
15. Neuroanatomy or neurophysiology	–	10.0	11.7	78.3	–
16. Mental-health education	0.8	3.3	33.3	61.6	0.8
17. Knowledge of individual psychodynamics	75.8	17.5	6.7	–	–
18. Knowledge of family or group psychodynamics	24.2	49.1	22.5	4.2	–

SOURCE: Hassler (1965).

basic turns out to be traditional psychoanalytic theory. The ideological and political tensions between traditional and community psychiatry are genotypically identical to those which characterized the relationship between clinical and academic psychology two decades earlier. It is an oversimplification to view these developments in terms of good-guy bad-guy, conservative-progressive dichotomies; these pejorative labels make for polarities that obscure the historical and the social forces which accompany institutional change. As we shall now see, such labels can effectively mask factors that cut across polarities.

A second problem encountered by community psychiatry was initially less a problem than a fact, namely its increasing association with government policy and its dependence on government funding. This fact had consequences for both traditional and community psychiatry, not the least of which was that psychiatry lost a degree of independence in building or renovating its own house. This alliance with the federal government, which began after World War II, far from being questioned or examined, was entered into quite enthusiastically. This was possible because federal policy and professional interests seemed to be identical. More important, both seemed to rest on two implicit assumptions which were as invalid then as they are now: these interests would remain identical or at least highly similar, and our economic system would no longer operate like a yoyo. Accepting, indeed failing to articulate, these two assumptions was a good indication of psychiatry's level of sophistication about the workings of our society. (In all fairness, it must be noted that other fields which should have known better did not.) Consequently, as it became clear that these interests were diverging, that divisions within psychiatry were emerging and that governmental policies and funding were changing radically in response to social crises, the conflicts and controversies within psychiatry sharpened in competition for the federal dollar.

The point is that all this happened with very little awareness of how it had come about and the dangers that could be expected. For example, one of the dangers was that it could become difficult for psychiatry to criticize federal policy and promises, and indeed this difficulty was not often surmounted. As Kaplan (1970) put it:

Since the man who pays the piper often calls the tunes, the direction and guidelines for program developments established in Washington frequently have become the way of life in practice. Inevitably, no matter what the intent of the central planning bodies, these practices became institutionalized. Geographic delivery of services become "catchment areas" not always following a sensible pattern of patient flow; standard outpatient services are called after-care, and rehabilitation facilities and an alcove off an inpatient ward become a partial hospitalization service. If nothing else, it behooves us to understand the governmental procedures in order to intelligently appraise new programs [p. 63].

This statement says quite clearly what could have been said, but was not, when the Community Mental Health Act was passed, to wit, that it called for more of the same even though the call was cloaked in new euphemisms. Kaplan went on to say:

However, I have not included this reference as a critique of the inevitable bureaucratic process of governmental machinery. I believe that the leadership taken by the federal planning groups was necessary and stems from the very complex problems of planning and finance in the entire medical care system. *There are legitimate difficulties that prevent medical institutions from being responsive to the rapid changes in medical care and medical management that are required to maintain a high quality of medical practice. Medical centers, particularly the teaching institutions, are undergoing a reappraisal of their commitments in which the relationship to governmental bodies is a critical factor* [p. 63].

This statement is interesting for the ambiguity in the sentences I have italicized. My interpretation of these sentences, upon which Kaplan does not elaborate, is that academic centers of psychiatry wish to reduce their intimate ties to government so that they can become less a service arm to it and can redirect their energies to those activities which contribute to "basic" knowledge. My experience suggests, especially in light of the recent cutbacks in funding (state and federal) that have produced large university deficits and reductions in academic staff size, that one should expect the process of "reappraisal" to have a greater adverse effect on the new accretions than on the older, more entrenched branches of psychiatry.

Another example of the danger of uncritically accepting government policies and programs can be seen in the degree to which psychiatry and government agencies managed to ignore the manpower issue. To fulfill the promise of the community mental health center program obviously required professional mental health personnel in numbers that did not and could not exist. This has been demonstrated quite clearly by Albee (1954, 1968a, 1968b) in the manpower analysis he made for the Joint Commission on Mental Health, but the new programming went forward as if "psychiatry for the millions" was in the realm of possibility. It is not unusual, and it is quite understandable, when political leaders promise more than they know can be accomplished. But should we not expect more candidness from an important profession, particularly when the justification for candidness existed? The answer lies less, I suppose, in the matter of candidness than in the social turmoil of the early sixties, when government and mental health professions formed a grand alliance to widen and improve the delivery of services. The very word "delivery," borrowed from the jargon of engineering and industry, typified the confusion, as if what was involved was not institutional change but a problem of resolve and efficiency.

Another problem encountered by community psychiatry was, in a substantive and procedural way, a direct consequence of its baptismal encounter with the community, primarily its black and other disadvantaged components. It was an encounter, far from over in many cities, which exposed psychiatry's previous isolation from the community and its insensitivity to social changes which were taking place within it. In developing and implementing the community mental health center concept, psychiatry proceeded in typical professional style: it planned *for* the community, it decided *to whom* its services would be available, and it made *itself* the ultimate decider of whatever things needed to be decided. Wasn't this the natural order of things, especially since it was all being powered, in the best spirit of professional *noblesse oblige,* by the desire for a more equitable distribution of mental health services? It was as "natural" as liking apple pie, and no less a reflection of culture and tradition. What psychiatry did not know, what its reading of the social pulse did not detect, was that a militancy had developed among the populations it wished to serve, a militancy that was anti-establishment and sought a decision-making role in all matters impinging on the militants' lives. More than that, some now familiar questions began to be asked quite loudly: could middle-class, white professionals understand blacks and other disadvantaged groups? Were the types of treatment and the theories they rested on free of color and class bias? Were the mental health professions and their services new ways by which society would treat the symptoms and hide the causes of social and economic injustice? Should not the community decide where facilities would be housed or built and what services the community wants?

It is hard to exaggerate the degree of shock experienced by psychiatry as it was made to confront the social forces within the central city. By theory and long experience psychiatry had learned a good deal about treating individuals in offices, clinics, and hospitals—that is, in settings set up and controlled by psychiatry with (for the most part) the acquiescence of those who sought its services. And a good deal had been learned about the individual's ambivalences, hostilities, and resistances, all of which were seen as understandable and, indeed, necessary for personal growth. But these theories and long clinical experience were a poor preparation for psychiatry's new community orientation.[4] As one psychiatrist put it: "It's a new ball game, but what is the game?"

---

[4] A glimpse of this can be obtained from Kaplan's (1970) brief description of what happened at Lincoln Hospital in New York, where the sharp conflicts broke out between psychiatrists and between psychiatrists and community groups. Kaplan's "psychodynamic" explanation of the behavior of younger dissident psychiatrists is a clear example of interpreting a complex social-political-cultural-racial situation in exclusively personality terms. For example: "Whatever their political convictions, it was not the intent of the psychiatric residents to subvert the teaching program or the capacity of their teachers to supervise their work. Nevertheless, this is what occurred to the detriment of all involved. Part of the explanation of the residents' behavior can be described as a result of their overidentification with the nonprofessional staff and the polarization of their ambivalent reactions into a good-bad object relationship projected upon the 'establishment,' personified by senior members of the faculty. I should make it clear that the residents who became involved are among the more highly regarded in the training pro-

The pressures were not only external because each psychiatric setting had a few younger psychiatrists who identified with the "community" against the traditional ways of the field. And there were, of course, those more traditional psychiatrists who looked upon these "goings on" (frequently described in detail in the daily newspaper) with a mixture of dismay and satisfaction, dismay because of the politicizing of the field and satisfaction because they had predicted well what would happen when psychiatry moved away from its base of competence by being unduly responsive to the needs of society. Several things began to happen. Some community psychiatrists became disenchanted with the new field, as much because of the personal turmoil caused by the community-psychiatry clashes as by the severe professional identity crises they crystallized. The traditional segments of psychiatry, particularly in the university, began to assert their power in relation to problems of distribution of resources and to the related problem of the nature of psychiatric training. The conflict between the old and the new, between the inside and the outside, in addition to the fact of limited resources, guaranteed internecine struggle. Toward the end of the sixties cutbacks in governmental support, which became increasingly severe, slowed down the growth of community psychiatry and seemed to provide the opportunity for more traditional psychiatry to assert its dominance.

Community psychiatry is too young a field, and we are still too close to events, to assess with any accuracy the dynamics of its present and the shape of its future. Although there is little in community psychiatry that is new theoretically or practically, the very fact that it has experienced what it has in the past decade will leave its mark on the field and may serve as a basis for more productive conceptualizations. As I see the field at the present, particularly in the university medical setting, which tends to dominate all psychiatric facilities in its area, the rhetoric about the

---

gram and who, in their supervised work, had not shown any propensity to these defense mechanisms in intensive long-term individual therapy or other therapeutic situations. However, because of their use of denial and rationalization and because of the reality of the political developments, it was not possible to discuss the issues with the residents objectively, or to turn their reaction to the advantage of the learning process" (p. 86). This is an article on teaching community psychiatry!

primacy of research and more rigorous training is returning with the force of authority and devotion to academic tradition. But the *act* of research is not productive, and its consequences do not influence a field, unless it is preceded by formulations that depart from the old and make us look at the world differently.

Social psychiatry has hardly commented on developments in community psychiatry, for this commentary would require the most searching analysis of psychiatry as a profession institutionalized in various parts of American society, identifying itself with medical ideology and practice, drawing its members from certain socioeconomic strata, adhering to theories primarily about the individual organism in its disordered aspects, and rarely examining its underlying values and social functions. Such analysis can only occur when tradition pays more than lip service to self-analysis and criticism, and this tradition has been notably weak in medicine in general and in psychiatry in particular. (Let us not forget that it took fifty years for academic psychiatry to recognize psychoanalysis.) This is not to suggest that nonmedical academic areas are models of open forums in which dissenters to prevailing opinion and values need fear no ostracism, or worse yet, silent rejection. They are not, but if I am right that medicine in general and psychiatry in particular differ discernibly in degree in this respect from other fields, then one has less reason to hope for revolutionary changes in theory and practice than would otherwise be the case. The development of a viable community psychiatry will have to be based on a searing examination of psychiatry as an institution. At the present time neither the conceptual tools nor the motivation for such a task exists within the field. As psychiatry has learned so well about the troubled individual, a good part of the battle for growth is won when the individual owns up to the fact that he is in trouble and then decides that he must change. The dynamics of individual change are not those of institutional change, but I employ the analogy because it serves to emphasize where one of the roots of trouble is buried.

Community Psychology

Community psychiatry was "legislated" into existence and its shape and funding represented explicit public policy. Community psychology had little or no separate institutional existence or independent relation to the public. That is to say, unlike a department of psychiatry clearly and formally providing clinical services to the public, a department of psychology viewed itself and was perceived by others as an academic department in which research and teaching rather than the rendering of a public service were its chief characteristics. Clinical psychology obviously was engaged in a public service, but this was predominantly within a psychiatric setting. Whatever its role and status in the psychiatric setting, clinical psychology was not viewed by public agencies as an independent profession, and it was certainly not seen in this way by legislatures, to whom community mental health programs were the responsibility of psychiatric physicians in particular and medical people in general. The most direct consequence of this was that most of those clinical psychologists whose interests shifted from the clinical to the community orientation played their new role in a familiar setting. It is my impression that these psychologists were among the most enthusiastic proponents of the new orientation and most ready to move in ways radically different than those of the past. This reflected in part their dissatisfaction with a secondary role, in part their disenchantment with the efficacy of psychotherapies, and in part their response to the increasing pace and seriousness of social crises. In addition, clinical psychology was a relatively new, if not infant, field which had not yet imprisoned its members within the walls of long-standing traditions to the degree that was true of psychiatry. It is also my impression that in moving to a community orientation the tension between psychiatry and clinical psychology was not eased at all because of the psychologist's perception of two familiar factors. The first was that the community orientation was creating sharp conflicts between psychiatrists, and that by taking sides the clinical psychologist ran the risk of being caught in the crossfire. Second, the clinical psychologist was, so to speak, a guest in someone else's house and this inevitably set constraints on what he could do. The psychiatric setting was far from being fertile soil for the growth of a distinctive community psychology.

There were clinical psychologists in the university who were not in a formal sense tied to the psychiatric setting and who moved toward a community involvement. For the most part they moved as individuals and focused on certain community settings depending on special interests and local factors. Some become heavily involved in the public schools, others in poverty programs, others in police and correctional agencies, and a few were able to be involved simultaneously in a few community settings. Precisely because these scattered efforts were usually initiated by one individual, who could gather some students and colleagues around him, they varied in size, scope, and orientation. In some instances, consulting to community agencies was the preferred model of giving service, while in others direct services were rendered. All of them were modest efforts and if judged by the criteria defining a community mental health center they obviously fell very short of that mark. The two factors common to almost all of these efforts was that those involved were focusing on community agencies to which they had never been exposed in their training, and whatever they were doing was being done in the natural setting rather than in their clinic or departmental offices. The label *community* psychologist referred less to any change in scope of activity than to the simple fact that psychologists were physically doing their work in a community setting around problems for which the traditional clinical role was deemed irrelevant. More often than not, these individual efforts were carried out as research projects in which services were either the objects of evaluation or the means by which new knowledge and conceptualizations might emerge.

Although the settings to which community psychologists (outside of psychiatric facilities) gravitated were diverse, as were their roles and goals in them, they were settings with which psychiatry had only tenuous relationships. Reformatories, institutions for the mentally retarded, schools, day care programs, neighborhood employment or service centers, and manpower training programs were some of the old or emerging settings in which community psychologists established new roles. And in light of clinical psychology's past experience with psychiatric guildism, it is not surprising that the community psychologist was in the forefront in developing training programs for professionally untrained people.

To get the full flavor of the range of activities in community psychology and psychiatry, the serious reader will have to consult Cowen's chapter, entitled "Social and Community Interventions" in the 1973 *Annual Review of Psychology*. He strives valiantly (but with saving humor) to organize the literature and define the area, with little hope that he can bring order out of chaos:

> What *is* a proper scope for Social and Community (SC) Intervention? For a fleeting, hopeful moment, the writer thought that he might answer this question via a lazy man's promenade in operationism. His reasoning, more defensible logically than empirically, was that the *Community Mental Health Journal* (CMHJ), regarded by many as a front-and-center exemplar of this new domain, had been in existence for about seven years, exactly the period of marked swelling of the SC tides. Should not a careful content analysis of the articles appearing in this journal provide the Talmudic wisdom —the blinding glimpse of the obvious—about the area's precise nature? Retrospection indicates that the foregoing assumption was, charitably speaking, an exercise in pious naivete.
>
> In the 7-year period between the first CMHJ issue and June 1971, 31 numbers appeared, containing about 330 papers. The chronicler would be able, whose conceptual powers allowed him, to "shoe-horn" these 330 papers into as few as 100 categories. By federating families of topics (e.g., mental illness, the mentally ill, mental hospitals, mental patients) one can eke out some 30–35 papers. Other gelatinous rubrics such as "programs and descriptions" and "planning" account for perhaps another score. Special topics that have attracted "one-shot" attention are numerous: e.g., articles about judges, unwed mothers, the dying, parents of preemies, and MH among the Eskimos each has its assigned space. The full spectrum of content baffles and defies most sophisticated machine factor analysis and the most perspicacious eyeball. Moreover, the ratio of speculation to research is alarmingly high. If one uses the liberal criterion of whether the author mentions a number or draws a chart, to classify a contribution as "research," about 3 of 10 CMHJ articles are "researchy." Of those, a fair number are simply descriptive (e.g., 30 percent of the dischargees from hospital X were ages 40–50, and 20 percent, ages 50–60.
>
> Although this brave venture in cataloguing failed abysmally to answer the intended "defining" question, it was informative beyond the points noted above. In infinite inno-

cence the writer had supposed that the word prevention would
be an important, high-frequency one in CMHJ. Accordingly,
he checked all titles for kindred words such as "prevention,"
"prevent," or "preventing." Ten such usages (3 percent of
all articles) were noted which, at first blush, is disappointing.
The second blush was worse, since of those 10 occurrences,
six were preceded by the word suicide, one by delinquency,
and two followed by "chronic illness" and "on campus,"
respectively [pp. 6–8].

If anything is clear in Cowen's review it is that the great bulk of
interventions reflect a clinical, or psychiatric, or psychopathological
orientation which on manpower grounds alone guarantees in-
effectiveness.

The core of the argument can be summarized as follows: However understandable the evolution and ascendance
of the medical model, however necessary that portions of it
survive, however much we can improve its efficiency, it fails
to deal satisfactorily with today's basic, nonpostponable mental
health problems, and as such can no longer stand alone as the
guiding frame for long-range planning. Reducing the flow of
dysfunction is appealing as a conceptual alternative. If we
cannot do this, we risk treading water until we drown! [pp.
23–24]

Elsewhere (Sarason, 1972) I have discussed this issue in terms of
"the myth of unlimited resources." The point I made is that as long
as "the mental health problem" is defined in a way so as to require
professional personnel for its solution, the situation is hopeless. The
prospect is made even more dismal by the tendency to look at the
community from the narrow perspectives of "mental health," a
tendency that will even subvert Cowen's plea that primary prevention (in contrast to secondary or tertiary prevention) be taken
seriously.

Community psychology was not fated to be more than a
miniscule part of academic psychology. Although clinical psychology had become an established but still conflict-ridden part of
psychology, there was nothing in the "public service" traditions of
either that would have facilitated new programs smacking of social

activism. Furthermore, clinical psychology had been developed and maintained by federal funding and there was comparatively little money available to help community psychology get started.

Just as social psychiatry came to be viewed (erroneously) as the basic foundation for a community psychiatry, one might have expected that social psychology would be similarly viewed in relation to a community psychology. From an uninformed standpoint one might have expected that social psychologists would make up a significant number of those who moved toward community involvement. The fact was (and is) that American social psychology was predominantly concerned with personality dynamics in its dyadic and small group aspects, or with the nature and measurement of attitude change. And if American social psychology took pride in anything it was the primacy it gave to experimental methodology as *the* way of contributing to knowledge. It was difficult to avoid gaining the impression that research which did not involve the manipulation of variables was the badge of misguided or second-class minds, or both. Few parts of American psychology were as laboratory-minded or adopted as super-scientific a stance as social psychology. There was precious little in social psychology that could serve as a foundation for a community psychology. The methodological and theoretical narrowness of social psychology insured not only that community psychology would have to go it alone but also that it would be ignorant of some highly relevant social psychological and sociological literature and traditions that never entered the mainstream of American psychology. If community psychology had a stunted growth, it was in part because its seeds were sown on barren soil. These judgments about social psychology and community psychology (as well as social and community psychiatry) should not be interpreted as a "writing-off" of these fields, as if they have accomplished nothing or contributed little to human knowledge. The thrust of my comments, as I will elaborate in later chapters, is that the guiding conceptions in these fields do not and cannot lead to a searching examination of *community*.

Community psychology, like community psychiatry, did not rest on any articulated formulations that would give meaning to the adjective "community." In fact, one can go through the recent literature without once encountering a serious discussion of how a community is conceptualized—the dimensions along which it is organized, the ways it has changed over time, sources of formal and informal power, the nature of relationships between its major institutions, the role of religious, ethnic, and social factors, and so on. There have been serious efforts to conceptualize a discrete setting like a school, or the nature and consequences of poverty, or the problems of race. But these efforts, however illuminating they have been, have not dealt with the complexity of the contemporary community. At the same time that these kinds of efforts riveted attention on obviously important problems they prevented recognizing the broader community context from which they had arisen and in which change was sought. We have responded to these problems because of their crisis nature, and in trying to alleviate them we have lost sight of the larger context characterized by forces and processes which, because we ignore them, defeat our efforts or set severe limits to what will be accomplished. Worse yet, by focusing on the crisis problems we are rendered insensitive to less overt ones which in the future will be our new crises. In working with the problems of individuals we have learned that the presenting symptoms are, so to speak, the tip of the iceberg, and that both the tip and the iceberg are the outcome of social-environmental dynamics near and far. We are far from viewing discrete community problems in this manner, and until we do, it borders on arrogance to describe our present forays as *community* oriented.

The failure to illuminate and define the parameters of community is not fortuitous. I consider this failure the root cause of unreflective and narrow responses to social problems, of the sterility and vagueness of attempts at theorizing, of the disillusionment which has already permeated these fields as they become aware of the discrepancy between problems and solutions, and of the likelihood that what has been creative and productive in these new fields will remain unrelated fragments in a welter of specificities. It is precisely for these reasons that an explanation of the failure must be attempted.

V

Some Neglected Pioneers: John Dollard, James Plant, and J. F. Brown

Amerian psychology in general, and community psychology in particular, have been uncomfortable with the concept of culture and its implications for theory and application. This may seem a strange statement, because even a casual perusal of the psychological literature would quickly prove that psychologists are vitally interested in man's environment and his social milieu. But interest in the environment is not the same as an interest in culture. For example, there have been thousands of studies on the classroom environment in which all kinds of relationships have been demon-

strated: name the variable and you can find scores of studies showing its impact on teachers, children, and performance. It may be the
style, age, experience, or technology of the teacher, or it may be
any one of scores of variables not provided by the teacher. For
both child and teacher there is an external environment, complex
and influential. But if one is interested in the culture of the classroom or school one starts with and then goes beyond the externals.
Let me illustrate this point by means of a device I employed in my
book *The Culture of the School and the Problem of Change*
(1971). Let us imagine that parked above a school on a space
platform is a man from outer space who, strange to the ways of
earthlings, cannot comprehend language and does not even know
that things go on inside their heads. But he is able to see and
record everything that goes on inside the school, and, possessed of
the most advanced types of computers, he can establish all possible
interrelationships among his observations. In effect, he can determine every type of regularity which exists in a classroom and in the
rest of the school. These regularities constitute much of what we
mean by environment or environmental variables. Now, let us
focus on what would probably be the first regularity the space man
would note: for five consecutive days the school is densely populated, and for two consecutive days it is empty. The space man,
of course, cannot account for this. But how would *we* account for
it? Is this five-two regularity a rational derivation from educational
theory or the consequence of a good deal of experience and experimentation? Obviously not. Is it a universal regularity? Obviously
not. Is it in some way related to characteristics and influence of the
dominant religions in this society? In part, yes. Is it in some way
related historically to changes in the economic structure of our
society? In part, yes. Was it always true that children went to
school? Obviously not. What on the surface appears to be a simple
question is not simple at all, and the more we would pursue an
answer the more we would find ourselves confronting a present
practice or structure which reflects an unrecognized past, unverbalized values, an unthinking acceptance of what is as what must
be, and an interrelatedness among institutions and social forces that
makes a narrow social focus untenable. Indeed, if we pursued the
five-two regularity we would begin to understand that one of the

distinguishing consequences of a culture is that it prevents most people in it from examining its basis, with the result that "what is," and "the way things are," seem "natural." Culture is a stabilizing force at the same time that it is an imprisoning one. It provides us with ways of thinking, categories of thought, values—a conception of what man and society are and should be—that are potent obstacles to individual and social change. Culture is not something one sees in the sense that one *sees* people and things, but rather a set of values and assumptions that give shape and force to our thinking and to our perception of ourselves and others. And equally as important and pervasive as culture is for the individual is the way it forms, interrelates, and justifies the characteristics and activities of social groups and institutions. Culture gives us our view of the world and if we come, as almost all of us do, to accept this view as natural and good it testifies not only to the fact that the culture antedates the individual but that it is absorbed by him unwittingly and powerfully.

Once we begin to grasp the nature and consequences of culture, and to take them seriously, they drastically alter how one looks at the individual and his surroundings. I say "drastically" because such a grasp demands that we control our tendency to focus primarily on individuals in order to sense how their surroundings are patterned, on what basis, and with what consequences. One can study thousands of individual school children, or myriads of types of groups that inhabit schools, without ever having to confront the deceptively simple question: why are our public schools closed on Saturdays and Sundays? Of course, I am not suggesting that such studies of groups and individuals are not and will not be important; some of them will be very revealing of the nature of man (*in our society*). But they are not likely to deepen our understanding of how schools are structured and function, their relationships to other institutions and forces, and how these shape our accustomed ways of thinking and perceiving—ways which seem "natural" and in no need of justification or explanation.

Culture is a Janus-faced concept. It directs our attention to what is outside of us at the same time that it requires us to look inward. The coherence we see "out there," as well as the more numerous external coherences that we accept but do not even reflect on, are consequences of an internal psychological coherence which is, so to speak, isomorphic with the perception of external coherence. It usually takes a dramatic event to force people to recognize that these internal and external coherences, these things that seem immutable and natural, are not universal truths or an objective description of reality. Such a recognition was forced on Americans when they learned that Russia had orbited the first space satellite. It was unimaginable that Americans would not be first in space. It was natural to expect that American scientists and technologists would lead man in outer space travel. But it turned out that their "natural" way of viewing themselves and the world was not truly natural. The immediate reaction was no more than raising the shade on the closed window to the internal aspects of culture, but the window was raised high when, after the initial reactions of surprise and anxiety, the clamor began for this country to reassert its primacy. If America was not first, it *should* become first regardless of the costs involved. And was not *that* goal a natural one? It is the hallmark of culture that it drastically limits the recognition and acceptance of a universe of alternatives to accustomed ways of thinking and acting.

It may well be a characteristic of a new field (as it is of a young person) to define itself in terms of the present and future and to regard the past as at best an interesting but irrelevant museum piece and at worst a burden never to be carried, let alone examined. That the past may be usable, that it may have contained individuals who transcended their times and perspicaciously saw the shape of the future, and that wisdom and insight are not the sole possession of modern man are cognitions not easy to come by when a new field struggles for an idiosyncratic identity. To search the past requires not only that one take distance from the present, but also that the search be from a height that permits the recognition of continuities.[1] I suspect the search is facilitated by

[1] An unusually instructive book in this connection is the Levines' *Social History of Helping Services* (1970) in which they describe innovative community interventions earlier in this century, and demonstrate the correlation between changes in modes of service and the social-political climate. These interventions and their rationales would be innovative even today, and the authors provide a detailed discussion of why and how these innovations were short-lived.

disappointment in, or failure of, or disillusionment with, the fruits
of efforts in the present. I consider community psychology and
psychiatry to be largely fields that have failed, or, perhaps more
fairly, have reached a point of arrested development after an
exciting, promising, but brief childhood. This is not my opinion
alone. I have talked with scores of people in these fields (in the
university, in federal agencies, and in the community) and overwhelmingly they express chagrin, or bitterness, or puzzlement about
the fact that the new orientation, as was the case with psychotherapy, was making practically no dent in the dimensions of the
overall problem. I wish to emphasize that this judgment should not
be interpreted to mean that nothing was accomplished, that people
were not helped, and that nothing new was learned. The disillusionment is rather a consequence of two things: the recognition
that by criteria traditional in the mental health professions the
new movement has been an ineffectual social band aid, and, more
importantly, the vague feeling that something is wrong somewhere
and a large part of it may be in the mental health professions
themselves. But one listens in vain for an answer that would explain
why things went wrong and also act as a conceptual compass to
new ideas and practices. I suggest that a significant part of the
answer resides in the failure of psychological theories to confront
certain issues by no means new or undiscussed. These issues were
raised and discussed long before there was community psychology,
community psychiatry, or social psychiatry. What I shall do in this
chapter is to select certain writings which have the following characteristics: they raised these neglected issues in a clear and compelling way, they challenged in a most basic way existing
psychological and psychiatric thinking, and with but one exception
they do not appear in the literature of community psychology and
psychiatry. In the case of the one exception, there is reason to
believe that it appears in a bibliography because it provides a pseu-
doscholarly gloss and not because it has been read and digested.
And aside from this one exception, the books I discuss have long
been unavailable, a rather objective criterion of impact. For each
selection I shall summarize those of its major points which, if they
had been taken seriously by psychology and psychiatry, would have
served as a far more productive and effective basis for the develop-

ment of a community orientation. There can be no doubt that, at
the very least, we would have a very different state of affairs than
now confronts us.

Dollard's "Criteria for the Life History"

This book was published in 1935. By that time Dollard was
by training and experience a sociologist, social psychologist, and
psychoanalyst. By virtue of his association with Edward Sapir,
who more than anyone else helped initiate and cultivate a relationship between psychiatry and the social sciences, Dollard was quite
knowledgeable in the literature of anthropology.

Although the title of the book accurately reflects its contents,
it is not the most illuminating title that could have been chosen and,
undoubtedly, probably conveyed to many people a "how-to-do-it"
orientation which would be more appropriate for clinicians and
social workers than for social scientists and psychological theoreticians. Far from being a technical guide it is an ingeniously searching
discussion and analysis of the "culture and personality" relationships. More specifically, Dollard sets out to test the seriousness and
adequacy with which these relationships are taken and employed.

> The taking of a life history is here viewed as a problem
> of the student of culture; it can, of course, be done by per-
> sons who do not formally acknowledge that they are students
> of social life, but this does not change the essence of the mat-
> ter; they are students of culture by definition if they attempt
> to deal with acculturated individuals. What particular "ist"
> they wear at the end of their field designation is merely tradi-
> tionally determined and unimportant. It is worth while to dis-
> tinguish the life-history view of the individual from the
> conventional cultural view of the individual. In the long-
> section or life-history view the individual remains organically
> present as an object of study; he must be accounted for in
> his full, immediate, personal reality. The eye remains on the
> details of his behavior and these we must research on, and
> explain. Here culture is bedded down in a specific organic
> locus. The culture forms a continuous and connected wrap for
> the organic life. From the standpoint of the life history the
> person is viewed as an organic center of feeling moving

through a culture and drawing magnetically to him the main strands of the culture. In the end the individual appears as a person, as a microcosm of the group features of his culture. It is possible that detailed studies of the lives of individuals will reveal new perspectives on the culture as a whole which are not accessible when one remains on the formal cross-sectional plane of observation. In pure cultural studies, on the other hand, the organic man has disappeared and only that abstracted portion of him remains that is isolated and identified by the culture pattern. If, in the "pure" cultural study, the organic reality of the person is lost, then we should expect that cultural studies would tell us little about individual experience and meanings. This, it is suggested, is the case. Since students of "culture" do not make our distinctions clearly and since they feel a pressure somehow to deal with the person, they will often accept uncritically the concepts of motivation nearest at hand, or, in other cases, go into business as social psychologists for themselves and invent them, without taking the trouble to study minutely the individual life. Such attempts will in most cases give inadequate results. Certainly we are only in a primitive phase of culture-personality study at the present time. The formal view of culture provides an indispensable backdrop for individual studies but via it we do not arrive at theories of meaningful action. As soon as we take the post of observer on the cultural level the individual is lost in a crowd and our concepts never lead us back to him. After we have "gone cultural" we experience the person as a fragment of a (derived) culture pattern, as a marionette dancing on the strings of (reified) culture forms. A culture-personality problem can be identified in every case by observing whether the person is "there" in full emotional reality; if he is not there, then we are dealing with a straight cultural or institutional study. If he is there and we can ask how he feels, then we have a culture-personality problem. It is stressed emphatically that there are no personality problems alone. Personality problems are always culture-personality problems [pp. 4–5].

Dollard describes and discusses seven criteria by which to judge the *conceptual* adequacy of a life history, that is, the seriousness with which the fact that one is always dealing with a culture-personality relationship is taken. It is obviously not possible in brief summary for me to do justice to each of these criteria and to convey the seriousness with which each of them is viewed by Dollard in the culture-personality context. For my purposes, Dollard's statement about the first criterion is most appropriate. In the following excerpts the italics are mine:

Criterion I. The subject must be viewed as a specimen in a cultural series. It is common in studies which refer to the growth of the person to indicate that he grows somehow in a "milieu," or perhaps the word "surroundings" is used, or sometimes "environment." Scholars who use such terms can only have a preliminary glimmer of the idea of culture. The terms above cited seem to imply that the "milieu" of the person is passive and negative in its value for him; the person does not grow up alone but he does have contacts with other people and this fact is indicated by some such term. Or it may be that a term like "environment" calls up a specifically physical image and seems to attribute potency in the shaping of character to the things surrounding the individual. *The criterion we have suggested above diverges emphatically from such an inadequate view; it suggests that the "environment" has a character, an historical, traditional character, that it is not a mere accidental aggregate of persons and things but that it is an ordered, configurated set of conditions into which the new member of the group comes.*

The importance of the criterion given above is best seen if we accept two units for our consideration: first, the group which exists before the individual; and second, a new organism envisioned as approaching this functioning collectivity. The organism is seen at this moment as clean of cultural influence and the group is seen as functioning without the aid of the organism in question. We will suppose that the organism is nearing the group through its intrauterine development and that it is finally precipitated into group life by the act of birth. Let us ask ourselves at this point what we can say systematically about what this organism will be like when it comes of age, sex granted. *All of the facts we can predict about it, granted the continuity of the group, will define the culture into which it comes.* Such facts can include the kind of clothes it will wear, the language it will speak, its theological ideas, its characteristic occupation, in some cases who its husband or wife is bound to be, how it can be insulted, what it will regard as wealth, what its theory of personality growth will be, etc. These and hundreds of other items are or may be standardized before the birth of the individual and be transmitted to the organism with mechanical certainty.

In order to make this idea clear to themselves some persons like to think of the society itself as the "living" thing; at one end, the new organic material is funneled in by birth, and at the other end of old age, the used up organic material is buried out of the society. If you reify a society in this way you can view it as an entity with an organismic stream flowing in and out of it. What is seen to persist are sets of folkways and mores which are only slightly altered from generation to generation in the normal course of things. In order to get this point of view you have to close your eyes slightly so that the individuals disappear but the connected sense of their habitual life remains. This point of view can show how the rough but powerful outline of the new individual life is forecast by the traditional life of the group itself.

A life historian, sophisticated in the above sense, can see his life history subject as a link in a chain of social transmission; there were links before him from which he acquired his present culture; other links will follow him to which he will pass on the current of tradition. The life history attempts to describe a unit in that process; it is a study of one of the strands of a complicated collective life which has historical continuity. The fact that an individual believes his culture to be "his" in some powerful personal sense, as though he had thought out for himself how to do the things which he actually does by traditional prescription, will not impress the observer who has the cultural view. He will regard this conviction as unimportant and will stress the point of uniformity of the subject's behavior with that of persons who have lived before him and who now live in the same group. In such a "march" of a culture through time the individual is seen as less than a phantom; in point of fact, the individual only appears in times of crisis when the mores are not adequate to meet some real life situation which the group faces.

We are stressing at this point the fact that the scientific student of a human life must adequately acknowledge the enormous background mass of the culture; and not as a mere mass either, but rather as a configurated whole. Before any individual appears his society has had a specific social life organized and systematized, and the existence of this life will exercise a tyranical compulsion on him. Seen from this point of view the problem of the life history is a statement of how the new organism becomes the victim or the resultant of this form structure of the culture. Each life history that is gathered will be a record of how a new person is added to the group. It will be a case of seeing "the group plus a person." To state the point in an extreme manner we can think of the organic man as the mere toy of culture, providing it with a standardized base, investing its forms with affect but creating very little that is new alone or at any one time. . . .

If our life historian is not equipped with the above criterion he will certainly fall into error by referring to accident, whims of individuals, or organic propulsion, much that is properly seen only as a part of the society into which the individual comes. These errors seem so chronic and immortal in social science thinking that it is hard to overdo the necessity of a very schematic statement of the cultural view. *Many individuals who are quite able to state the point, after one fashion or another, are persistently unable to work it through into their manner of dealing with problems. One of the marks of an effective grasping of this point is the stated or implied "in our culture" whenever one makes any point in connection with individual behavior; it is a good thing to get into the habit, for example, of saying "men are more able than women to exhibit aggressive behavior in our culture." One might venture that to the social psychologist the three most indispensable letters in the alphabet are I.O.C. (in our culture* [pp. 13–17].

The bulk of the book is devoted to an examination of seven published case histories. Dollard's catholic view is best conveyed by the following chapter headings:

The Criteria Applied: The Case of Miss R, by Alfred Adler
The Criteria Applied: "Thirty-one contacts with a seven-year old boy," From *The Dynamics of Therapy*, by Jessie Taft

> The Criteria Applied: "Analysis of a phobia in a five-year
>   old boy," by Sigmund Freud
> The Criteria Applied: "Life-Record of an immigrant," From
>   *The Polish Peasant in Europe and America,* by W. I.
>   Thomas and Florian Znaniecki
> The Criteria Applied: *The Jack-Roller,* by Clifford R. Shaw
> The Criteria Applied: *Experiment in Autobiography,* H. G.
>   Wells
> A Reference to *Crashing Thunder, The Autobiography of an
>   American Indian,* Edited by Raul Radin; and to Jung's
>   Psychology

All of the histories were found wanting in their systematic use of
the criteria, albeit in varying respects. Dollard demonstrates beyond
cavil that the psychiatric type of life history suffers from two
major defects. The first is that the psychological theories which
give the life histories their distinctive character, far from being
general statements about human behavior, are themselves in many
ways a product of a particular culture, but of this the theorists are
not aware. The second is that although each of the writers of the
psychiatric life-histories has a concept of culture and society, it is
vague, undifferentiated, and does not reflect the configurated,
continuous complexity of culture that the anthropologist and sociologist had already demonstrated so well.

It is not until Dollard takes up Thomas and Znaniecki's
Polish Peasant in Europe and America, the only life history that
does justice to the first criterion, that we begin to get a more clear
picture of what it means to take the concept of culture seriously,
and to see how it is reflected in community structure and dynamics.

Even a cursory reading of the Thomas and Znaniecki
volumes, or for that matter any good anthropological account of a
particular people and locale, makes clear that a community is a
highly differentiated and configurated set of relationships, things,
functions, and symbols, grounded in implicit and explicit traditions
which in turn reflect geographic, economic, religious, political, and
educational factors. Dollard is quite correct in maintaining that
when the psychologists and psychiatrists use such words as "milieu"
or "environment" or "social factors" they recognize the inextricable
relationship between culture and personality at the same time that

they expose their ignorance of the dimensions by which the culture becomes comprehensible. When the psychologist or psychiatrist sees an individual he literally *sees* a palpable, concrete, distinctive human being. He does not see culture the way he sees the individual and, it is Dollard's point, he does not have a conceptualization of culture that would allow him to understand or relate the individual's immediacies or behaviors or characteristics to the culture pattern. As a consequence, the individual always remains "figure" and culture always remains "ground," perpetuating the illusion that the constancy of the figure-ground relationship is only a reflection of the "out there" which the psychologist passively records.

From time to time Dollard seems to despair that a unified conception of culture and personality will emerge, and as a sophisticated student of culture he does not base his despair on the characteristics of individuals, or on partisanship, or on motivational factors, but he bases it on the structure and traditions of the academic culture. In the following excerpt Dollard makes clear that the character of the problem of a unified conception is not only determined by individual theoreticians (the way each thinks, formulates, and handles the problem) but also by the structure and traditions of the university.

As a matter of fact the coinage of the terms culture and personality at just this time indicates a kind of victory for the formal students of culture. Their researches and concepts have progressed to the point where they are mastering the minds of all social science students. We begin dimly to see that psychology begins wrong end to if it starts to study the individual mental life apart from its social contexts. The idea of culture is winning such control in the social science field that every problem, formerly posed without relation to this idea, has to be reexamined in the light of the new concept. It puts a new demand on the field of psychology; we must have a psychology which is not only independent and vigorous in an academic sense, but one which is oriented from the standpoint of the systematic study of culture. Any other kind of psychology will shortly be an historical curiosity.

If it is clear that the use of the terms culture and personality is a euphemistic device which permits an approach to a problem that would otherwise be more difficult to study, we can use the terms with comfort. After all, we do not object to the specific configuration of letters or syllables which are pronounced when we say culture and personality; we are only concerned that we shall not be deluded by our own terms and that we do not make another false start on one of the crucial social science problems. We are still talking about psychology when we say personality, and we are still referring to the systematic views of sociology and ethnology when we treat of culture. The essential problem, that of a psychology which is serviceable from the cultural standpoint, can just as well be discovered without using the terms at all.

If blame were to be attached to the use of the terms culture and personality we have laid ourselves wide open to it, for we have used them freely in the preceding chapters of this book. It will not have escaped any reader that the study of the "life history" is a problem in the field usually called "psychology," nor that this same life history can, even must, be seen as a cultural event. The fact of scientific importance is that neither psychology nor sociology gives a significant portrayal of the individual life and what seems to be demanded is that the life of the individual be taken as an object of study by both fields. We cannot say what such an attempt would do to the present definition of these two fields of knowledge; it might be found that the difference between them was one of emphasis, a difference so slight that it would no longer be desirable to study their object in two departments; perhaps a division of labor as yet not surmised would be discovered. The one scientifically intolerable state of affairs is the supposition that either can make much sense of its data without the other and that we are dealing with two discrete levels of useful observation. It may be we shall eventually have to go the whole way and state that there is a single social science and that what now seem like discrete fields or sciences are really shadings and points of emphasis in a unified field of scientific observation which is only distorted when we try to abstract "sciences" from it as we do at present [pp. 274–276].

Unfortunately, Dollard's plea is as urgent in 1973 as it was in 1935, and this unpleasant fact helps us to understand why when community psychology (and psychiatry) emerged in the university it was a reflection of psychology and not culture or community, of the individual and not the collectivity, of psychological structure and not community structure, of psychological dynamics and not community dynamics. One should, I suppose, be thankful that these fields were forced to look at the community, but this positive is more than cancelled by several negatives: the new look taken was through the misleading lenses of psychopathology; it addressed only those problems which phenomenologically seemed the most immediate and pressing; and it brought to bear on these problems actions, techniques, and interventions guaranteed to ignore or deemphasize the community structure and dynamics out of which these problems emerged.

Plant's "Personality and the Culture Pattern"

This book was published in 1937 when Dr. Plant, a psychiatrist, was the director of the Essex County (New Jersey) Juvenile Clinic.[2] Interestingly enough, but not surprisingly, the book is "an outgrowth and expansion of a short series of lectures before the Seminar on the Impact of Culture on Personality assembled at Yale University during the academic year 1933–34. Nor would it be complete without an expression of profound gratitude to the Director of that Seminar—Professor Edward Sapir of the Department of Anthropology." (John Dollard came to Yale to assist Sapir in that seminar.) Aside from the fact of his directorship of the clinic, the only other thing the book tells us about Plant's background is that he worked in industry for several years. From another source we learn that Plant was a key participant in the Second Colloquium on Personality Investigation held in 1929 under the joint auspices of the Committee on Relations of Psychiatry and the Social Sciences of the American Psychiatric Association and the Social Science Research Council. Reading the Proceedings of the Second Collo-

[2] After I had finished writing this book I learned that Plant's book was reprinted in 1966. At the very least its re-publication indicates that there are people who regard his book as highly as I do. There is no evidence that its re-publication has had a general impact, general acceptance, or increased recognition. That it was republished in 1967 obviously suggests that some people considered it to be as highly relevant to events of that time as it was to events of the thirties.

quium (1930) (and of the first one, held in 1928) reveals how wide a gulf there was between psychiatry and social science. The colloquia did little to bridge this gulf and the participants seemed aware of it. Conceptually, Sapir dominated the proceedings, aided (not that he needed aid) by Plant, Lawrence Frank, and Harry Stack Sullivan—who at one point said that the proceedings were contributing to confusion. Of the psychiatrists and psychologists at the second colloquium, Plant made the most distinctive and conceptually radical statements, the significance of which he more clearly elaborated in the book I attempt to summarize.

Whereas Dollard's book was a kind of focused *tour de force* and, therefore, not difficult to summarize, Plant's is more sprawling, broad, and speculative-theoretical, and it is far more difficult to summarize briefly. I shall not attempt to do justice to all of the major issues he raises or to convey the scope and depth of his erudition. Suffice it to say, he had a sense of social history and a working knowledge of the literature of social science that few people in community psychology and psychiatry have today. I cannot hope to convey through summary Dr. Plant's ability to take distance from the culture in order better to see its regularities. Nor shall I emphasize the fact that this meaty volume is a dispassionate indictment of psychiatric parochialism in terms both of its theoretical and practical absorption with the individual, and its ignorance of the ways in which the structure and dynamics of our society and communities shape personality. I regard this book as the best statement ever made about the possibilties of and the need for a community orientation. What I shall present will be, I fear, dull brass compared to the intellectual gold contained in this book.

(1) The culture-personality relationship. Plant discusses the conceptualization of the relationship in much the same way as Dollard did. He, too, states that dichotomizing the relationship to the extent that we do does violence to how it actually is manifest in reality. "Perhaps with increased knowledge we can accept the free permeability or even the disappearance of the wall between the personality and the environment as we have been accepting the disappearance of the walls between the physical and the mental, between the present and the past, between the conscious and unconscious. Still, man thinks in dichotomies and clings to them, and

in spite of our feelings that possibly the terms environment and personality are little more than general and specific modes of speaking of the same thing, we will continue to use them with the ordinarily accepted distinctions" (p. 16). When Plant discusses how environmental forces can influence and change personality, he does this via examples which reveal a penetrating sensitivity to the nature of community forces and characteristics.

> There is . . . (another) way in which the environment affects the personality. The discovery of steam as a motive power has "mechanically" forced the close packing of abodes, the dispersion of the functions of the family, the odd phenomenon of persons working and living in close proximity without the development of intimacy ties. Indeed—without too much sophistry—one may follow Ogburn to a tracing of all the far-reaching changes of the industrial era back to our inability economically to transmit steam as power. Another example is closer at hand—the dual set of forces that operate upon individuals living in or near New York City. There is the centralization on Manhattan Island of an enormous agglomeraion of socio-economic interests—these operating as a centripetal force of great power. There is a centrifugal force impelling these same persons towards more comfortable living conditions. Steam, electricity, the automobile—in ruthless succession these throw their power towards one or the other side of this tug-of-war. Individuals are impelled in one or the other direction, giving for the whole area that queer stability of the beehive built upon the ceaseless restlessness of each individual.
>
> Such forces have previously been recognized but that they actually color and alter the personality has been little more than asserted by the sociologists—and ignored by the psychiatrists. The exploration which we propose, has, therefore, two important goals. It seeks to cover that part of the field of knowledge where the social and individual disciplines must commingle. It also envisages the beginning of a form of social planning based upon the real and discovered needs of the individual. Society is, and has been, aroused over its misfits and the mass of human breakdown that is in the wake of its progress. It has erected every conceivable type of agency to study, salvage, or merely sweep up this debris. As the wreck-

age mounts, new agencies are demanded or "better standards of service" asked of those existing. The folly of believing that happiness and goodness can be fabricated by machinery (agencies) will be exposed only when we understand that the ills, corruptions, and hypocrisies of a cultural pattern flow into the child and man and "become a part of him for the day, for the year, or for stretching cycles of years." If it is true that the triumphs and tragedies of the street flow into and become a part of the child, then all programs of personality change must manage somehow to change the street. In other words, we need an individual-centered culture—a social pattern in which the components, good or bad, will be evaluated on the basis of the changes they produce in, and the goals they offer to, the personality [pp. 17–19].

Plant understood well that mobility was an increasing and crucial factor in the lives of people and that far from being understandable only in motivational terms, it was a reflection of distinctive economic characteristics of certain communities in relation to each other. Earlier than most people he saw how the characteristics of Manhattan would shape the surrounding area (Northern New Jersey, Long Island) in ways that would literally determine quality and structure of community and family, and the kinds of problems the individual personality would encounter. For Plant, Manhattan and Essex County were not simply adjacent points on a map, or areas in two different states that were obviously different in countless ways, but rather two areas who differences could only be understood by what brought them into relationship with each other.

It is a recurring theme in the book that social and community planning must be based on the most careful knowledge of the different points at which the cultural pattern creates undue stresses on the individual. But these points can never be discerned by a psychiatry whose theories and practices are not based on a confrontation with the culture-personality relationship. From Plant's standpoint the traditional bases of clinical psychiatry are major obstacles to new knowledge and productive social action. "The student of the personality, then, finds that his subject stretches out beyond the limits of the present into all of the past and that the here is nothing but a marked-off portion of the there. To understand the personality, it is not enough to be a psychiatrist; one must be historian and sociologist as well. If the ever-present, ever-growing, ever-controlling unconscious makes the individual one with his past, so do the psycho-motor tensions and the 'mechanical' forces of sociological influences make him one with his total environment" (p. 23).

(2) The "casual breakdown." How, Plant asks, can we develop a method which would allow us to locate and study the points at which personality and the culture pattern collide, and at the same time provide the opportunity to alter the pattern (not the individual)? Plant's answer is generalized from the principles, practices, and experiences of his "juvenile clinic," which was embedded in a school system.

> We use the term "casual breakdown" to describe the individual who is presenting a short and dramatic dislocation of his usual relationships with any given social institution or social pattern. . . .
>
> An example of the way the casual breakdown may show what the environment means to him is to be found in the experience of the churchgoer. One who is a regular Sunday school or church attendant answers all questioners (including himself) as to what the religious life means to him, in platitudes which sound well but have scarcely been tried in the fire of the issues of life. (Admittedly many individuals who seriously question leaving the church answer these queries in such a way as not to appear overtly as casual breakdowns. Our experience on a parallel situation suggests, however, that when the psychiatric clinic is organically attached to an institution the "pre-breakdowns" of that institution are soon at its doors.) A considerable amount of psychological investigation as to the relationship of the individual to the church has been already carried out on older people who have not been for a long time attending church or who as church members have various other problems. Such material, we have found, fails to throw into relief what we are looking for, namely, the contribution which a given sector of the environment makes to the personality and the consequent emotional reverberations. But when the individual first begins to break his formal contacts he does so because he has come to some decision—and

the reasons for that decision are available at just that time if they ever are to be. While the actual overt break is relatively incidental in relation to his total mental life, we have become so institutionalized that it seems to the individual a very critical step.

The minister or (in the school) the teacher is not the one to handle the problem at this point. He has too much at stake. The man can no more tell him that his sermons are stringy than can an adolescent boy discuss his interest in pictures of nude women with his parents. The observer of the casual breakdown can never be the individual carrying the social responsibility within the institution involved. The latter never learns more than the "delinquent" thinks he ought to know. The specialized observer must be close to the institution to be worked with, but his lack of institutional responsibility gives him in the eyes of the casual breakdown the objectivity that encourages frankness. We say "lack of institutional responsibility" because there must be adequate social responsibility— the observer who merely champions the individual in some new-found freedom is as useless as one who would but tie him back again into some particular institutional form [pp. 58–60].

Plant clearly argues against traditional thinking and practice in which clinics are geographically, socially, and conceptually distinct agencies, capable only of "seeing" the individual and robbed of the opportunity of observing the actual points of clash between the individual and the social institution. As a consequence, action for change is action to change individuals, and whatever in the particular institution contributes to the problems of individuals is left unchanged, guaranteeing an overwhelming case load. Plant's conception can be understood superficially as a serious commitment to primary prevention, which indeed is true. It is also true that Plant is in favor of a role geared to action for institutional change. What gives a distinctive thrust to these truths, indeed what powers them conceptually, is the seriousness with which Plant takes the personality-culture dynamics.

(3) Consequences of urbanization and mechanization. A long chapter entitled "Psychiatry and the Pressures of the Environment" is no less than a sophisticated discussion of the consequences

of increasing urbanization and mechanization and their mixed
effects on the developing child. Crowdedness, mobility, the role
of radio and the movies, changes in family functions and structure
are some of the factors he discusses. These consequences had been
noted and discussed by countless social analysts long before Plant.
Plant's contribution is to highlight the conflict between psychiatry's
emphasis on personality *integration* and the culture pattern's
production of personality *disintegration*. Psychiatry assumes that
integration is an individual need, but, he asks, what if this is not
the case? "Perhaps the psychiatric assumption that integration is
needful is in error. If not, these various threats to the integration
of the personality represent individually an unhealthy trait or
tendency, and if these social forces of increasing urbanization are
forever fostering them, we are presented with a grave problem,
predicting early and serious human breakdown, unless compensating
ways of attaining this necessity can be found" (p. 138). In closing
this chapter, after discussing the radical ways in which the traditional family structure and functions seemed to be changing, Plant
states that for him the heart of the matter is psychiatry's conceptual parochialism, which results in practices guaranteed to contribute to the overall confusion. *It would be more correct to say
that Plant views psychiatry no less than its patients as a victim of
specialization.*

> And what of the psychiatrist? Is he to build an even
> more impressive structure upon something which is vanishing
> into thin air? As the family in the sense in which we have
> known it is rapidly disappearing, is he to go on stressing its
> importance in the determination of all the adjustments of
> individuals?
> If the formulations of modern psychiatry are dependent
> upon the theory that the child's adjustment is the response to
> the interplay of family relationships and if these social forces
> of increasing urbanization are increasingly dismembering the
> family, we are presented with the serious problem that the
> most intimate and fundamental of the child's needs cannot be
> satisfied or that the psychiatric formulation as to the impor-
> tance of the family pattern is in error.
> The classical psychiatric approach—preoccupied with

the structure of the individual in vacuo—thus seems to us inadequate to a situation facing frankly the sociological forces [as illustrated in this chapter in the problems in an urban area]. This approach, rigidly adhered to, would predict nothing but rapid and widespread mental breakdown throughout our area. Possibly this will occur but our experience to date does not indicate that. We are suspicious that psychiatric theory demands considerable reformulation after it has had a much more extensive experience with individuals actually adjusting in a certain milieu. As long as we center our interest in hospitals—and will study our patients at ten, twenty, or hundreds of miles away from their actual homes, psychiatric theory must suffer from a certain parochial sort of individualism that quite lacks in realism [pp. 142–143].

It is no wonder that psychiatry, then and now, has managed to ignore Dr. Plant, for his social psychiatry (a term he used) had a conceptual, historical, social-science clarity that truly gave direction to action and practice.

(3) The "brutalizing" effects of poverty. This discussion takes place in a chapter entitled "Personality and an Urban Area." It is remarkable that a separate chapter should be devoted to this problem, and in light of when the book was written the degree of insight provided in it is somewhat amazing. If Plant's understanding and conceptualizations had ever entered the mainstream of psychiatry, the direction and viability of community psychiatry would have been discernibly different. At the very least, psychiatry would have viewed the War On Poverty with less shock and ignorance.

Most of the chapter is devoted to the effects of crowding on the individual. Four effects are discussed: lack of self-sufficiency, destruction of illusions, sexual maladjustment, and negativism and irritability. Plant does not discuss race in this chapter, which is somewhat surprising because he is talking about Newark, New Jersey, which had long harbored a large and scandalous black ghetto. The one time in the book he does discuss the question of race it is briefly, non-judgmentally, and insightfully handled.

(4) The individual-centered culture. The latter part of the book is an examination of how certain major social institutions and organized practices (the family, school, recreation, law, social

work, medicine, industry, church) define and illuminate the culture pattern and how through the method of the "casual breakdown" we can discern how they must be changed if they are to meet the needs of the individual personality.

When Plant "saw" an individual he saw him in the context of a changing but structured community. When he "saw" the community or any of its parts, he saw it in the context of a "psycho-osmotic" process in which there is no conceptual wall between personality and culture pattern. Plant does not criticize traditional psychiatry because it endeavors to help troubled individuals but rather because it fails to see that the problems of individuals are always related to and reflect the culture pattern, and the failure to recognize this (or the failure to develop procedures sensitive to these relationships) robs psychiatry of the possibility of changing the culture pattern—the only kind of change that has social promise. Plant is not a wide-eyed activist, or do-gooder, or crass environmentalist, or antiprofessional, or superficial social commentator and critic. He is also no advocate of the simplistic notion that increased services and material resources are the most important means of attacking widespread mental health problems. For Plant the two top priorities are a conceptual reorientation that would permit the development of new methods for locating the "casual breakdowns," and an understanding of "casual breakdowns" that would lead to action against the cultural pattern. Plant would have looked with pain on our community psychology and psychiatry because they reflected little or no change in thinking and they focused predominantly on changing individuals and not the culture pattern. Plant's ideas are truly radical; they attack the roots of traditional thinking in psychology and psychiatry. But in his insistence on systematic conceptualization, in his knowledge and use of the previous literature, and in his desire to avoid repeating the mistakes of the past, or to justify something new simply because it is new, Plant was working in the best conservative tradition.

Brown's "Psychology and the Social Order"

This book was published in 1936. Although it had little or no lasting effect on the "mainstream" of American social psychology, it was not without impact when it was published. The impact was due not only to the book's scope and directions but also to the shattering effects of the Great Depression, which by the middle thirties had not yet found a bottom. If Brown had written the book in the euphoric twenties, it is doubtful that a publisher would have paid any attention to it. Who in psychology would be interested in a book that attempted systematically to bring together the theories of Marx, Freud, and the Gestaltists? Who in psychology was interested in the structure and dynamics of the *social order,* in the idea that society is a dynamically (ever-changing) structured affair with genotypic and phenotypic properties that shape individual and group behavior? Who in psychology had a grasp of the concept of culture that would have led them in a time of presumed "prosperity" to see the disintegrative forces that would culminate in the Great Depression and expose the inadequacies, if not the bankruptcy, of American social science? (Bankruptcy does not mean one is without assets, but rather that one's assets are insufficient to sustain the business, and that one needs help and reorganization.) But by the middle thirties American society had so changed, and American social science was so shaken and bewildered, that Brown's book received a fair amount of attention, if only quite briefly. In the middle thirties psychologists could not easily dismiss Brown's disdain for existing social psychological formulations:

> The older texts which presented the psychological mechanisms supposedly governing social behavior in a broad and inclusive fashion are methodologically hopelessly outdated. The newer workers, on the whole, are so concerned with not making the methodological errors of the Instinct School of social psychologists that they neglect first principles altogether. They have little or nothing to say about the great social problems created by the economic and cultural crisis that all competent observers realize is now at hand. Furthermore, most of them are so filled with detailed accounts of the results of so-called experiments and measurements, of which the implications are never clear and actually often contradictory, that they could be of interest only to the specialist. It seemed to me that a course in social psychology should do two things for the general student. It should, first, attempt some clarifica-

tion of the methodological issues involved even in speaking of
a science of social psychology and it should indicate the relationships between social psychology and the other sciences,
like sociology, anthropology, and political economy, which are
also concerned with social behavior. Secondly, it should
present, in all their implications, those positive findings of
modern psychological research and theory which may be considered basic to social science and social philosophy. This
second point seems particularly important in these times of
economic and political stress, when scarcely a month goes by
without the appearance of some very pretentious social philosophy based as a rule on a faulty psychological premise.

For my purposes I shall single out from this meaty book
some major emphases that have bearing on a community psychology.[3] The first of these emphases is on the economic system,
which in any society reflects and reinforces values and ideology,
requires differentiation in labor, and shapes the nature of groups
or classes and their interactions. The relation of individuals and
groups to the processes of production shapes their "psychology,"
which is a fundamental point in Marx's writings. To understand
individual or group or social-class behavior without considering its
relation to the processes of production is to ignore a crucial variable.
That it took the Great Depression to make this point clear only
emphasized how ideology and culture had served to mask some of
the basic properties of the economic system, or, more correctly, how
the view that economics is economics and psychology is psychology
was a form of conceptual disaster that made the later social disaster
the surprise it was. The following quotation is interesting in several
ways: for revealing the social psychological significance Brown
attaches to the economic basis of class membership, for illustrating
his capacity to criticize the wish-fulfilling tendencies of the Marxist
and capitalist proponents, and, for showing quite cogently, how

---

[3] I shall have little to say about Brown's sympathetic but critical
remarks on Freud, which are basically similar to those made by Dollard and
Plant. The same will apply to his handling of the culture-personality relationship. The reader should be aware that by focusing only on those points in
Brown that neither Dollard nor Plant discuss, I do an injustice to his heroic
effort to fuse heretofore disparate theories.

the failure of academicians to recognize Marx's existence reflects *their* relationship to the conditions of *their* work.

Now before we go on to a more precise analysis of the concepts involved and attempt to define classes in terms of their underlying dynamic situations it is important to point out one fact immediately. In a great deal that is written on social classes it is quite obvious that very definite and precise wishes are often the fathers of very indefinite and hazy thoughts. This is certainly true of most of the bourgeois apologists for capitalism and preachers of cooperation; it is decidely true of great sections of Pareto's *The Mind and Society,* the one bourgeois attempt at a truly scientific sociology, and it is true of many single Marxist analyses. With few exceptions those who deny or gloss over the problems of classes and the class struggle, dynamically have membership-character in groups which would ultimately stand to lose a great deal by the class struggle, did it exist. And in these groups must be reckoned certain individuals who pay lip service to the cause of the workers but whose actual bread is very thickly buttered by the capitalist system and whose fare would be crusts alone under any other. I include here the professional leaders of the British Labour Party and of the American Federation of Labor. That such individuals deny the class struggle is only explainable on the basis of individual psychological factors, which will be introduced in Part III. On the other hand, those (there are individual exceptions here, of course, too) who most vehemently insist that the class struggle is basic to all contemporary politics, social philosophy, and economic theory would have the most to gain from a successfully conceived and executed proletarian uprising. This fact alone, looked on from the standpoint of a "disinterested" scientist, gives considerable support to the Marxist position. *One of our chief conclusions in this work will be that membership-character in a social field is the chief single determiner of the individual's aims and ambitions, his fears and hopes.* It has also been shown that threatened destruction of an organized social group increases the degree of organization for group self-protection. Since it is the avowed aim of the Marxist practical program to destroy the capitalists as a class and to further the class struggle, it is scarcely surprising that apologists for the existing order begin by denying antipathies to it, sometimes even denying the existence of classes themselves. Unpleasant thoughts about ourselves, as the Freudians have shown, tend to be pushed into the background. Naturally the comfortable bourgeois denies the "class struggle." Even the Marxists do not expect him to affirm it.

Some of those who insist on class struggle as being ever present fall into errors nearly as serious as do those who constantly deny it. Certain Marxists made laughing-stocks of themselves throughout the later nineteenth century by predicting in the fall of every year the successful conclusion of the class struggle through revolutionary mass action in the following spring. Leon Trotsky after his expulsion from Russia for attempting to further his doctrine of the permanent revolution has made mistaken prediction on mistaken prediction concerning sociological historical events. Certain American radicals saw in the election of Franklin D. Roosevelt and the ensuing "Roosevelt Revolution" a second Kerensky revolution, which regime they predicted might fall before Christmas, 1933. It is, however, quite obvious that the "American Proletarian Revolution" is still far in the offing.

In this vast confusion of rival opinions the "academic" social scientist is inclined to hold his tongue, because he pretends a neutral disinterested attitude and protests that social science is not yet in a position to solve such problems. I cannot refrain from pointing out that such a glossing over of this highly important problem is quite indicative of academic "social science." The position of the scientist in both endowed and state tax-supported institutions depends not only in the long but also in the short run on the existing social order. His membership-character is in the bourgeois region and consequently he usually does not even so much as mention the class struggle. Amongst these individuals Marx, whose opponents, those of them who were intellectually honest, at least, have always considered him a thinker of great import, is the victim of an at times conscious, at times unconscious conspiracy of silence. Most texts of social psychology completely ignore his theories, other mention them only in very distorted fashion. But it is daily becoming more obvious that despite certain methodological limitations of the Marxian system, the time is past when social science may ignore Marx. Let us start

our discussion of social classes with emphasis on the following
statement: Marx is undoubtedly the most important social
psychologist of modern times on the question of the effect of
social class membership-character on the social psychology of
the individual, when the class struggle exists [pp. 167–169].

One does not have to be a Marxist or even agree with
Brown's partial acceptance of the dynamics of the "class struggle"
to recognize either the inextricable relationship between economic
and psychological systems or the validity of his claim that Marx
was a most insightful psychologist. In recent decades there has been
a resurgence of interest in Marx, particularly in relation to his
psychology, and the reader unaware of this aspect of Marx should
consult Fromm (1961) and Bernstein (1971), the latter a philosopher, whose recent book *Praxis and Action* is the most penetrating
discussion I have read.

A second emphasis in Brown, stemming primarily from the
Marxist stance, is on social conflict. Put most simply: communities
in our society are not, as American ideology and political rhetoric
used to put it, one big happy family cooperating on the basis of
equal opportunity to achieve common goals; they are instead highly
differentiated on bases which make for conflict. Communities have
been born out of conflict, religious and political, and increasing
differentiation within communities frequently has been a result of
conflict. This, of course, was no longer news to Brown's readers who
were in the midst of the Great Depression, but up until that
catastrophe such an emphasis was rarely taken seriously.[4] Related
to this general emphasis are specific conflicts stemming from
differences in religion, race, ethnicity, minority status, political
affiliation, social class, and rural-urban locale.

Brown does not emphasize social conflict in the social
order because it is frequent and influential but rather to understand

[4] The nature and sources of conflict within the American community
were clear but not stressed in the first Middletown study by the Lynds
(1929), done in 1925, but they were crystal clear and stressed in the second
Middletown study (1937), done in the midst of the Great Depression. And
when one reads Robert Lynd's *Knowledge For What?*, published in 1939,
one can see why community conflict became an inescapable problem for
some social scientists.

how the different sources of conflict are related to each other and how in turn they reflect major characteristics of the larger society, of which the manner in which the economic system determines social relationships is very important. (Brown is not an uncritical economic determinist; he criticized Marxism for its gross underestimation of the influence of "national membership" on behavior.) Brown, for example, does not discuss black-white conflict only in terms of its psychological and moral aspects but attempts to demonstrate how the conflict and its severity (as in lynchings) vary as a function of changes in the economic status of both races. The phenotypic aspects of a social conflict, be it a race riot, labor strike, or religious or ethnic discrimination, should never be confused with its genotypic characteristics, which alone permit one to see the larger picture.

The books by Dollard, Plant, and Brown were published about the same time, but the first two make only passing reference to the Great Depression, and it is only Brown for whom it is a major event requiring drastic changes in thinking in the social sciences. Whatever other factors may have contributed to Brown's emphases, it is certainly true that the social and psychological theories he utilized lead him to look broadly at the contexts in which human behavior is embedded and developed. The fact that Brown attempted systematically to integrate three major, ostensibly different, theories is more important than the partial success of his efforts, because the effort not only exposed the incompleteness and inadequacies of traditional social psychology (as a basis for explanation and prediction, let alone control) but also demonstrated how what C. Wright Mills later called the sociological imagination is the most potent weapon we have against the disease of academic parochialism. After one reads Brown one cannot look at society in general, and its communities in particular, as a vague conglomeration of groups and functions that in some equally vague way shapes the lives of people; one will not easily confuse its phenotypic appearance with genotypic characteristics and dynamics; one will not pretend to understand a community by focusing only on narrow aspects of it; one will be less likely to assume that "treating" the problems of individuals has any bearing on changing those community characteristics which play a role in creating those problems; and finally, it makes it more difficult to forget that one's own thoughts and actions are no less a reflection of society than the thoughts and actions of those whom one observes or attempts to change, and that unless one understands this, one's grasp of social and personal reality will unduly restrict the already narrow limits of change.

Brown is no visionary or utopian or prescriber of solutions—witness the concluding sentences of his book: "Man can choose and can effect change, but both what he will choose and how much he will effect the change are very limited. All signs indicate that the next few years will be years where change occurs with extreme rapidity. The final outcome of these changes is quite uncertain. It is hoped, however, that the material presented in this book will help the reader to understand these changes and view his own role in them with greater equanimity. Any social psychology which does not do at least that much is worth nothing at all" (p. 460). But to understand "with greatest equanimity" obviously did not mean for Brown the passive acceptance of change but rather the satisfaction that follows from the feeling that one has unshackled oneself from those aspects of tradition that are imprisoning. And Brown was an amazing exemplar of this point in that he was able to view American society and social science in general, and social psychology in particular, from the vantage points of three "foreigners" (Marx, Freud, Lewin) who in 1936 were not at all close to the substance of American social science traditions. That he was able to do this helps explain why Brown has remained unrecognized and why when community psychology and psychiatry emerged as a consequence of the social turmoil of the sixties, a turmoil in its own way almost as severe and unsettling to the society as the Great Depression, there was no feeling of "understanding with equanimity" but rather bewilderment with fear. This would not have surprised Brown, whose analyses made it quite clear that traditions change very slowly and that the university in our society is so dependent on the society, and its internal organization of specialities so bureaucratized and rationalized (like industry), so as to have the effect on its members of making examination of self and society virtually impossible. Brown did not need Marx to make this and some others of his major points. Veblen would have served him as well. In the

case of the university, Veblen's *The Higher Learning In America,*
first published in 1918, was in 1936, as it is today, the best description and interpretation of how the university reflects and is dependent on the dominant society and its ideology, a fact which helps
explain why Veblen received so little reward and recognition during
his career in numerous academic settings. The most recent analysis
I commend to the reader is Gouldner (1970).

In his 1935 foreword to the *Handbook of Social Psychology,*
Murchison said:

> The social sciences at the present moment stand naked
> and feeble in the midst of the political uncertainty of the
> world. The physical sciences seem so brilliant, so clothed with
> power by contrast. Either something has gone all wrong in the
> evolution of the social sciences, or their great day in court has
> not yet arrived. It is with something akin to despair that one
> contemplates the piffling, trivial, superficial, damnably unim-
> portant topics that some social scientists investigate with
> agony and sweat. And at the end of all these centuries, no one
> knows what is wrong with the world or what is likely to hap-
> pen to the world [p. ix].

In 1969 Nisbet comments:

> It is the massive transformation of the American social
> scene since the Second World War that has focused attention
> upon the relative poverty of resources in the social sciences.
> Vast industrial relocations, redevelopments of central cities,
> city and regional planning, community organization, serious
> efforts on the part of civic agencies to prevent, rather than
> merely punish, crime, the innumerable social and psychological
> problems involved in the administering of both governmental
> and private social security systems—all of these and other
> problems have led to an almost desperate turning to social
> scientists for help.
>
> Of a sudden, a good deal of so-called social science
> was proved empty or irrelevant despite the public pretense
> to the contrary of some academic intellectuals. It became evi-
> dent that more reliable knowledge—slim though it was—
> frequently lay in the experiences of social workers, business-

men, architects, city-managers, and politicians than in whole
volumes of the social science journals. Several generations of
social thought based upon determinism had produced very
little of value to society. The familiar prescriptions of governmental ownership or management, by which liberals had for
decades salved their social consciences, began to turn sour
in the mouth when it became apparent that the real problem
often was not whether the government shall render aid, but
how [pp. xvii–xviii].

I do not regard Brown's *Psychology and the Social Order*
as a conceptually successful book, but I do regard it as a deliberate
effort to face the significances of certain social realities (particularly the Great Depression and Fascism), to acknowledge the bankruptcy of traditional social science theory, and to construct a new
theoretical base. Brown was not trying to be fashionably "relevant"
from the standpoint of social action and participation; in fact, he
has little to say or recommend about action or program, and was
quite the opposite of fashionable relevance in that he challenged
the most cherished assumptions of his field and proposed a radically
different theoretical alternative. In his recent book Gouldner (1970)
has discussed why a social scientist like Brown would have, at best,
a temporary impact, and why even today Brown's emphasis is not
in the mainstream of American social science. And Gouldner's
analyses indicate why this mainstream, in which Talcott Parsons,
who is referred to most frequently in the literature of community
psychology and psychiatry as a basic conceptualizer for these fields,
has been the chief navigator, leads one away from rather than
toward social reality. Parsons' *The Structure of Social Action* was
published the year after Brown's book and its difference from it
can be seen in Gouldner's judgment:

> Seen as a conservative manifesto of antideterminism
> and antipessimism, Parsons' earliest work should no longer
> appear so utterly disconnected with the calamitous events in
> the surrounding society. If one were to regard it as a Shavian
> piece of "Advice to Intelligent Patriots in the Midst of Social
> Disaster," it might be thought of as a remonstrance not to
> despair, but to take heart, to believe that they may yet work

their way out of the impasse in which they find themselves, to believe that their own energies and effort do make some difference, and to believe that they should not surrender to false theories that prophesy an end to their way of life. For all its detachment, then, Parsons' early work is very much a response to the crisis of his time.

But it is not a response from the standpoint of those whose deprivation was near destitution; it does not, in short, resonate to the suffering of the bankrupt small farmer or the unemployed worker. Indeed, it is only if we expect that a response to social crisis must express sympathy with suffering that we will fail to see Parsons' work as a response. Parsons' reponse, however, is singularly insensitive to the sheer suffering of the desperately afflicted. Nowhere is the word "poverty" mentioned in *The Structure of Social Action,* although it is written in the midst of a national experience with breadlines, unemployment, and hunger. Instead, Parsons' response is concerned to avoid institutional discontinuities and to maintain traditional loyalties; that is, he is concerned with discouraging radical social change [pp. 195–196].

I shall assume that those community psychologists and psychiatrists who refer to Parsons have rarely read him. Certainly none of them has ever indicated in what way he or she depends on and uses Parsons, and none of them seems aware that in recent years some leading Parsonians are looking more appreciatively at Marx than heretofore (Gouldner, 1970, p. 362). Gouldner makes much more sense out of Parsons than I have ever been able to, although Gouldner is at pains to point out that one can never be sure what Parsons is saying.

The Chicago School of Sociology

In the recent literature on community psychology one finds (not always) some reference to the Chicago department of sociology which for most of the earlier decades of this century dominated the field, both by its research activities and by its students who subsequently made distinctive contributions elsewhere. It would be more correct to say that the reference is usually to one or two of the leaders (Burgess, Faris, or Park, for example) and the reader is

left to his own devices if he wishes to know why the activities of
the Chicago department might be relevant today.[5] In fact, when
I query psychologists and psychiatrists about the Chicago school
rarely am I told more than about three characteristics: the department was interested in the city, mental disorder, and juvenile
delinquency. One is left with the impression that reference to the
Chicago school is a token gesture to scholarliness, an acknowledgement that in the museum of scholarship there are some interesting
antiques.

The interest of the Chicago school in the city was not a
reaction to specific events or to the sudden eruption of conflicting
social forces, as was the case in the recent emergence of community
psychology and psychiatry. On the contrary, the interest reflected
a long-standing focus in American and European sociology on the
nature and consequences of industrialization and urbanization in
capitalist society. That society was becoming urbanized; that this
process was a reflection of economic-political-social values and
processes; that the human flow to the cities (in America, at least)
was comprised of ethnic and racial groups which affected and were
affected by existing physical-geographical and social class factors;
that social and family disorganization were outstanding concomi-
tants of urbanization; that the city was an everchanging, highly
differentiated social organism that could not be comprehended by
paying attention to isolated fragments or problems; that knowledge
of this organism was superficial and therefore could not serve as

---

[5] As I indicated in an earlier chapter, George Herbert Mead is
referred to far less frequently, and yet from a theoretical standpoint his
writings provided the underpinnings for much of the work done at Chicago.
Indeed, one of the most cogent points Dollard (1935) makes earlier in this
chapter is identical to one that Mead constantly emphasized: "We are not,
in social psychology, building up the behavior of the social group in terms
of the behavior of the separate individuals composing it; rather, we are
starting out with a given social whole of complex group activity, into which
we analyze (as elements) the behavior of each of the separate individuals
composing it. We attempt, that is, to explain the conduct of the individual
in terms of the organized conduct of the social group, rather than to account
for the organized conduct of the social group in terms of the conduct of the
separate individuals belonging to it. For social psychology, the whole
(society) is prior to the part (the individual), not the part to the whole;
and the part is explained in terms of the whole, not the whole in terms of the
part or parts."

a basis for productive social action; that the city was the arena in which the future of American society was being shaped in an unplanned, haphazard way that increasingly diluted any personal sense of community—these were not new ideas in American or European sociology. What was distinctive about the Chicago school was that they attempted to take the totality of these problems seriously, and deliberately mounted a multifaceted research program on the basis of which they hoped sound programs of social planning and amelioration would develop.[6] To the leaders of this school the city was a phenomenon as fascinating, complex, and ever-changing as the human personality was to the psychoanalyst. To grasp the interrelatedness in this phenomenon of its social, historical, and physical characteristics, the ecological theory and method were employed, and here too the principles of ecology were taken quite seriously. The combination of a comprehensive and historical view of the city, an ecological sensitivity to its human flow and composition, and a focus on changes in and relationships among geographical or neighborhood or "natural" areas conveyed a sense of the city and its dynamics that has yet to be rediscovered by community psychology and psychiatry.[7] There is hardly an urban problem today that was not recognized and conceptualized by the Chicago school within a broad and dynamic conception of the city. They were interested in mental disorder, but primarily as an index of social disorganization and the withering sense of community. They were interested in juvenile delinquency and other forms of deviance not only because they were significant social

[6] For an account of the Chicago school the reader should consult Faris (1967) and Burgess and Bogue (1967). They describe how interest in the city was shared by many people in different departments at the University of Chicago, long before the 1920s when the department of sociology launched a formal urban research program. In fact, when one reads the history of Jane Adams' Hull House, started in 1889, some of its strongest supporters and participants were University of Chicago faculty members, not the least of whom was Albion Small who founded the department of sociology, the first in this country. John Dewey played a similar role. The school which Dewey started in 1896 is one example among many in which a faculty member engaged in some community venture to implement and test ideas.

[7] Here is a *small* sample of some of the things studied: the family, strikes, black culture, immigrants, the Chicago Real Estate Board, prostitutes, delinquents, hobos, voluntary associations, street corner society, police, hotel life, gangs.

problems but also because they illuminated the nature of urbanization. They studied racial and ethnic groups in the community not only because they were intrinsically interesting but also because they were part of the urban culture, that is, one could not understand the urban community without coming to grips with these groups and their relationship to each other. The use of the life history was far more than a way of understanding an individual or a clinical document pointing to a therapeutic remedy. It was a window through which one could get glimpses of community dynamics. The life history was a cultural document.

There was a roving, scanning curiosity about the city that would rest on groups and places ordinarily overlooked or unstudied. Let us listen to Burgess (Burgess and Bogue, 1967):

> I recall Nels Anderson telling me he was greatly bored by his landlady, in the roominghouse district where he was studying the homeless man, telling him her life history. I told him, "Why, this is valuable, you must get it down on paper." I still have this document; it is most revealing. Who becomes a roominghouse keeper? What are the problems of a roominghouse keeper? Who is the star boarder: How do you keep a roominghouse orderly against all the tendencies toward disorder in a roominghouse district? Out of this one document you get more insight into how life moves in the roominghouse area, and especially from the standpoint of the roominghouse keeper, than you do from a mountain of statistics that might be gathered [p. 9].

Dollard was a product of the Chicago school of sociology, Plant was strongly influenced by it, and the fact that both of these men have gone unrecognized is symptomatic of the lack of understanding by community psychology and psychiatry of what the Chicago school stood for and did.[8] If such understanding had

---

[8] In psychology Dollard has been recognized for his work in personality and learning theory, particularly in his collaborations with Neal Miller (1941, 1950). In taking this direction Dollard was seeking to employ learning theory as a possibly fruitful way of studying in minute detail how culture is acquired by the individual, that is, as an intervening set of mechanisms or processes or "glue" which explained how personality and culture are inevitably and permanently fused. I do not regard this to have

existed these "new" fields would have had, at the very least, to confront several questions: how is community being conceptualized?
Can one justify using the word community when one's major focus
is on a particular physical area or on a particular set of human
problems? Is it possible to understand the structure and workings of
a community in terms of an individual psychology or one which
focuses on presumed personal pathology? If the presumed pathology
of individuals and the problems of particular groups are in part
manifestations of social and cultural factors, how are these factors
embedded in community institutions? Can one justify dealing with
social pathology without altering community institutions? If a
community is an everchanging (albeit relatively stable) social organism, how does one become aware of these changes so that their
possible consequences can be critically assessed? Is it possible that
psychological and psychiatric theory are in principle inadequate for
conceptualizing a community and, as a consequence, can never
do justice to its structure and workings? Are these fields doomed
by this possibility to the role of reactor instead of actor, always
missing the forest because we only see trees? Is the use of the label
"community" based on some kind of systematic conceptualizing
(as, for example, personality is in psychoanalytic theory) or is it a
euphemism for a desire to be socially relevant, to be better as
firemen putting out social blazes not knowing where the next fire
will erupt or whether the embers of old fires will get renewed
strength?

    Towards the end of his career, Burgess (Burgess and Bogue,
1967) said:

> It is my firm conviction after a quarter-century of
> urban research, that the conceptual system for urban studies
> should take in the whole field of sociological theory. Social
> organization with its class structure; social change as the result
> of technological discoveries and inventions; collective behav-
> ior; social control, ecological studies, and population studies,
> all give us clues. But whatever is done in one of these fields

been an illuminating effort, although it grappled with an important problem.
Few psychologists know of Dollard's earlier works which led up to this
effort, and which are still excitingly relevant to the issues of our day.

should not fail to acknowledge principles established by research in other areas of urban life. Personal and social disorganization are of peculiar interest in the study of the city because of the fact of change, because of the change of tempo of city life. But social disorganization needs to be studied not so much from the standpoint of social pathology (although that also requires certain attention) but as an aspect of an interaction and adjustment process that eventually leads into social reorganization. Many trends in social disorganization lead to personal disorganization, community breakdown; but others are attempts at community reorganization. Some of the reorganizational efforts are successful and these of course need to be most carefully observed and studied as they occur. Merely charting past trends, and extrapolating them into the future can never suffice for an entity so dynamic and adaptable as the urban community! [p. 10]

The Chicago school of sociology was not the last word in bold or imaginative theorizing, or in scope, or in the depth of its social analysis and proposals for change, or in its use of social action as a vehicle for comprehending the nature and strength of cultural values and institutional traditions—that is, to use efforts at change as a deliberate method for experiencing the nature and dilemmas of social change. Nevertheless, it represented a pioneer effort to understand the composition, structure, and dynamics of communities, the principles of their growth and change, their sources of conflict, disorganization, and stability, the subcultures they contained and their interactions, and the ways in which the political and economic values and factors operated as cause and effect in urban living. They tried to breathe life into the abstractions "city" or "community."

If social psychiatry, community psychology, and community psychiatry had been able to identify meaningfully with what the Chicago school stood for and did, they would have been provided a vision, a fund of knowledge, and a way of thinking that would have liberated them from the constrictions of an individual psychology, of an ahistorical stance, and of a superficial grasp of the nature and strengths of societal values and urban culture. But as Dollard, Plant, and Brown state, American psychology and psychiatry were not in a basic sense rooted in the concept of culture, certainly not in the sense that sociology and anthropology were. If such roots had existed, psychology and psychiatry would have "discovered" the community long before the nineteen sixties and they would have been better prepared, in theory and practice, to understand the dynamics of urban life and to avoid some of the dangers and discouragements of reactions to crises and to the symptoms rather than to the causes of human misery. They would have been less prone to develop theories of personality so devoid of the facts, structure, and influence of the culture pattern. They would have, perhaps, become more self-conscious about how their role and place (as individuals or as fields) in the community—who entered these fields, where they were located, the people they served or studied, and the relation between these and economic factors—were themselves illuminating facts of community structure, not fortuitous or self-evident, or not in need of justification other than on the basis of professional tradition and wisdom.

If the roots of psychology and psychiatry had been in the soil of the Chicago tradition, they might have seen that what powered interest in the contemporary community was a sensitivity to what may be considered the single most disintegrating aspect of contemporary life: *the withering, attentuated psychological sense of community.* What powered the sociology of that time was a poignant awareness of the depth of modern man's psychological sense of anonymity and alienation. But to psychology and psychiatry, rooted in the psychology of the individual and the supremacy of intrapsychic factors, the cultural context was at best seen as background noise and at worse ignored. Although in their work with troubled individuals psychological clinicians were aware of the consequences of a weakened sense of psychological community, they could not place this in the larger context, and when in recent years they have been literally forced to recognize that it existed and that they were being asked to, or on their own wished to deal with it, it was no wonder that they felt and were found to be wanting. As Plant predicted several decades ago, to help troubled individuals who bring you their problems requires no special defense, however much one may disagree with how it is done and with what benefits. The defining characteristic of a clinician is that he does the best he can on the basis of whatever he knows to help someone who comes to him with his troubles. But when the psychological clinician enlarged his role to include the community and its problems, he should have had the wisdom to be humble before the recognition that he was faced with what for him were new conceptual and practical problems of a scope and complexity for which his accustomed ways of thinking and acting would in most respects be a hindrance. The degree of culture shock he experienced was the hallmark of his parochialism. Ironically, in dealing with the culture he was confronted with the very thing of which he had been an unwitting victim.

VI

The Perception
and Conception
of a Community

Taking the concept of culture seriously requires facing two sets of
related general problems. One is social, in the sense that it concerns
the structure, functions, and interrelationships between institutions.
The other is psychological, in that it concerns how this external
culture patterning is assimilated by individuals, providing them
with a blend of values and categories of thought that "explains"
their world—indeed, a blend which has the effect of avoiding the
need for explanation and justification. If only because this book is

130

concerned with *community* psychology, we must give priority to the question of what this label for a field encompasses and the concept of external culture patterning it reflects. What is meant by a community? What institutions comprise it? How are they seen to be related? What are the formal ways by which a community recognizes and responds to problems? How does one determine the distinctive characteristics of a particular community; how does it differ from other communities? What is the significance of geographical factors? What constitutes and who possesses formal and informal power?

We can ask other questions but the overall thrust is clear: a community is more than a political or geographical area. It contains a variety of institutions which may be formally or informally related to each other—or not related at all. It is made up of myriads of groups, transient or permanent, which may have similar or different purposes and vary in size, power, and composition. It possesses resources and vehicles for their disbursement. Its groups and institutions vary considerably in size, purposes, and the power they possess or seek. And a community has a distinctive history which, although it may no longer be relevant in a psychological sense, is crucial for understanding some of its present qualities and social, political, religious, or economic characteristics. A community has changed, is changing, and will change again. How and why this occurs will in part be a function of what happens in the larger society, but only in part; its own characteristics will always play a role in how it responds to external forces. Communities have many characteristics in common, but each in some ways possesses distinctiveness.

How complete a community is, the degree to which its parts are functionally related, the extent to which change in one part brings change in other parts, the sensitivity of a community to the facts and directions of change, the relationships of change to alignments of power—these make a set of related issues no less difficult to study and comprehend than the nature of the atom or the workings of the human body. I shall return later to the significance of this complexity, but one of its significances must be stated now: *The complexity of a community will in large part determine the fate of efforts to change that community in any respect. The fact*

*that individuals or groups in a community desire to effect a change
is saying something about that community. What happens to the
effort will in large measure be determined by the degree to which
it is based on a realistic conception of the complexity and distinctiveness of that community.*

Let us turn to a listing and brief discussion of a few dimensions or factors which would begin to reflect the composition and
structure of a community. Any one of these dimensions is quite
complicated and its detailed interrelationships with the others raise
the level of conceptual complexity exponentially.

Religion in Two Communities

Although religion and its institutions are an obvious feature
of a community (in our society), social scientists have given them
little attention. It is as if the constitutional separation of church
and state had in its own ways been taken seriously by social science.
The fact that religion has played a decreasing role in the lives of
individuals, particularly among scientists, undoubtedly has made
it an unfashionable area for study, but what is unfashionable should
never be confused with what is unimportant. What may be unimportant to an individual scientist may be quite important to
others and play a very significant role in the community. Few social
scientists would deny that religion is an ubiquitous feature of our
communities, that communities vary in the extent to which they
bear the stamp of religion, and that the dilution in the strength
of religious belief in the past two centuries has had pervasive effects
on the nature of social life—such as an effect on the psychological
sense of community. Whether it be for the purpose of understanding
a community or because one wants to understand how it is or should
be changing, the community psychologist cannot ignore the role of
religion. I shall illustrate this point by some experience which I and
my colleagues had in the role of community psychologists.

A number of years ago a superintendent of schools called
me, as Director of the Yale Psycho-Educational Clinic, to ask about
the possibility of obtaining school psychological services. The town
in which he was superintendent was old, industrial, and unattrac-

tive (Town A). I went to see him and within five minutes was told that the services he sought were for both the public and the parochial schools, neither of which had psychological service of any kind. The inclusion of the parochial schools struck me as odd, if not illegal. I knew that this was an overwhelmingly Catholic town and the superintendent made it clear that this was so. For reasons completely unrelated to religious considerations, it was not possible for us to arrive at a mutually satisfying arrangement. I was, in fact, interested in a relationship precisely because our clinic (which was then a training and research center) had no experience with parochial schools. This superintendent died the following year. Two years later I was contacted by the new superintendent, who was young, vigorous, and eager to make changes, none of which, however, involved the parochial schools. This young man was a native of the town, quite aware of the intimate ties between the church and the public schools, and intent on husbanding all resources for, and only for, the public schools. A contract between this school system and our clinic was quickly and successfully negotiated.

At about the same time a similar relationship was started with the adjacent town (Town B), which was, so to speak, a twin town. Both towns looked identical and they were perceived by residents and nonresidents alike as peas from the same pod. But not too long after we began to work in the two school systems, particularly in their high schools, we became aware of differences. In Town A the high school was akin to a military establishment with scores of published rules about dress, conduct, and general comportment; and these rules were enforced by a principal who was no less than a petty tyrant. The high school in Town B was much looser and anarchic, with numerous problem students and generally poor morale among teachers and students. The differences between the two high schools were marked in the extreme and in no ways compatible with our guiding assumption that we were dealing with highly similar towns. If these two towns were as similar, as we and everyone else believed, how did we account for the extreme differences? If our assumption was correct that characteristics were directly and indirectly reflected in its schools, we had to conclude that the two towns were not all that similar, external appearances and popular belief to the contrary notwithstanding. And so we began to look afresh at the two communities, asking new kinds of questions and using new sources of data.

What we found was that in Town A well over 90 percent of students and teachers were Catholic. Approximately 50 percent of the teachers had received their training at a local teachers college and 40 percent had received their training in one of three Catholic colleges. A conservative estimate would be that 70 percent of all school personnel were native to the town. Town B was significantly more varied on these same factors. In addition, whereas Town A was essentially white, Town B had a growing black population. Furthermore, the military characteristics of Town A's high school met with the enthusiastic approval of parents, who received the principal as a worthy defender of their traditions. In fact, the new superintendent had been a student of the incumbent principal, and despite the fact that he did not approve of the principal's outlook and practices he made it quite clear to us that the community would resist any effort to remove him. Nothing like this kind of relationship between school and community existed in Town B; indeed, it was hard to discern any close and direct relationships between school and community.

These findings were as puzzling as they were interesting. Although they pointed to differences in the schools in religious and racial composition, we still did not understand how this could happen in two contiguous communities so highly similar to each other. We then met separately with the top administrators of the two school systems, told them precisely what was puzzling us, and asked them to try to tell us how these differences between schools might become more comprehensible. Our relationships with the administrators were cordial and they were prepared to talk candidly. They tried hard, but the more they talked the more they talked of the similarities. With one exception: near the end of the second meeting one of the administrators pointed out a difference that, to his surprise, he had failed to bring into the conversation. Whereas Town A was overwhelmingly Catholic and Italian, Town B was far more heterogenous in religion, running the gamut from numerous Protestant denominations to Greek and Russian Orthodox ones. This religious variation was, of course, related to ethnic variation, but the point this individual went on to stress was that the religious heterogeneity very much influenced the social structure of the community, the workings of the political system, and the schools. For example, he pointed out that whereas Town A had never had a school referendum turned down, and had just opened a magnificent new high school, Town B had just voted down a school building referendum for the second time, and this was in no small part due to the opposition of different religious groups. (Not surprisingly, when the era of teacher militancy began, the possibility of a teachers' strike in Town A was next to nil, and there has been no strike. There has been one major strike in Town B and each of its yearly contract negotiations have been marred by major conflicts and animosities.)

The point of this example is *not* that religion explains the differences between the schools or even that it accounts for some of the important differences between the two communities. Such explanations are much too simple and rest on a cause-and-effect type of thinking that shortcircuits sensitivity to the interrelationships between factors. The obvious point I wish to make is that institutionalized religion is a major characteristic of a community, an organizing and ramifying force, a force not only significant in the lives of many of its individuals but also significant for other community institutions and forces. To understand individual students and teachers in Town A requires far more than attending to their religion; but, similarly, in order to understand the culture of their school, to comprehend what they absorb and how they absorb it, we cannot ignore the role of religion in their community. One can, of course, ignore it because ordinarily one cannot *see,* and by law one is not *supposed* to see, religion in public schools. But the controversy about prayers in the schools, and about celebrations of religious holidays, reveals that in schools and their communities religion is both an organizing and a divisive factor. And if one follows the modern history of the issues surrounding the use of public monies to support parochial schools, it is impossible to deny that religion is an ubiquitous factor in our communities, and one that interrelates with other factors basic to an understanding of a community.

To say that religion is a factor and that it interrelates with

other factors is to offer a glimpse of the obvious, even though we
are far from understanding what this means for the present and
future of communities. The role of religion today is not what it was
in the past or what it will be in the future. To understand these
changes we ordinarily invoke the role of social forces and processes
in the wider society, as if change in the local community is a simple
consequence of those external forces. This is a way of thinking that
permits one to say that changes in the role of the Catholic church
in a particular community are due to Pope John and the Vatican
Council he convened. There is, of course, some truth to such an
explanation but there is also truth to an explanation that says that
what led up to and what happened at that council reflected prior
changes in countless local communities in which the church was a
part.

Although significant changes in a community almost always
reflect happenings and events "outside" of it, those factors which
we perceive as external already reflect some aspect of change in
the community—for example, what happened at the Vatican Council reflected and reinforced changes that already had taken place in
countless communities. Our tendency to think in simple cause-and-
effect terms, as well as in terms of simple internal and external
relationships, are potent obstacles to being sensitive to the early
signs of change. Yes, it is a glimpse of the obvious to note that
religion is a factor in the community and that it interrelates with
other factors, but what is not so obvious is that just as the interrelationships (in a particular community) have not always been
what they are now, they will in the future be different again.
And that is the whole point: how do we look at these obvious interrelationships at the same time that we take seriously the fact
that the obvious is time-bound? How do we look at each of these
factors and their interrelationships in order to discern the ways in
which they are changing? How do we transcend the consequences
of the fact that inevitably each of us is narrowly embedded in a
community, perceives it in very restricted ways, and sees its future
as a continuation of its present? It seems true that although one
part of us knows that our community is different today than it was
in the past, we cannot imagine its future being much different from
its present.

It is likely that for many readers religion means the Catholic, Protestant, or Jewish religions. Although in some vague way we realize that none of these religions is composed of people who are homogeneous in belief, or of congregations that are similar in all matters of ritual and observance, we are usually far from clear about how these intrareligious differences are reflected in a community and are part of its dynamics. These intrareligious differences would lack general interest were it not for their relationships to social-class factors, residential concentration, population shifts, ethnicity, and sponsorship of community service agencies. That these differences are of significance for the larger community is well-known, if not obvious, to anyone who has participated in the collection and distribution of United Fund money. In fact, my experience persuades me that if one traces over time the changes that have occurred in the religious affiliation of those responsible for dispensing United Fund money, and the changes in the agencies and programs receiving this type of community support, one would begin to grasp the past and present significances of the religions (changes within and between them) in the life of the community.

It could be argued, with a vast array of statistics and observations, that the three major religions are no longer the force they were in our communities, and are even less influential in the lives of their members. The implication is that over time religion will cease to be a major factor in understanding the nature and dynamics of a community. But this argument obscures several issues that are central for a community psychology, one of the more obvious being how we understand this change and its consequences for the community. Not so obvious is the question: what has begun to replace (or may replace) the function of religion as a group-organizing force and as a way of providing meaning in one's life?

How one thinks about this question is very much a function of the type of community one is looking at and the groups within it. If one is in a community where Jesus movements of varying kinds have become prominent, one might conclude that far from being weakened, religious commitment is increasing. In other communities one might well be impressed with the increasing interest of young people in mysticism and Far Eastern religions, just as in some black communities adherence to the Moslem religion seems to be increasing. One of the characteristics of the counter-culture among young people is not only a rejection of the tradi-tional religions but a groping toward substitutes which would serve similar functions for the individual and the group.

What all of this suggests is that the role and force of the major religions is changing, but that the pace and content of change will vary considerably among communities. It also emphasizes that a community psychology which is not seriously concerned with these issues is as shallow and ludicrous as a theory of personality would be if it gave short shrift to the role of sex.

Age Groupings and Characteristics

In the normal course of living we are unaware of how much our perception and conception of our community is a function of the characteristics and distribution of its age groupings. As in the case of religion, it frequently requires a dramatic event or the eruption of a problem or conflict to remind us of these factors; sometimes, however, they are forced into our awareness by "ab-sence." For example, in the summer New Haven is for me a very different community than it is during the rest of the year. As soon as the Yale graduation is over, New Haven takes on a deserted air. Because it is smack in the middle of New Haven, dominating the downtown in numerous ways, the sudden flight of several thousand students is almost impossible to overlook.[1] As a colleague once put it: "For a week or so after graduation I feel sad the way I did when my older child went away to college. You don't realize what their presence means until they're not there."

It could be argued that my example is an inappropriate one because I am a Yale faculty member interacting constantly with students, and my response to their absence says more about me and my position than it does about the significance of this particular

[1] Yale has never had a summer school, but beginning in 1975 there will be one. All Yale people are aware that the introduction of a summer school will have effects in Yale, but few Yale people think about the ways it will effect New Haven or how the character of the summer school will be affected by the fact that Yale is in New Haven. The summer school repre-sents a major break with a Yale tradition, and it is inconceivable that this will not produce change in Yale and its relationship to New Haven.

group of young people for the larger community. Because this group is part of my conception of New Haven and is an organizing force in my life does not mean that it plays a similar defining role for the non-Yale community. There are several ways of responding to this argument. The first is to note that there are several segments in the community for whom the student group is an essential ingredient of their conception of New Haven. There are the police, numerous shops and businesses, scores of schools, social agencies, and institutions with which Yale students have meaningful and sustained contacts. I am not now talking about Yale as a corporate or entity abstraction but rather about the countless interactions that for nine months of the year take place between Yale students and non-Yale people. The conception of the community which these people have surely includes Yale as a geographical area, possessing distinctive architecture, having corporate characteristics and purposes, and comprised of diverse groups. But in their daily lives the non-Yale community sees and interacts with students, diverse in numerous ways, but all sharing the characteristic of youthfulness. It is not until the students are absent that they can note the difference in the community. To some, the students are an ingredient that lends a positive tone to their conception of the community. To others they are quite dispensable. In either case, the reaction concedes that to talk about New Haven without talking of Yale students makes no sense.

Another way of responding to the argument is to imagine that the land on which Yale stands is occupied instead by a large prison or factory. This, of course, would mean a very different kind of New Haven, but would not part of the difference lie in differences in age groupings and their characteristics? Ordinarily we do not examine how our conception of our community is influenced by its age groupings and their characteristics. And yet these factors are always present, however silent and unrecognized they may be; an unusual turn of events will thrust them into community awareness. It is difficult to make age groupings and their characteristics a part of our conscious conception of a community because we tend to see and react not to groups but to individuals—or at least we think we are responding only to individuals. One does not *see* age groupings, just as one does not literally *see* a population explosion.

But age groupings and their characteristics are a defining feature of a community, part of that "ground" which gives shape and substance to our experience of the community.

The significance of these factors would not have to be emphasized to anyone who has knowledge of small midwestern farming communities which have been losing their younger people to the cities. The economic consequences of this for the older generations and their community are of course enormous, and this is what has received emphasis; but no less significant have been the psychological and social consequences. The older residents are keenly aware that their community has changed, that their individual lives have been altered, and that they must deal with a future they did not anticipate. Their conception of their community as well as their psychological sense of community, intertwined as they are, have changed. Such changes do not occur suddenly, of course. They go on for decades, but so slowly and subtly that our perception of stability is not challenged until the consequences of the change become so general that we can no longer ignore the fact that change has occurred—and then we know what our earlier conception of the community took for granted, but should not have.

Although my examples have been about young people, I have discussed them in terms of consequences for older people (and from the standpoint of a particular older person). We should recognize that these factors are no less significant for younger people. For example, up until a few years ago, I never had a student, graduate or undergraduate, express an interest in old people. Recently, however, a number of students have spontaneously come to me to discuss a study they would like to do with aged people. Young people have always known that there were "senior citizens" but very few, if any, ever conceived of them as an important part of their community—important, that is, in terms of numbers, problems, use of community resources, and changes occurring over time in all these respects. They may have had experience with older people like grandparents but there was nothing in their thinking to help put the experience into a community context.

But all this has changed in recent years. It is rare that the daily newspaper does not have an article about older people or their activities. Nursing homes for the infirm aged, new senior citizen

housing, community centers for meetings, programs, and activities—
these are only some of the visible signs that make it likely that young
people will be aware that there are older people in numbers and
with characteristics that have required a certain community action.
They may not know how or why that community action came about,
what its relationship is to existing resources, or how to judge its
quality; but in some vague way they know that old people are part
of the community, and however vague this knowledge is, it is much
clearer to them than it was to young people ten or twenty years
ago. And, it should be noted, today's young people understand
quite clearly that the aged have problems and that it is a responsibility of the community to help them with their problems. *This
was not always part of the young person's conception of a community.* The problem, both in size and substance, is not new. What
is new is the recognition that our past conception of the community
did not alert us to what was in it and was happening there.

A Major Obstacle: The Psychological Orientation

By self-selection and training, psychologists "naturally" think
in terms of motivation, attitudes, personality, and a host of other
factors that we think explain human behavior. Consequently, when
they attempt to answer the question: "What is my conception of a
community?" their answer inevitably refers primarily, if not exclusively, to psychological factors. This prepotent way of thinking
about human behavior has been very productive, but it also has
some built-in disadvantages depending on what one is trying to
understand. Barker (1968), who has thought and studied more
about behavior and ecology than anyone else, describes and illustrates some of the disadvantages:

> How does one identify and describe the environment of
> behavior? Students of perception have been centrally con-
> cerned with this problem, and they have had some success in
> dealing with it. When perception psychologists have turned
> from the nature of perception to the preperceptual nature of
> light and sound, they have discovered something very im-
> portant about the ecological environment of vision and hearing:
> it is not random; it involves bounded manifolds of individual

elements with varied and unusual patterns. The environment of vision and hearing has a structure that is independent of its connections with perceptual mechanisms. All science reveals that nature is not uniform; the environments of atoms and molecules, of cells and organs, of trees and forests are patterned and structured, and this greatly facilitates their identification.

It would appear that students of molar behavior might profitably emulate students of perception, and consider the ecological environment of the behavior with which they are concerned entirely aside from its connection with behavior. This requires, in fact, a new science which stands with respect to molar behavior as the physics of light and sound stand with respect to vision and hearing. An analogy may help to make the problem clear.

If a novice, an Englishman, for example, wished to understand the environment of a first baseman in a ball game, he might set about to observe the interactions of the player with his surroundings. To do this with utmost precision he might view the first baseman through field glasses, so focused that the player would be centered in the field of the glasses with just enough of the environment included to encompass all the player's contacts with the environment, all inputs and outputs: all balls caught, balls thrown, players tagged, etc. Despite the commendable observational care, however, this method would never provide a novice with an understanding of "the game" which gives meaning to a first baseman's trans-actions with his surroundings and which, in fact, constitutes the environment of his baseball-playing behavior. By observing a player in this way, the novice would, in fact, fragment the game and destroy what he was seeking. So, also, he might by observations and interviews construct the player's life-space during the game: his achievements, aspirations, successes, failures, and conflicts; his judgments of the speed of the ball, of the fairness of the umpire, of the errors of his teammates. But this would only substitute for the former fragmented pic-ture of "the game" the psychological consequences of the frag-ments, and thus remove the novice even further from the ecological environment he sought. Finally, the novice might per-form innumerable correlations between the first baseman's achievements (balls caught, players tagged, strikes and hits made, bases stolen, errors, etc.) and particular attributes of the ecological environment involved (speed of balls thrown to him, distance of throw, weight of bat, curve of balls, etc.). But he could never arrive at the phenomenon known as a baseball game by this means.

It would seem clear that a novice would learn more about the ecological environment of a first baseman by blotting out the player and observing the game around him. This is what the student of light and sound does with elaborate instrumentation [pp. 15–16].

Barker's illustration demonstrates that a narrow focus on the behavior of an individual is productive at the same time that it limits and even distorts one's understanding of his behavior. But what if the Englishman did blot out the first baseman and then observed the game around him? Certainly he would learn more about the game of baseball, but I suspect that he would be unlikely to note certain features of the game because they are not psychological, even though they have obvious psychological consequences for the players. Indeed, changes in these features would change the game. Why are the distances between the bases the same? Why that particular distance? Why are the running paths of dirt and the rest of the field of grass? Why is the pitcher's mound elevated (assuming he would note that it was)? Why does home plate have certain dimensions and why does it have a plate instead of a base like first, second, and third base have? The game of baseball is not understandable by looking at all the players and their interactions. These are necessary things to know, but they are not sufficient. No less important is that "preperceptual structure" of which we ordinarily are not aware but which nevertheless is playing its role. If we rivet on people as individuals or groups, we can never be aware of the non-psychological background.

Barker's example of baseball and the Englishman, and my prediction that he would fail to note certain nonpsychological features of the game, are based on the assumption that most Americans understand the game of baseball. This is true as long as game is defined in terms of the behavior of the participants and the rules governing them. It is not true if we mean by "understand" that the relationship between behavior and the nonpsychological features of the environment are comprehended. I have asked many people to assume that I knew nothing about baseball and to explain the game to me. No one ever described the significance of the non-psychological features as basic data for understanding the game of baseball. My prediction about the Englishman may be grossly in error precisely because he has a different cultural background and when he looks at a baseball game he could note relationships that we, in our culture, have never needed to note, just as we might see things quite differently than the Englishman in our efforts to understand cricket.

What I have been saying about the baseball example is in principle applicable to the way in which we ordinarily try to understand a community in terms of people, however differentiated they may be in terms of groups, functions, locale, interactions, age, religion, and so on. If we see a community through the eyes, so to speak, of a particular group (first basemen), we get one view of the community (baseball as a game). If we enlarge our scope to include other related groups we learn more about the community. But as long as we stay on the "people level," employing traditional psychological theory and technique, we cannot see other basic factors and processes that explain the community.

Let me illustrate what I am getting at by pursuing the baseball game example. Let us assume that our Englishman has seen several major league games. What if he were to ask us why he had to pay to get into the baseball park? We could answer by saying that someone or some group "owns" the park and has paid a large sum of money for the franchise. But, asks the Englishman, who has the right to dispense a franchise and what restrictions and privileges come with it? How do the owners determine how much to pay their players? Do they all get the same amount? To maximize his profits why doesn't he have them play the game all year? If we were asked why some games are played at night when expensive lighting equipment is required, the answer would be primarily an economic one: it will pay off in increased attendance. *Baseball is both a game and a business, and the two are not unrelated.* Indeed, one cannot understand certain changes in the game of baseball unless one understands the dynamics of its economic structure (for example, changing the rules to speed up the game and make it more interesting and so increase attendance).[2] One cannot understand the psychology of baseball players *qua* players by ignoring baseball as a business—for example, the negative attitudes of players to night games, to certain types of doubleheaders, to travel arrangements, to unionization and militancy, and to pensions.

If baseball has an economic base and dynamic, it has also had a foundation in law and tradition. How would we explain to a foreigner that if he were watching baseball two or three decades ago, he would see only white players and that the bulk of black spectators would be sitting mainly in certain parts of the park, that is, in the cheapest seats. And how would we explain to him why he does not see women players? I could raise many more questions but the point remains: as long as we view baseball in purely psychological terms we will fail to see how ostensibly nonpsychological factors and processes are part of the background of what we see and experience; how our experience of the game is shaped by business considerations, tax policies, and benefits, by the economic requirements of the communication media, and by law. It is no different when we are trying to understand a community. There are countless things in a community and there are innumerable ways in which they can be categorized and interrelated. An economist's description and analysis of a community would appear to be set forth in language and arranged in categories that are very nonpsychological, but does anyone doubt that his description and analysis of the community have enormous psychological significances for those who live in it or for those who want to understand those who live in it?

When we talk about the "urban crisis" we usually refer to a cluster of social and clinical psychological factors and problems. We are aware *now* that there are direct and indirect relationships between this cluster and the character, structure, and distribution of the community's public and private economic resources. In part, at least, this crisis is a consequence of economic factors and processes which have been at work for a long time but whose psychological

[2] The economics of baseball have had less impact on the game as a game (its basic rules and procedures) than it has had on the experience of the game on the part of players, owners, and fans. In the case of professional football, however, economics have affected the rules of the game much more directly. That is to say, changes in rules have been stimulated by the aim of making the game more "lively" and catering to the needs of television.

consequences were ignored. Why they were ignored is quite complicated, but part of the answer is that the effects of economic factors,
processes, and interrelationships are frequently slow, cumulative,
and indirect. I am not maintaining that the economic characteristics
of a community in some simple direct way have psychological consequences, although in the lives of individuals this frequently happens. What I am maintaining is that economic characteristics of a
community and changes in them have a dynamic that is always a
factor in how people conceive of the community. They may be
unaware of this relationship, just as we are visually aware of
"figure" and not of "ground" and do not note the background unless something happens that forces us to do so. They may at times be
aware of some small aspect of the relationship, an aspect which has
meaning for them and which therefore inevitably prevents recognition of the general nature of the relationship. When by virtue of a
crisis or catastrophe a community recognizes the general relationship
between "economics and psychology," it is testimony to how unaware they had been of what had been going on. The crisis is made
not by a change in the relationship but by a change in our awareness. Put in another way: studying the "psychology" of individuals
in a community may never lead one to comprehend how it is related
to economic characteristics of that community. If someone's job is
eliminated his "psychology" will change and only then will he
realize that impersonal economic processes and changes had been
going on that would effect him.

Let me illustrate the point by describing something that is
at this moment producing quite an uproar in Connecticut communities, and in many other places throughout the country. As
usual, it is in the form of a crisis, centering around the distinct
possibility that public bus transportation will die or be curtailed
even more drastically than it has been in recent years. To many
people bus transportation is an essential feature of their community:
it exists, it should exist, and without it their community would be a
very different kind of place. Many who feel this way have not used
public transportation for years and would have difficulty recalling
the last time they were on a bus. Others have used buses once or
twice a year when their car was in for repairs. Those who depend
on buses, of course, know what is at stake. But it makes no differ-

ence: all those with whom I have talked maintained that bus transportation is a necessary feature of the community. Now how come the crisis? Nobody has "willed" it, and given the public clamor it is likely that bus transportation will continue to exist in reduced form and with public subsidy. The fact is that the crisis has been "there," brewing and developing, for several decades. It is not necessary to explain in any detail how it developed. Suffice it to say that several factors have been at work: increased use of cars; high-speed, limited-access highways; population shifts to the sprawling suburbs; increased costs of labor and equipment due to an inflationary spiral; a steady increase in fares, and so on. If one goes back two or more decales one finds that public officials in the community, reflecting no doubt a sizeable portion of community opinion, fought for some of these factors that have contributed to the crisis because they felt they would be good for the community: the bigger and better highways, increased parking facilities, new public housing away from the central city, for example. Those who clamor against the demise of bus service had once clamored for the various programs which contributed to the present "crisis." This is a good example of what Murray Levine called problem creation through problem solution. The important point is that most people were unaware that a crisis was brewing, that something they viewed as an essential feature of their community was being affected and that the change would some day alter their psychological view of their community. They were unaware that their "psychology" in part rested on a foundation of community characteristics and processes that were not psychological at all.

For most people, perhaps, the demise of bus service, or a drastic reduction in service, would be akin to losing a convenience. For many others it is to lose a necessity. Young people, poor people, and old people would be most adversely affected. What the near- and long-term consequences would be for these groups is no trivial question either for them or for the larger community. Just as there were few people who understood what would happen to public transportation and saw the coming crisis, there are few today who pursue the psychological consequences of the present crisis and how it can effect the community. I have never met a psychologist or psychiatrist with a "community" orientation who was even interested in the problem of public transportation or who understood its differential relationship to various groups in the community. And in the present crisis I am not aware that any group of mental health professionals has taken a public stand or in any way attempted to demonstrate what might face the community if public transportation were further reduced or eliminated. And is it not ironical that many of these community psychologists and psychiatrists are seriously interested in young people and poor people? (They have much less interest in old people!) It may be ironical, but it is quite understandable. As long as one has a purely psychological orientation, as long as one focuses primarily on the individual, as long as one conceives of the environment narrowly or in interpersonal terms, one can never comprehend how much of an individual's "psychology" reflects nonpsychological factors and processes.

The principle I am stressing is quite familiar to psychologists working in such fields as perception, audition, and vision. They know that what we see and hear cannot be understood without knowledge of a structured background of which we are not aware. We respond to what we see and explain our subsequent actions as if there is no background. We take it for granted and, indeed, we are quite surprised when we learn that what we did not "see" was as essential determinant of what we did see. This principle is no less operative when we look at a community. If one looks at a community in terms of people, there is a good deal one can learn about it: the groups that comprise it, their interrelationships, how and at what they work, their recreational activities, their modes of transportation, and so on. But if one stops there, as most of us do, we cannot become aware of "background factors" until changes in them force us to recognize, first, their existence and, second, their structure. *Now* we know that in earlier decades we "saw" public transportation as no more than that: a form of transportation. We did not see that its existence and viability rested on certain givens like housing patterns, population density and stability, location of work sites, wage rates and price levels, etc. If what we saw seemed stable it was because the background factors were relatively stable or changing slowly. Now we can see how these background factors are functionally related. And we have come to see one other thing: although these background factors are or become functionally interrelated, this is not because they are planned that way. Indeed, what has characterized our communities, both in terms of public and private sector decision-making, is the lack of concerted planning. Twenty or more years ago very few people in a community would have questioned the right of different interest groups, public and private, to take actions which were in their self-interest. This questioning stance is today more frequent because it is recognized that a significant change in one aspect of the community, wittingly or unwittingly, has consequences for other aspects. However unrelated these aspects may be substantively or psychologically, they are presently or will soon become functionally related.

When a psychologist looks at the community by virtue of his work with individuals or particular groups, his "looking" is like our hearing a symphony. What is figure for most of us is the melodic line (which may be equated to the individual or group or setting)— that which forces itself into our awareness. That melodic line may change, or now one section and then another section of the orchestra may take it up, but we rivet our attention on that melodic line. Most of us do not hear anything else. If forced to reflect, we recognize that we are hearing only a sample, and usually a small sample, of the sounds of the orchestra, and we know that most of the instruments are not playing the melody. And if we are forced to change our set and disregard the melodic line in order to hear what else is going on, we become aware that what we ordinarily hear literally depends on a complexly structured background. The melodic line can exist without that background—we can play it on a harmonica, for example—but then we are not experiencing a symphony. Similarly, we can deal only with individuals or discrete groups, but that does not constitute a community orientation. The psychological concepts and theories we use in working with individuals or groups or discrete settings are not adequate to conceptualizing and understanding a community. This is to state the limitations of psychology and not to criticize them. What is subject to criticism is the failure to recognize these limitations and to attempt to explore what would be required to transcend them.

It is, I hope, clear from my discussion that to transcend these limitations requires that we begin to pay attention to community processes and characteristics that on the surface lack psychological substance but which have enormous psychological consequences. This will not require that a community psychologist become expert in land values and usage, the political system, housing, taxation, religion, transportation, pollution, health services, education, race and ethnicity, recreation; economic policy, process, and organization; the diversity and history of modern communities; architecture, demography; and law and the law enforcement system. These are community features or processes functionally related in varying degrees, although few people may be aware of this functional relationship. Depending on time and circumstance, usually a crisis, there may be general awareness and an attempt made to increase order or control, or to plan on the operation of these variables. No, the psychologist cannot be expected to be expert in these matters, but he should be expected to be knowledgeable at least to the degree that he understands and accepts the fact that what members of a community are, their differences and communalities, are in part shaped by features and processes that on the surface may appear to be quite unpsychological.

No psychologist would purport to understand a person without reference to his family which, he would say, is his most potent environment, the shaper of his destiny. There is truth to this, but it is not the whole truth. There is a wider context in which this family is embedded, a context which has put its usually unrecognized stamp on it. This wider or community context may not be salient for the psychologist in terms of what he wants to do with or for the *individual*. If, however, the psychologist pins on himself the label of *community* psychologist, his scope and perspective must shift from seeing the individual in terms of his family and other types of group membership to seeing all of them in the context of community features, processes, and history.

This shift is not a matter of choice; it is a consequence of confronting the question, What does one mean by a community and how does the community determine the behavior of its members? If the community psychologist shrinks from this conceptual confrontation, it is understandable because he is entering new territory in which adaptation requires unlearning some (by no means all) accustomed ways of thinking, and learning new facts and concepts. Faced with such a task, the psychologist's tendency, shared by the rest of the human race, is to translate the new in terms of the old, and the result is old wine in new bottles. It is like the joke about the sick man who on a very wintry day went to see a doctor who after examining him told him to go home, take off all his clothes, stand in front of an open window, and breathe deeply. In horror, the patient said to the doctor, "But if I do that I will get pneumonia." To which the doctor replied, "*That* I know what to do about."

There is one other way in which a purely psychological orientation can be a major obstacle, and it arises by virtue of the community psychologist's concern with and involvement in bringing about change. In later chapters I shall be dealing more fully with the relationship of the community psychologist to community change, that is, to the objects of change, the dilemmas of action. Suffice it here to note two things. First, although by and large the community psychologist is dealing with individuals, groups, and problems that were long neglected by psychologists—problems that are truly community problems—in practice he has dealt with them as if he was to pour old wine into new bottles. Concretely, community psychology has become a "mental health" psychology. More specifically, it has become a "mental disorder" psychology, attempting to help more people with their problems. The point is not that this has happened, but that many psychologists have become disillusioned by their perception of the ever-increasing discrepancy between need and available service. It is obvious to them that far from effecting some change in the community, they have become more overwhelmed than ever before with the number of troubled people who, they think, need their help. They know they have had little or no impact on the community, nor will they if they continue as they are. As one community psychologist said to me, "If I really wanted to make an impact, I should go into politics or become a social activist." He knew rather dimly that his professional way of thinking and practicing had led him to set quite superficial goals and had been based on a superficial view of a community. The fact that he concluded that going into politics was the "real" answer was but another indication of his oversimplified view of what a community is and how it changes.

The second thing that should be noted about the relationship of the community psychologist to community change is that he brought to this new field a clinical psychological orientation which, by its very nature, deals with problems that already exist, and usually in severe form. Of course, serious problems of people should be dealt with, but if that is all those in a field "think about" they can never engage in preventive action. They can never look at the community in terms either of heading off serious problems or of seeing how its resources can be developed and used in innovative ways. As long as one's work is in the nature of putting band aids on psychological wounds, and band aids are in horribly short supply, preventive action is always viewed as a luxury, if not an irritant. And so the faster one runs the more stationary one's position; some people, of course, would say that far from standing still we are falling further and further behind.

A Major Virtue: The Psychological Orientation

The federal government and many states have enacted legislation which requires that certain types of new buildings cannot be erected (or types of equipment used) until their effects on the environment are first determined (see, for example, *The New York Times,* October 8, 1972). Such legislation is usually in the form of an environmental quality act. Analogously, the major virtue of the psychological orientation is that it requires (or could require) that any change in any significant aspect of a community—be it in terms, for example, of land use, housing projects, new industry, highways, a new school, recreational facilities—be scrutinized from the standpoint of what its possible effects would be on the psychological sense of community. I do not have to justify the assertion that when we look back over the past we see that one of the consequences of the ways in which our communities have grown and changed is that increasing numbers of its members, far from feeling themselves to be part of the community or sensing that they understand and approve of it, feel set apart from it, unimportant to its functioning and well being, and impotent to affect it. Let us not view the past idyllically. Our communities have had (and will always have) their sources of tension, controversy, and alienation. There have always been people and groups who felt apart from the larger community, whose psychological sense of community in no way included the larger community (spatially and personally). Just as many students no longer feel identified with their college or university, an identification which once had deep psychological meanings and ramifications for most students, so in our communities more and more people feel unrelated to and disinterested in what their community is and does. The psychological sense of community does not require that there be a homogeneous population, because even where there is homogeneity there can be a diluted sense of being a willing part of the larger community.

One could argue that the positive sense of belonging to the larger community was easier to achieve in the past because communities were so much smaller, more face-to-face contact was possible, it was not difficult to know a lot about how the community worked, and it was not hard to see with one's own eyes everything that existed within the community's boundaries. But this argument begs the most important question: how did it happen that our communities permitted a type and rate of growth that destroyed for so many people the psychological sense of community? It was not growth per se but a type of growth not governed by the value of maintaining or bolstering the psychological sense of community.

The psychological sense of community can have many referents, ranging from a family or a gang to a professional organization with members across the nation. I shall use the concept of referents to mean those groupings (families, fellow workers, friends, neighbors, religious and fraternal bodies) which give structure and meaning to our daily lives and whose quality and force are in some ways a function of the legal-political-administrative entity: the city, town, or village. It is that entity in which these groupings are embedded, an entity whose characteristics provide the "ground" to the "figure" which consists of these groupings. In borrowing the concepts of figure and ground I want to convey, first, that they are always related and, second, that we normally are not aware of ground.

It is possible for these groupings to provide us with a positive sense of community. My experience suggests that it is extremely rare, particularly in cities, for people to have such a positive sense from more than one or two such groupings, and that however strong such a sense might be there is hungering for a more enlarged sense of community. When one looks at the divorce rate, the declining force of institutionalized religion, high-rise living quarters, changing neighborhoods, and a fantastic rate of moving, it is no wonder that the absence of a stabilizing sense of community has been pinpointed as one of the most frequent and significant features of our society. As someone once said: "we may be becoming *one* world but we seem increasingly to suffer from feeling that each of us is *one* person *alone*." This feeling is peculiarly individual and psychological, and that is precisely how it has been "treated": as a characteristic of the individual, having diverse intrapsychic origins. This makes as much sense as saying that meningitis is a characteristic of the individual who has it. Of course *he* has it, and of course we should do whatever is possible to help *him*, but this is no basis for conceptualizing meningitis as an individual problem.

Some might agree that the absence or dilution of the psychological sense of community is the most frequent and poignant feature of life in our communities, that in the context of social living it gives rise to intrapersonal and interpersonal dynamics that heighten rather than lessen the sense of aloneness, that it acts as both cause and effect of disordered thinking and acting, that it nourishes the experience and strength of ineffable anxiety—and while agreeing that all of this may be true, as countless writers have maintained, they may still ask, what can the psychologist or psychiatrist do except help individuals cope more effectively with this problem? Of course, the argument continues, when we work with individuals, we know and they know what it means to feel alone, to feel that there is little or no basis for identifying with their community, or even with their family or neighborhood, but what can we do except help them cope less destructively with the problem? Who can listen to our patients describe their desperate efforts, through work and play, to feel part of some larger entity, to break through the barrier of aloneness, to feel part of and wanted by others—who can listen without agreeing that all of this in some ways reflects how our communities have changed, diluting rather than reinforcing a sense of community? But what can we do about it?

This was the question which in the past two decades came to haunt psychology and gave rise to the new field of community psychology. The question was answered in different ways by different people, but there were, nevertheless, some underlying agreements: focus had to shift from an emphasis on intrapsychic factors to understanding and changing larger social contexts; adapting such a focus would require new conceptualizations and tactics; and the major criterion by which these new efforts would be judged was the degree to which they led to a greater psychological sense of community. As Cowen (1973) so well noted, the literature in community psychology does not lend itself to easy generalizations. As I read this literature, however, there is one theme, not always articulated clearly, which runs through it: the most important criterion by which to judge these efforts is whether they have produced or sustained a more positive psychological sense of community. Whether it be a headstart program, a neighborhood council, schools, senior citizens, drug abuse programs, or any of the scores of community settings in which the community psychologist has found himself, his goal has been to create the conditions in which people can experience a sense of community that permits a productive compromise between the needs of individuals and the achievement of group goals.

As these efforts proliferated, and particularly as many of them encountered failure or a disappointing level of success, it was recognized (by some at least) that community *structure* (in which were embedded the settings the community psychologist was endeavoring to change), as well as community *forces,* could not be ignored. One could ignore them when one began; but at some point, and it was usually early, community structure and forces, heretofore part of the ground, intruded into the figure. One might begin, for example, by being interested only in a headstart program, but one could not remain interested *only* in that program. What the community psychologist was learning was not only that "everything seemed to be related to everything else" but also that the witting or unwitting effect of one community force on another was to lessen the psychological sense of community of all concerned. Everything was seen as interrelated but practically nobody felt interdependent, a kind of absolute zero in the psychological sense of community.

It is understandable if some community psychologists retreated, conceptually and in action, from this staggering complexity, for which traditional psychological theory and practice were quite inadequate. How does one decide where to intervene and what resources would be necessary to have some intended effect? Was this a legitimate part of psychology? Even if one grants that what happens in a community and what is planned for it will have consequences for its members' psychological sense of community, and granted that so much of these activities seem oblivious to the significance of this sense, and granted that as psychologists we know the alienating consequences of these developments; still, on what basis do we arrogate to ourselves a problem of this scope, and how do we justify any actions that our conceptualizations would suggest? We are *psych*ologists not *community*ologists. Our stock in trade is mind and behavior, not the dynamics and structure of communities. We know a good deal about individual behavior, a good deal less about group behavior, and somewhat less than that about how to alter behavior; but whatever it is we know seems a frail reed with which to attack these larger issues.

This argument is not without merit even though it suffers from the very disease we are discussing. Town planners plan towns, architects design buildings, political scientists study political systems, highway engineers design and build roads, sociologists study groups and social process, values are the domain of the philosopher (if he is not studying the logic of scientific inquiry and the nature and sources of knowledge), and psychologists rivet on the human psyche —is it any wonder that the phrase "community of scholars" tends to be used with derision? Everybody has a piece of the action at the expense of everyone's enlarged sense of community. Psychology can retreat into its intellectual ghetto, content with the hope that others will deal with the larger social issues and satisfied with the knowledge that it is doing what it does best. It is an uneasy retreat because it is a retreat from a problem that will not let psychology alone, because psychology will always have to deal with its consequences.

The concept "psychological sense of community" is not a familiar one in psychology, however old it may be in man's history. It does not sound precise, it obviously reflects a value judgment, and does not sound compatible with "hard" science. It is a phrase which is associated in the minds of many psychologists with a kind of maudlin togetherness, a tear-soaked emotional drippiness that misguided do-gooders seek to experience. *And yet there is no psychologist who has any doubt whatsoever about when he is experiencing the presence or absence of the psychological sense of community.* He luxuriates in its presence and despairs in its absence. As long as the psychologist experiences this as peculiar to him as an individual, not something that is characteristically human and shaped in different ways in different societies, not something that he has in common with the janitor in his building or his auto mechanic, he exposes his ignorance of his culture and his imprisonment in an individual psychology. He also is demonstrating that he always has two theories, one which he applies to himself and one that he applies to "others." In response to these thoughts a student of mine once said in class: "Aren't you saying in a figurative way that people should have more of the experience that blood is thicker than water, a bigger sense of kinship?" And before I could answer another student said: "No, I thought he was asking why there is so much water and so little blood."

Precisely because we all experience the presence or absence of a psychological sense of community, however restricted it may be in terms of the size of the referent group, some of its characteristics are not hard to state. The perception of similarity to others, an acknowledged interdependence with others, a willingness to maintain this interdependence by giving to or doing for others what one expects from them, the feeling that one is part of a larger dependable and stable structure—these are some of the ingredients of the psychological sense of community. You know when you have it and when you don't. It is not without conflict or changes in its strength. It is at its height when the existence of the referent group is challenged by external events, by a crisis like the air war over London in 1940, or a catastrophe like an earthquake; it is also at its height, for shorter periods, in times of celebration, during a political victory party or an Easter mass. It is one of the major bases for self-definition and the judging of external events. The psychological sense of community is not a mystery to the person who experiences it. It is a mystery to those who do not experience it but hunger for it.

My suggestion that the psychological sense of community

is the overarching criterion by which one judges any community development or plan stems from more than my personal values and needs. Indeed, as I have pointed out in earlier chapters, community psychology arose because so many social scientists were jolted into recognizing that our communities were riddled with conflicts and conditions symptomatic of the loss of a psychological sense of community. They saw their task as how to bring things and people together, how to achieve agreement on some overarching value, or, for some who thought this is not possible in our present society, how to create a new society that had for its major aim the attainment by its members of a psychological sense of community. If there was no agreement about how this had come about or how it might be remedied, if the sense of crisis led people into all kinds of actions to repair the disintegrating seams of the community or to destroy them so that a new community garment could be designed, there was agreement that the sense of community had all but vanished and that its reinstatement was the top priority. And as never before, developments within a community began to be scrutinized and criticized in terms of how they would effect this sense of belonging.

Community control, community participation, communes, the fantastic popularity of the group dynamics approach with its emphasis on "groupiness and togetherness," and the counter-cultures themselves—all of these should in part be seen as an expression of the need for a psychological sense of community. A harbinger of what was to come was Skinner's *Walden Two* (1962), which continues to have a wide appeal not explainable by Skinner's behaviorism, which is not all that popular within and without the field of psychology. Its appeal in large measure stems from Skinner's passionate and derisive analysis of modern society and his equally passionate plea for a society which would restore in its members a psychological sense of community. In fact, the psychological sense of community is the overarching criterion by which any development in *Walden Two* is viewed and judged. There is very little in Skinner's *Beyond Freedom and Dignity* (1971) that is not said in *Walden Two*, except for an increased emphasis on the point that the welfare of the community must take precedence over that of individual, because it is only through a shared sense of community that the creative potential of the individual and the community will reach expression. It may seem surprising that Skinner, whose "science of behavior" is in the longstanding narrow tradition of American learning theory (which has always been a theory of the individual rat, pigeon, or human), should be such an articulate pleader for the psychological sense of community. It is surprising only if one assumes that a psychologist in our society is immune from what is a central problem in our society.

The remainder of this book is largely concerned with illustrating how an acceptance of the psychological sense of community as an overarching criterion will determine the tactics of the community psychologist as he involves himself either in institutional change or in the creation of new settings. It will become apparent that far more is involved than criteria and tactics, not the least of which are the functional interrelatedness of community characteristics, conceptions of human resources, the nature of work, and professional traditions.

Many readers have had little first-hand contact with most of the specific settings (special classes, institutions for the mentally retarded or juvenile offender) I use to raise and discuss the significance of the psychological sense of community. Community psychology has shown little interest in these settings, although this degree of interest is far greater than that found within community psychiatry. This situation reflects interrelated historical-traditional roots in psychology and the larger society, but at the very least it is a consequence of the failure to confront the question What is a community? After all, when we talk about these settings we are not talking about small numbers of people or small amounts of money. Far from it, for when we think, as we must, in terms of families, resources, services, and personnel, we are faced with a sizeable portion of a community. And yet, the social sciences (with the exception of sociology in regard to criminology) have shown little interest in these settings. Race, poverty, the "normal" school populations, alternative school settings, the nature and structure of the delivery of health services, the training of paraprofessionals—these are some of the fashionable problems to which community-oriented psychologists have gravitated. At the same time that they are fashionable they are also important problems, and if they do not occupy center stage in subsequent chapters, it is not because I wish to downgrade their significance to the community. I chose the settings I did because they permitted me—more than my experiences in other community settings would have—to state and discuss the reasons I consider the psychological sense of community to be the overarching value by which to judge efforts to change any aspect of community functioning. I hope the reader will have no difficulty comprehending the major thrust of these chapters and relating it to the settings with which he is more familiar. Although some of the settings I discuss may be unfamiliar to many readers, I urge them to bear in mind that phenotypic differences among settings (and people) in our society are, unfortunately, effective barriers to the perception of genotypic communalities. Nowhere is this more true than when one deals with a concept and value like the psychological sense of community.

VII

The Residential
Institution: The
Consequences of
"Humane" Segregation

▉▭▭▭▉▭▭▭▉▭▭▭▉▭▭▭▉▭▭▭▉▭▭▭▉▭▭▭▉

Few things are as destructive of the psychological sense of community, in its narrow and broad aspects, as the tendency to segregate the atypical person, to place him in a special geographical area where he will be with his "own kind" and receive "special handling." The mentally retarded, the mentally ill, and the juvenile offender are among the most frequent recipients of this form of community "care," which despite the vast expenditures these insti-

161

tutions require, is seen as both necessary and humane. In this chapter, I shall attempt to demonstrate why the existence of these institutions virtually guarantees that they will become self-defeating for all those within them, at the same time that they rob the community around them of an opportunity to reinforce the psychological sense of community among its members. It will become obvious that the positions I take do not start with consideration of the nature of deviance or its remediation, either in their scientific or professional aspects, but rather with the value that any proposed change in the relationship between an individual and the community must be scrutinized from the standpoint of how it may strengthen or dilute the psychological sense of community. Community policy always rests on values about what is good or bad for the community. The policy will always be buttressed by some set of facts which makes it appear self-evident that a basic community value must be reinforced. As I shall attempt to show, the value may change, the old set of facts may become irrelevant, and a new set sought. It may also happen that the value remains constant but it becomes evident that its relationship to a set of facts was wrongly interpreted.

The Special Class

I shall deliberately not begin with instances of segregation that involve removal from the community. Rather, I shall start with practices in regard to another class of instances that are viewed as obviously progressive and humane. Indeed, I assume that almost all readers will find it difficult to reorient their thinking because their mind-set in regard to these instances seems so unassailable and natural, a sure sign of the force of our culture. And if this initial difficulty is overcome, the consequences for action and change are so enormous that one should be prepared for an upsurge in the internal and external sources of resistance.

Particularly in our urban centers, school systems have been divided into two parts, the regular and the special, and over the past two decades the special part has been steadily growing in size. The special part is comprised of a heterogeneous assortment of groups: the mentally retarded, emotionally disturbed, perceptually handicapped, those with learning disabilities, brain injury, and so forth. And within each of these groups finer differentiations are often made, usually accompanied by expressions of satisfaction that the small classes into which these children are put will enable them to receive the individual attention they require. By far the largest number of special classes is devoted to the mentally retarded, and it is around them that I shall focus my remarks.

The stated purpose of the special class is to provide conditions for learning and personal growth not possible in the regular classroom—small class size, which makes individualized instruction more likely and appropriate, reduced frustration due to unfair competition, and a teacher specially trained to work with these special children. This stated purpose, however, obscures the historical fact that the primary argument for the special class was far less the special needs of these children than it was the needs of normal children to progress academically at a "normal" rate, unhindered by the presence of the retarded child. It seemed unassailable and self-evident that the needs of normal children should have precedence over those of retarded children, because the presence of the latter, even when very few in number, interfered with the pace of learning of the former. It is in no way doing violence to this history to say that most educators had little or no interest in the retarded child, and looked favorably on institutionalization as the program of choice. If matters have changed in the past two decades it is not because the values and attitudes of educators have remarkably altered but rather because of the organized pressures exerted by parents of retarded children, which have given rise to legislation requiring and funding expanded programs in schools.

This fragment of the history of attitudes toward the mentally retarded should sensitize us to the possibility that the stated purpose of present practices of educational segregation is not as benevolent as the rhetoric may suggest. Indeed, within the past few years a number of states have begun to set up special schools to which the retarded child is bussed daily, the ostensible reasons being those of efficiency and comprehensiveness of program. In my discussions with some of those who have led in the development of these regional schools, they quite candidly said that a major factor in their thinking was the social isolation of the special class in the regular school—the generally inhospitable atmosphere, in which the special teacher and her pupils felt unwanted and unneeded. As one put it: "Let's face it: the schools have never accepted the mentally retarded. They suffer them. At best they tolerate them as if they were the deserving poor, and at worst they view them as lepers. Why not face the fact that we are not and never have been wanted. Better we should have our own ghetto than live in alien territory." This picture is somewhat overdrawn, but not by much. Although most educators have learned (or they have been told) that mentally retarded persons do not require institutionalization and are capable of being maintained in the community, they have difficulty accepting the idea that retarded children really belong in a regular school.

One consequence of this state of affairs is that the special class teacher rarely feels at home with regular class teachers in the sense of feeling part of a common enterprise. She feels "out of it," well aware that she is frequently not regarded as a "real" teacher but rather as a kind of custodian or babysitter who only tangentially or superficially deals with the heart of the educational process. Whereas initially she regarded the title "special class teacher" as a badge of honor signifying dedication to children with special needs, she slowly but surely begins to view herself the way the bulk of her colleagues do: a second-class citizen who by virtue of background, interests, and competence is not and cannot be part of the mainstream. She feels neither understood nor valued. She may be respected as a person and she may even be made to feel that she is performing an important function (babysitting with handicapped or troubled youngsters is important, after all) but she is not regarded as indispensable; one cannot eliminate first-grade classrooms, but one can eliminate the special class. The principal of the school (and I have never known a school principal who had ever been a special class teacher) does not regard himself as competent to supervise the special class teacher, a task usually assumed by a central office person who occasionally visits the school—a relationship that reinforces the feeling of everyone else in the school that the special class is indeed quite special.

What the special class children experience is much the same as that of their teacher. It could hardly be otherwise. Why he is in the special class, why he does not partake of many school activities, why other classrooms appear different, why he remains in the same physical location for a period of years, why his siblings or neighborhood friends seem to have a different school experience— these are puzzling questions to the child, and however he answers them, or others (parents, teachers) provide him with answers, the result is that he feels different and apart. Countless times I have observed the process whereby a child was transferred from the regular to the special class, and it was rare indeed to see it handled in a way that reflected a sensitivity to the needs and thoughts of the child. More often than not, there was a diluted sensitivity to the fact that the transfer would not sit well with the child, but any or all of three factors insured that this sensitivity would not be appropriately manifested: a fear of saying the truth as the individual saw it, the expectation that the child could not comprehend the explanation, and the assumption that an explanation given once suffices to to help the child understand and accept the new state of affairs. It was not infrequent that a teacher or principal was surprised and angry that a child resisted the transfer which, they felt, he should have accepted gladly because it was in his own best interest, because "he would learn more and be happier." This insensitivity to the plight of the child was understandable to me because I had handled similar situations in much the same way. My first professional job was in a new residential institution for the mentally retarded. It was in its day a magnificent set of home-like structures, beautifully appointed, and based on an educational rationale that was then innovative and exciting. That this institution was in the middle of nowhere and, therefore, defeating of its basic rationale is not central to the present discussion but quite relevant to the overall theme of this chapter.[1] As soon as its doors were open communities began to send to it their children, many of whom were from underprivileged backgrounds. None of them came

---

[1] The story of this institution has been described by Sarason, Grossman, and Zitnay in *The Creation of a Community Setting* (1972). This book also deals with the consequences of the lessons learned by those who developed this new institution—that such an institution was a self-defeating venture which should be "replaced" by small regional centers. I shall discuss the self-defeating nature of these regional centers in Chapter Nine.

willingly and a number ran away. We could not understand it: here we were providing an environment that in every respect, we thought, was superior to their own and they were rejecting it. I shall never forget one young woman, a frequent runaway, whose case record rivalled anything in *Tobacco Road* for experience with rural poverty, indignity, and sexual promiscuity. For example, her father "sold her mother to a neighbor for an alarm clock." Why was Ruth always running away to return to such an environment? It took me a long time to recognize the obvious: when we remove a child from the only reality he has experienced and is familiar with —even a reality suffused with anxiety, cruelty, and deprivation— we should not expect her to jump for joy at the prospect of the separation. The anxiety and anger that accompany feeling pushed toward the unknown have their source in the security one feels with what is familiar. If it took me a long time to recognize the obvious, I could not be uncharitably judgmental when observing the insensitivity of those whose responsibility it was to explain to children why they were being placed in a special class. In any event, the point is that the child in the special class does feel apart from all other children in the school, and this is precisely how he is viewed by other children in the school. The psychological sense of apartness is no less a fact than that of physical apartness. The two facts are remarkably isomorphic.

For the parents of the retarded child, special class is a mixed blessing. On the one hand, they welcome the opportunity for their child to be in a smaller class where he can receive more attention and help; on the other hand, they recognize that it is only another context where his difference sets him apart from others, an apartness they have usually grappled with before in the family and neighborhood. As they have had to do before, they must explain to the child and others why he requires special treatment. From the standpoint of school personnel, the parents, like the children, are expected to be grateful for the special class that has been provided, and here again there is an insensitivity to the fact that the special class frequently represents to the parents another reminder of their own feelings of social isolation and private grief. The poignancy of parental feelings stems not only from events in the past and present but from a concern for the future: when the parents are no longer alive who will care for their child in ways that will counter rather than reinforce his social isolation? The parents may be young, but the fact that they have a retarded child forces them to be concerned with the consequences of their death for that child. To the parents the question is not only who will take care of the child, but will it be done humanely? And humanely means being embedded in a social context that approximates family living in the community. It does not mean institutionalization, which like the special class isolates the child and drastically reduces the range of social experience. Just as the aged person resents being treated differently and being placed away from the mainstream of social living, the parent of the retarded child fears that his child will ultimately be segregated—that he will not be seen as having a legitimate place in community living. The parent knows the difference between care which derives from and takes place in a psychological context of belongingness, and care which is ritualistic, contractual, and impersonal. It is the psychological difference between being sick at home and sick in a hospital.

The special class teacher, the regular class teacher, the retarded pupil, the nonretarded pupils, the principal, the parents— one of the major effects of the special class on each is to accentuate their sense of apartness and aloneness. Far from feeling a part of a mutually dependent and interactive community of people, they are aware that they are isolated from each other, despite their presence in the same building. And yet it all seems so "natural" that it rarely occurs to anyone to ask if the price being paid is not too high.

That question ordinarily cannot be raised for two reasons. First, the assumption that the retarded child needs a special place and program for his educational needs and personal happiness is seen as obviously true and humane. The very way in which this assumption is formulated, concerned as it seemingly is *only* with the retarded child, diverts attention away from its consequences for everyone else at the same time that it cloaks the present and future consequences for the retarded child in the garments of altruism and efficiency. The second reason, related to the first, is that an alternative to the special class is literally inconceivable to most educators. Do you mean, I have been asked, that we should leave the retarded child in the regular class where he experiences failure and frustration and interferes with the education of others? Isn't *that* an unconscionable price to pay, a far higher price than we are now paying? What I have learned in these discussions with educators and parents is that, with few exceptions, they are not challenging the validity of the consequences I have described: very few special class teachers deny that they feel special in a second-class citizen kind of way, very few regular class teachers assert an educational and professional kinship with the special class teacher, and the same is true for principals. What emerges clearly from these kinds of discussions is that the justification for the special class is not only that it is "good" for the retarded child but also that it protects the other children from what would be a source of educational interference. In short, the rationale for the special class is a variant of the "separate but equal" argument: groups (white-black, retarded-normal) should be kept apart for the good of each.

Any alternative way of dealing with this problem should reflect values different from those on which present practice rests. That is to say, if I conclude that the existence of special classes gives rise to a quality of social relations that I deem undesirable, it is because I consider the development and maintenance of a psychological sense of community a value coequal with any other educational value and goal. We run into an ironic paradox here because educational rhetoric has long maintained that a major goal of education—coequal with that of educational learning in the narrow sense—is to create conditions in the school and classroom that reflect a democratic ethos in which tolerance, cooperation, and mutual respect are primary values. How this goal and its underlying values are to be implemented have varied over time. The Supreme Court desegregation decision in 1954 was at its heart concerned with practices which it deemed inimical to the achievement of a psychological sense of community—the practice of segregation interfered with narrow educational goals precisely because of its adverse effects on the attainment of a psychological sense of community. The decision did not involve values new to education but rather a recasting of the relationship between accepted values and traditional practices.

I am maintaining that the rationale for the special class is precisely the same as the one which the Supreme Court decision ruled unconstitutional, and it should surprise no one if people would have great difficulty giving up this rationale, just as they continue to have difficulty adjusting to racial integration. And one should expect that every argument, practical and theoretical, employed against racial integration will have its counterpart in the arguments against the elimination of the special class; for example, the retarded child will be unable to compete, the education of the normal child will be diluted, educational standards will be lowered, school personnel will not be able to deal with the new range of ability in the classroom or the difficult interpersonal problems which can be expected, the normal child will be adversely affected psychologically by the presence of some retarded children who will look strange and have obvious physical disabilities, and the community can be expected to take up arms against such a mix in the classroom. What is valid in these arguments is not their specific content but the recognition that what is being proposed will alter the nature of life in the classroom. If people can discern no good whatsoever in the proposal it is less because of a clash of values than because of the understandable difficulty we all have in distinguishing between what is natural and what is merely traditional. If we have been brought to accept special classes as natural, or humane, or just, we should be pardoned if we think someone is irrational or worse if he tells us they are inhumane, inequitable, or unthinkingly traditional.

Let us imagine the situation in which special classes must be eliminated. What are some of the specific issues the classroom teacher would confront and how would we want her to think about them? One of these issues is how to discuss with the class the consequences of the obvious fact that there is now a heterogeneity among the children greater than anything they *and* the teacher have previously experienced. That obvious fact will produce both known and unknown consequences. One of the known consequences is the questions it will raise in everyone's mind about why people look different, learn at different rates and in different ways, and require different kinds of help. Another consequence is that some of us have a tendency to react unfavorably toward people who are different than we are—what we do not understand we tend to put down. Still another consequence may be that a person will not be getting as much attention or help as he needs or wants. Indeed, what we will have to figure out are new ways of learning to help each other so that we are all "teaching" each other. But why should we do all this? Why should we think that we should learn to understand and help each other? Why don't we say that each person is responsible for himself and only himself, and that he should not feel obligated to give his time, thought, feeling, and energy to someone else who would benefit from them?

How one "explains" all this to the children—the words one uses, the frequency of explanation, the vigilance required, the vehicle for mutuality and discussion that would be necessary—is less important for my purposes than it is to convey to the reader how a teacher has to start to think and act if engendering a psychological sense of community is a major goal. Far from this being a matter of making a virtue out of necessity, or a pious articulation of values devoid of experienced meaning, it can produce those conditions that drastically enlarge the range of everyone's cognitive and affective experience. The major task is not to get agreement on verbally stated values (that is relatively easy) but to act on them in ways that confront the inevitable conflicts and problems that arise when a group acts on the basis of verbally stated values, and this is only possible if there is a heightened self-consciousness that going from values to action in a consistently appropriate way is always to be traveling on an obstacle course. To engender and maintain a psychological sense of community in this classroom would involve everyone, teacher and pupils, in problem-solving behavior around issues of learning, resources, rules, mutuality, and goals. The concept of the psychological sense of community is not ritual or empty rhetoric. It is no less than a basis for confronting the realities of social living, and the fact that we are discussing it in terms of a particular kind of classroom should not make for an arbitrary and misleading distinction between the learning process and the social context in which it is taking place. Classroom learning is always social. The question is the value basis on which the social organizations rests and the degree to which both enlarge the range of conceptual experience.

But, someone could legitimately argue, what I am recommending for this imagined classroom contains nothing new—John

Dewey, for example, said it all (and better). When Dewey said that school is not a preparation for life, it is life itself, he was emphasizing the point that the major problems of social life in the "real world" were also present in the classroom, and to the degree that this was not recognized and dealt with it insured that the classroom would be unstimulating, unreal, and maladaptive for life in the "real world." So, this person might add, Dewey probably would have agreed that the increasing tendency to segregate children into special classes increased the artificiality of the regular classroom (making it special). It is absolutely correct that what I have said about the imaginary class is what has long been said should be characteristic of any real classroom. I did not say anything that would be idiosyncratic to a classroom with a wide range of abilities and handicaps. There are not two "learning" psychologies, one for retarded pupils and one for regular ones. There are not two "social" psychologies, one for retarded pupils and one for regular ones. And on whatever values a classroom should be organized, they are as relevant to retarded pupils as to regular pupils.

It would appear, therefore, that the task confronting the teacher of our imagined classroom is not one that requires learning new principles or adopting new values. The fact is, however, that very few classrooms in our public schools are organized and conducted on these principles and values. I have sat in hundreds of classrooms and it was the rare one indeed in which the psychological sense of community was present. Why this is so I have discussed in my book *The Culture of the School and the Problem of Change* (1971). The major reasons are several and complicated, but it suffices to say here that the usual discrepancies between the teacher's stated values and actual behavior stem from the teacher's concern with technical matters, pressure stemming from the need to meet narrow criteria of academic progress, and an inability to forge between pupils and herself agreement on values, the nature and limitation of available resources, and vehicles for conflict resolution —in short, to confront the realities of the classroom and the "constitutional issues" they pose for those who will be living there. This failure has enormous consequences not the least of which is that as children grow older the classroom becomes an increasingly uninteresting place in which the sense of personal growth and a satisfying interpersonal mutuality is absent. If our schools today are seeking desperately to become more interesting places, to give children in them a greater sense of belonging, and to reduce the artificial barriers between learning and living, it is a reflection of a long-standing state of affairs in which the classroom and the school became increasingly differentiated, specialized, and professionalized —all of this in the pursuit of efficiency and humaneness. And few of these efforts seemed as educationally efficient and humane as the rise of all kinds of special classes. There literally was no awareness of two possible consequences: the regular classroom would become increasingly special and artificial itself, and a greater number of pupils, teachers, and parents would come to feel apart from each other.

The shock and disbelief with which most people react to the idea of eliminating special classes deserves further emphasis, because it illustrates the lip service paid to the concept of the psychological sense of community, as well as the strength of the tendency to segregate, physically and psychologically, people who are "different." For the past two decades educators have publicly expressed great pride in the dramatic increase in the number of special classes (of which those for the mentally retarded were but one type). This presumably testified to the ability and willingness of our schools to be responsive to the needs of all children. Although this was undoubtedly the sincere belief and goal of some educators, for most others the expressions of pride were hardly justified, because in fact the increase in special classes took place not because of but in spite of traditional school attitudes and policy. It came about primarily because of pressures from outside groups, the force of legislation, and special funding. Although special classes have long been in our schools, the number was always small and deliberately so; schools were primarily for those who could benefit from the regular classroom, and they were not equally appropriate for those who needed special conditions. Furthermore (and there was a furthermore), "they" would be far happier in institutions where they could be with their own kind.

I am talking here of attitudes I once had to deal with. Over thirty years ago when I went to work in a new state residential institution for the mentally retarded we were inundated with special class children. In fact, some school systems eliminated their special classes, and those that could not would have dearly loved to. Therefore, when I suggest that the more recent expressions of pride on the part of school personnel may not have been as genuine as the rhetoric would suggest, I am not being perversely critical or uncharitable. I am merely taking seriously what is a central historical attitude in the culture of the school (which, in turn, is a reflection of something which has been central in our society). Unfortunately, the validity of my position is now being buttressed by an increasing tendency (explicitly a matter of public policy in New York and Connecticut and probably elsewhere) to set up not just special classes but special *schools* for the mentally retarded. If, as is likely, this tendency spreads we will have another example of the maxim that the more things change the more they remain the same.

It would be an absurd oversimplification to explain the history of special classes and attitudes toward them in terms of a single concept like the psychological sense of community. I have used the special class only for the purposes of illustrating the consequences of ignoring the psychological sense of community, of employing it in rhetoric but not implementing it on practice, and, perhaps most important, for the possibilities it provides for new solutions to old problems. I have long believed that solving one problem creates others, predictable and unpredictable, and so do not entertain the illusion that if we ever get to the point of eliminating special classes we will have an educational paradise. Getting to that point would in itself create problems, involving as it would the necessity of changing cherished beliefs and combatting vested interests. It may even be that the elimination of special classes will turn out to be a mistake in terms of developing, strengthening, and maintaining the psychological sense of community in one of our most vital community institutions. Obviously I do not think that will happen. Equally obviously, I would not accept any *a priori* set of arguments as a basis for not seriously pursuing the matter. If we pride ourselves in our devotion to unfettered inquiry and the experimental spirit, and if we truly accept the psychological sense of community as a basic value by which we wish to judge the quality of our individual lives and social living, we cannot continue to accept unthinkingly the special class as natural and good. These "ifs" are easy to state, but they are inordinately difficult to recognize and act upon, precisely because we are products of and actors in communities structured in ways increasingly inimical to that very sense of community for which we seek recognition and acceptance.

Many readers of this book will have little knowledge of special classes. The very fact that many readers will have had no experience with a sizeable minority in their community is symptomatic of a community structure which dilutes or restricts a broad psychological sense of community. We will see a similar state of affairs when from the same perspective we view those state institutions charged with the responsibility of caring for or rehabilitating atypical people: the delinquent, criminal, psychologically disturbed, and mentally retarded populations. The size of these institutions, the monies involved, and the families affected have enormous effects on our communities, and it is the rare citizen who is not conscious of how he is affected, if only in terms of his pocketbook.

The Residential Institution

The rationale for removing someone from his family and community is identical to that of placement in a special class, except, of course, that it is a more drastic form of segregation. In the case of the juvenile or adult offender, or of an individual with a severe psychological disturbance, there is no attempt to obscure the fact that the protection of the community is considered as important as the rehabilitative needs of these individuals. However, one never hears institutionalization justified only in terms of protecting the community; it is always tied to the ostensibly humane goal of rehabilitating the individual to the point where he can again become a nonthreatening member of the community. It is not my purpose at this point to examine critically the assumption that the goal of community living can best be achieved by removing the individual from his community for long perdiods of time. Nor shall I discuss the welter of factors—historical, psychological, professional, economic—which have made it seem natural that these institutions should exist.[2] In short, I shall not focus directly on how

[2] Some of these factors are taken up in Chapter Nine.

the existence of these institutions reflects the psychological sense of community of those in the community from which the individual has been removed. When a person is removed from a community, especially when the removal has the force of law, something is being said about the quality of its citizens' psychological sense of community, even though what is being said is that the range of that sense of community is extremely limited or that it hardly exists at all.[3] My focus here will be on the psychological sense of community of all those, patients and employees, who make up the institution. And the question I shall address is why the people in them are quite aware that they share little or no psychological sense of community.

Compared to the residential institution, the school with its special classes is a model of interpersonal mutuality. Hardly a month goes by in this country without the appearance of some published account exposing in one of these institutions horrible living conditions and brutality. Convalescent hospitals accelerate the process of dying by obscuring the difference between death and living death; correctional institutions prepare individuals for a new career in crime; mental hospitals recycle the ingredients of madness; and

[3] I remind the reader that the psychological sense of community can vary in terms of the number of people encompassed by the word "community," that is, one's immediate family, or extended family, or those with whom one works, or all or most of those living in a particular geographical area. Regardless of the number of people or their geographical spread, the psychological sense of community can vary phenomenologically in strength. One can feel completely alone in this world, and one can feel a psychological kinship with a vast number of people. When I discussed the psychological sense of community in relation to the special class, I was using the concept to refer to the degree to which those who populated the school were conscious of and acted upon feelings of mutuality, interdependence, and belonging, that is, of feelings which weld rather than separate. In the present discussion I am using the concept with two referents: to the legal-political-geographical entity in which one resides, and to the residential institutions to which people are sent. About the first, most of us have little or no psychological sense of community. We live there but we do not ordinarily feel that we are needed or are wanted there—it is a physical residence that ordinarily does not embed us in the tasks, processes, and responsibilities of the bounded political entity. I live in North Haven but I have little or no psychological sense of community with what it is and does as a geopolitical entity. As I hope to show, the lack of a psychological sense of community among all those who are sent to or work in our residential institutions is in part a consequence of a diluted or nonexistent psychological sense of community among those residing in the geopolitical entity.

training schools for the mentally retarded neither train nor school except for a cattle-like, custodial existence. But it is not my purpose here to document the failure of these institutions to accomplish their rehabilitative goals. That failure is obvious enough if one only reads the newspaper. Professionals know it. Many of them avoid contact with these settings. A few write about it in the impersonal language of research and theory. And a few (very few) write that not only is the emperor naked but he also has the visible signs of dreaded terminal disease. It is rare that a professional has devoted a large part of his career to exposing the social cancers that our residential institutions are. One of these rarities is Dr. Burton Blatt and his colleagues whose publications have documented with exceptional clarity what life is like in different types of residential settings (Blatt and Kaplan, 1970a; Blatt, 1970b; Biklen, ed., 1970; Blatt, 1973; Biklen, 1973). His first publication was a "pictorial essay"—words were not necessary to elaborate on what the pictures signified. As with earlier crusaders against human injustice and indecency, the initial publication received a good deal of attention, but little action. Subsequent publications by Blatt and his students were much more comprehensive in scope and substance. Concomitant with these publications were newspaper exposés of institutional conditions in numerous states around the country. The courts became involved, sometimes to the point where the judge specified the precise number of each type of employee the institution immediately had to hire if contempt charges were to be avoided. In all of these instances, and they represented only the tip of the iceberg, there was complete agreement about one thing: the institution was necessary. The problem was how to clean out the Augean stables or how to build new ones that would not become morally hideous.

If we examine the residential institution in the same way we looked at the special class, we may begin to see why its existence should be seriously questioned. Again we are confronting the justifications for and consequences of the segregation process:

(1) The resident requires special treatment in a special place.

(2) The community from which he comes cannot and should not cope with the resident, and if it were required to do so its normal functioning would be impaired. The community needs

to be protected against such interference and danger; otherwise its social fabric would begin to deteriorate.

(3) If the health of the community is protected, and the special needs of the resident are met by special treatment in special places by special people, it makes it very likely that most of these residents will be enabled to become again part of the community fabric.

These are the basic justifications for the residential institutions, justifications which continue to be accepted despite the obvious fact that they have never had the desired consequences, except that the community is "protected." This is a noteworthy exception because it suggests, as in the case of the special class, that the needs of the atypical person are quite secondary to those of the "normals." But let us go on by focusing not on postinstitutional consequences but on how the institution effects and is perceived by all who are part of it.

(1) Removal from family and community accentuates the patients' feeling of being different and rejected. Separation from what is familiar and, therefore, contains the only known sources of belonging—literally separation from the only interpersonal world one knows—weakens whatever psychological sense of community the individual may possess. A readjustment process begins, new bases for a psychological sense of community are found, but with the result that the sense of loss remains, the bases for the old sense weaken or disappear, and the bases for the new sense are far more restricted than the old.

(2) The psychological sense of community that the family felt with the patient (and in the populations served by these institutions one can assume that it was frequently fragile) is further attentuated. The very fact that these residential institutions serve a large geographical area and thus tend to be in hard-to-get-to places are for many families major obstacles to (and sometimes excuses for neglecting) social contact with the patient. Since every therapeutic and rehabilitative program assumes that the individual's difficulties are in part a function of family factors, the location of most of these institutions obviously renders it difficult, and in reality impossible, to act in accord with that assumption, since the theoretical rationale for these programs also assumes either that community

characteristics may play a role in the development of the individual's difficulties or that the community has a crucial role to play in the rehabilitative process, or both. The distance factor here too becomes an obstacle to or an excuse for not dealing with the community. But these remarks assume that these institutions have programs that deserve the labels *therapeutic* or *rehabilitative*. Generally speaking, it is a grossly invalid assumption as exposé after exposé has indicated. Programs and rhetoric are, after all, not the same things.

(3) The professional staffs in these residential institutions are perceived by their community colleagues as second-rate people, the proof of which is simply that they have chosen to work in settings which basically lack programs, are part of a large public bureaucracy, and contain a high degree of "hopeless" causes. Increasingly, as these residential institutions become related to and dominated by large university-based centers (medical and others), the perceived second-class status of the institutions' professionals is underlined. Not surprisingly, these professionals perceive themselves as second class. But even in those rare instances where the professional does not view himself, or is not viewed by others, as second class they voice two conclusions: the disparity between goals and resources is scandalous, and "no one really gives a damn," by which it is meant that no one in the outside world is really interested in what is going on in the institution. The professionals, like the residents, feel apart, rejected, and the recipients of undeserved abuse. They rarely enjoy any feeling of satisfaction or growth in their work with the residents. And in this catalogue of unpleasantries a prominent place has to be given to the conflicts, rivalries, and struggles that characterize professional interrelationships in these institutions. These internecine battles have no simple explanations but their strength and destructiveness are fed by the absence of any intrinsic job satisfaction as well as by the knowledge that there are very limited resources—they are in a win-lose (zero-sum) game with each other.

(4) The residential institution tends to have little or no relationship to the community in which it is physically embedded. There is always an economic relationship: citizens of the community may be given employment, purchases are made from local stores and industry. However, the local community has no sense of

responsibility for the institution and its residents, there is no positive identification with its residents. It is a place where one may work with strange, deviant, and perhaps dangerous people. Not infrequently, the local community fought the erection of the institution and continues to feel it is endangered by its presence. As most of its citizens see it, a major task of the institution is literally to contain its residents, and although there may be no walls, there are social barriers between those within and those without these invisible walls that are quite impermeable. When one says that the institution is an alien body in the local community it is, of course, but another way of emphasizing the absence of a psychological sense of community.

There is no point in further laboring the obvious. The residential institution has always been, at worst, a "humane" equivalent of a Nazi concentration camp and, at best, a well-run animal farm. If this characterization seems uncharitable to some, I will be content if they will accept the conclusion, hardly disputable, that our residential institutions have been failures, overwhelmingly and consistently so. And by failures I mean their inability to become places where those within them experience a psychological sense of community. On the contrary, they dilute the strength of the residents' and employees' psychological sense of community so that when the residents return to their own communities they frequently are less able to cope with community living than they were before they were institutionalized.

My characterizations would be stupidly uncharitable if I were blaming the institution for the evils it contains and its failure to meet its objective of restoring its residents to a satisfactory life in their home community. That would be another example of Ryan's (1971) description of how we tend to "blame the victim." The fact is, of course, that these institutions exist because of a variety of historical and cultural factors in our society, as well as the impact of these factors on theory and practice in the relevant professions. If these institutions have been largely failures it is not because of something peculiar to these institutions but rather to the nature of their relationships to the surrounding society, the values underlying these relationships, and the justifications provided by the relevant professions for these values and relationships. If only a particular type of institution (for example, the mental hospital) were a failure, or if it were the case that the exposés we read about in the newspapers and professional literature were not typical of institutional life, we might be justified in focusing narrowly on the institution. But that is not the case and no one, in my experience, knows that better than those who have direct professional responsibility for these public institutions.

Each exposé has predictable consequences: public indignation, scapegoating of one kind or another, a clamor for increasing funding, some kind of reorganization within the institution, public satisfaction that evil has been conquered, and then silence as the buildup for some future exposé begins. In the entire process there is no questioning of the assumption that the institution should exist, or any discussion of the possibility that the very fact of the institution's existence is symptomatic of what is wrong in society's view of the problem. As in the case of the special class, it is inconceivable to people that the institution need not exist. It becomes conceivable only if one recognizes that for any social problem there is not one and only one solution but rather a universe of alternatives from which one can choose, and, crucially, that choosing among alternatives always forces one to choose among different values, that is, to decide by what values one wishes to live. The obstacles to and the productiveness of this process were forced on me several years ago in the course of working with groups of individuals who had helped create and build public residential institutions (the details of what emerged from these groups will be found on page 240). It is not, I think, fortuitous that when these individuals were forced to consider the universe of alternatives they came up with possibilities that rested implicitly (sometimes explicitly) on the psychological sense of community as an organizing value. They knew well how socially isolated the institution was from the communities from which their residents came; they knew well that they felt these communities looked upon the institution as a "dumping ground"; they knew how difficult it was to get these communities to devise settings and programs which would enable many of their residents to remain in or return to their communities; and, finally, they were quite aware of the subtlety and insidiousness of the process whereby community irresponsibility leads to feelings of hopelessness and boredom among the institutional staff. Thus it is not surprising that when some of those institutional administrators were forced to consider alternatives to present practices their responses were determined by values which were directly opposed to those which justify segregation. Different problems within the community were seen in relation to each other, and different groups within the community were seen as necessary to each other—not in the sense that parts of a mechanical system are necessary to each other but in the sense that each can contribute to and enlarge the other's sense of belongingness.

One could point to certain developments within the past few years that rather clearly suggest that the attitude toward the traditional residential institution has gone beyond disillusionment to serious experimentation with alternatives. The increase in halfway houses for different groups (drug addicts, mentally retarded, psychologically disturbed, juvenile offenders); one state (Massachusetts) in the process of dismantling its institutions for juvenile delinquents; numerous states adopting the policy of not building any more institutions; some prisoners being allowed to spend part of each week with their families in their own communities; community responsibility for its senior citizens being accepted—these are among the recent developments that can be viewed as signalling the beginning of the end of the traditional residential institution. That these developments represent a rejection of the traditional institution is testimony to man's capacity to learn from past mistakes, although it would be unwarranted in the extreme if we viewed this rejection as one that is generally shared either by the population at large or the bulk of professional groups. Public attitudes and policies are still overwhelmingly supportive of the traditional residential institution.

Raush (1968) found forty halfway houses for psychiatric patients in 1963. He estimates that by mid-1967 there were probably more than 100 halfway houses in the United States. Although this represents a sizeable percentage increase, it is miniscule in terms of the numbers that should be developed. This is in part, as I indicated above, due to public attitudes, but it is also due to professional inertia and ignorance.[4] I am not aware of any psychiatric or clin-

---

[4] Sometimes, of course, public attitudes are far ahead of professional

ical psychological training program which concentrates on the
rationale for the development and maintenance of halfway houses.
Indeed, very few mental health people are aware of Raush's book,
which is basic in this area. If they were aware, they would learn
that for Raush the psychological sense of community is a central
justification for halfway houses:

> The diverse models presented in our studies offer
> possibilities for a range of social settings gauged to a range of
> psychological disturbance—from the adolescent who needs a
> temporary relief from the intensity of his family life to the
> schizophrenic whose massive and diffuse psychopathology
> requires him to have help in all aspects of living. It would be
> wrong, however, to think of the halfway house as a smaller,
> or more humane, or more individualized, or more efficient
> mental hospital; it would be wrong to think of it as requiring
> fewer resources than the hospital. It is not a hospital at all.
> It provides arrangements for living through a structure de-
> signed to make daily experiences useful rather than harmful.
> But equally important is its service as liaison between the resi-
> dent and community resources. Unlike the hospital which
> gathers all resources under its wings—and whose size is in part
> related to this—it is important that the halfway house is
> limited. Because of its limitations the halfway house must call
> upon the resources of its members and of the surrounding

---

ones. See, for example, an article in the *New York Times,* July 12, 1973,
with the heading "28% of State's Mental Patients Return Within 6 Months
After Being Released." (A month before, the same newspaper, in a page one
article, reported its own investigation and found a number of former patients
"jammed" into unlicensed and disapproved foster homes.) In the July 12
article "The basic reason for the 'revolving door' admissions, as seen within
the State Department of Mental Hygiene, has been the failure of the released
patients to follow up on the necessary medication and aftercare appointments.
'The inherent nature of mental illness,' an administrator who is also a psychiatrist said, 'is that patients feel better and stop their medication. It is
hard to engage them in an ongoing case.'" This statement deserves some
kind of prize for stupidity and/or ignorance. In the same article a group of
relatives of patients demanded that the "state rescind its directives to empty
the hospitals until it has properly provided for decent conditions in the
community . . . To assert the noble principle of 'community treatment'
without making adequate provision for proper housing, follow-up care and
treatment, rehabilitation, and job training is an immoral and malicious
mockery of these helpless and ill people."

community. For a halfway house to function properly it needs to find and work with its community, by which we mean not the local neighborhood but that community which consists of shops and services, of employers and job opportunities, of psychotherapists and clinics, of recreational and social facilities. The halfway house cannot stand alone and the usefulness of its transactions with its residents is based on the fact that it does not stand alone. Neither it nor its residents can be isolated from the community [p. 209].

Raush then goes on to say:

The halfway house needs the hospital. Hospitals are traditionally specialized emergency facilities capable of providing care, security, and technical competence in cases of physical or physiological crises. Some equivalent is needed for psychological crises. It is likely that many who are mentally disturbed will suffer at some time or another disruptions which are so acute as to demand the total protection which hospitals can provide. If hospitals were freed from responsibility for long-term incarceration and if hospital staff and patients were freed from the stigma which comes from this function, crisis episodes might be dealt with far more effectively. Intensive emergency short-term service, responsive flexibly to need, could be part of urban general hospital facilities. Professional resources could be maximized for intensive professional work. There would be a dignity and an excitement to such work not presently found in hospital practice [pp. 209–210].

Two things are unclear in the second quotation. First, why is the hospital needed? Raush provides no convincing argument. Second, if the potential of the halfway house were truly developed, what *kind* of hospital would be needed? Raush states that it would bear little kinship to existing mental hospitals. I would maintain that as long as there was any kind of mental hospital it would end up perpetuating some of the worst evils of the traditional one. Raush assumes a mental hospital is needed. That assumption, one which our culture makes seem so "natural," I question and will discuss later in this as well as other chapters. I am quite aware of the arguments that could be advanced against doing away with all

mental hospitals. Precisely because all of these arguments derive
from experience with the mental hospital, and not from serious
attempts to try other vehicles based on radically different assumptions, I remain unconvinced that a mental hospital is necessary.
Let us not forget that all of these arguments were once directed
against the concept of the halfway house and, we should remind
ourselves, against the idea that mentally retarded individuals could
and should remain in their communities. If thirty years ago someone had predicted that the time would come that the need for
residential institutions for the mentally retarded would be seriously
questioned and that there would be growing acceptance of the
idea that these individuals could and should be maintained in their
communities, he would have been viewed as an ignorant fool. The
fools, of course, are those who can only envision a future that bears
striking resemblance to the present. But they are not so much fools
as unwitting prisoners of a culture at a particular point in time.

Nevertheless, efforts at change within the past few years are
more numerous, serious, and successful than earlier efforts so that
one is justified in suggesting that we are finally witnessing the
beginning of a very long process which will culminate in the disappearance of the traditional institution. It is not fortuitous, I
think, that these new developments began to be considered and
tried at approximately the same time that community participation
and control became issues in education, neighborhood councils
became vehicles for a variety of urban renewal programs, and communes and other forms of communal living became numerous and
fashionable.[5] All of the developments I have mentioned seemed to
reflect three characteristics of the social atmosphere: disillusionment
with bigness and centralized authority of any kind, struggle against
the feelings of anonymity and impotence, and striving for some
psychological sense of community. These are not new characteristics

[5] Relevant here is the fantastic spread of the group dynamics movement which, in the tradition of most new movements, was presented and
accepted as a solution for practically every major personal and social problem. The important point is not the different rationales which different parts
of this movement articulated but rather the number of people who eagerly
sought to get a "group experience," that is, to break out of their feelings
of lonely insignificance by becoming part of a group which, however transient,
promised the experience of community.

of our social atmosphere, but what seems different about them is their strength, generality, and their expression in new social forms.

The Residential Institution: It Exists, Therefore It Should Exist

In 1973, Rosenhan published a study which deservedly received national attention. The title of the study was "On Being Sane in Insane Places." In the first part of the study each of eight "pseudopatients" was admitted to a mental hospital:

> In order to generalize the findings, admission into a variety of hospitals was sought. The twelve hospitals in the sample were located in five different states on the East and West coasts. Some were old and shabby, some were quite new. Some were research-oriented, others not. Some had good staff-patient ratios, others were quite understaffed. Only one was a strictly private hospital. All of the others were supported by state or federal funds or, in one instance, by university funds.
>
> After calling the hospital for an appointment, the pseudopatient arrived at the admissions office complaining that he had been hearing voices. Asked what the voices said, he replied that they were often unclear, but as far as he could tell they said "empty," "hollow," and "thud." The voices were unfamiliar and were of the same sex as the pseudopatient. The choice of these symptoms was occasioned by their apparent similarity to existential symptoms. Such symptoms are alleged to arise from painful concerns about the perceived meaningfulness of one's life. It is as if the hallucinating person were saying, "My life is empty and hollow." The choice of these symptoms was also determined by the absence of a single report of existential psychoses in the literature.
>
> Beyond alleging the symptoms and falsifying name, vocation, and employment, no further alterations of person, history, or circumstances were made. The significant events of the pseudopatient's life history were presented as they had actually occurred. Relationships with parents and siblings, with spouse and children, with people at work and in school, consistent with the aforementioned exceptions, were described along with joys and satisfactions. These facts are important to remember. If anything, they strongly biased the subsequent results in favor of detecting sanity, since none of their histories

or current behaviors were seriously pathological in any way
[p. 251].

The pseudopatients were never detected. "Admitted, except in one
case, with a diagnosis of schizophrenia, each was discharged with
a diagnosis of schizophrenia in 'remission.'" A second study was
then done.

> The following experiment was arranged at a research
> and teaching hospital whose staff had heard these findings but
> doubted that such an error could occur in their hospital.
> The staff was informed that at some time during the follow-
> ing three months, one or more pseudopatients would attempt
> to be admitted into the psychiatric hospital. Each staff mem-
> ber was asked to rate each patient who presented himself at
> admissions or on the ward according to the likelihood that
> the patient was a pseudopatient. A 10-point scale was used,
> with a 1 and 2 reflecting high confidence that the patient was
> a pseudopatient.
>
> Judgments were obtained on 193 patients who were
> admitted for psychiatric treatment. All staff who had had
> sustained contact with or primary responsibility for the patient
> —attendants, nurses, psychiatrists, physicians, and psycholo-
> gists—were asked to make judgments. Forty-one patients were
> alleged, with high confidence, to be pseudopatients by at least
> one member of the staff. Twenty-three were considered sus-
> pect by at least one psychiatrist. Nineteen were suspected
> by one psychiatrist and one other staff member. Actually, no
> genuine pseudopatient (at least from my group) presented
> himself during this period [p. 252].

These results are, as Rosenhan states, not surprising. Neither, for
that matter, are Rosenhan's vivid descriptions of the depersonaliza-
tion process experienced by patients, the degree of segregation
between patient and staff, the insidious consequences of the institution's hierarchical organization, the insensitivity of staff to patient-
initiated contacts, and the witting and unwitting callousness and
cruelty.

> So what is to be done?

I do not, even now, understand this problem well enough to perceive solutions. But two matters seem to have some promise. The first concerns the proliferation of community mental health facilities, of crisis intervention centers, of the human potential movement, and of behavior therapies that, for all of their own problems, tend to avoid psychiatric labels, to focus on specific problems and behaviors, and to retain the individual in a relatively nonpejorative environment. Clearly, to the extent that we refrain from sending the distressed to insane places, our impressions of them are less likely to be distorted [p. 257].

Several *caveats* are in order here but I must first express my agreement with Rosenhan that the new community-based service settings do represent a potential improvement over the mental hospital. I say "potential" because these new settings were created explicitly on the assumption that removal of an individual from his family and home community was in itself countertherapeutic and that it became even more so when removal meant entering the mental hospital. The idea that seriously distressed individuals could and should be maintained in the community is revolutionary when viewed in light of psychiatry's history, theories, and practices. It is an idea the importance of which cannot be overestimated. However, there are several considerations which should caution one against uncritical enthusiasm about what these settings are or may become. For example, when these new settings were conceived and implemented there was no serious discussion of what was meant by a *community* center. Indeed, in none of the several centers I observed did the word community mean other than what professional groups would create and do in a particular building. If there was any inventiveness in their thinking it was in their attempts to devise new types of service and to give help to more people. But there was no question in their minds that the new centers were *their* responsibility and no one else's. In short, these centers in actuality were based on a traditional conception of *professional* responsibility rather than on some substantive conception of community responsibility—in no way different than the basis on which the mental hospital was founded. Clearly the result of the narrow conception of responsibility were the consequences that several of these centers experienced as they became actualities. They met a storm of protest from different parts of the community precisely on the grounds that the community had no role in the planning of the centers and their activities.

The reaction of many mental health professionals ranged from puzzlement to anger at ingratitude. Who were *these* people to tell *us* what the problems were and how we should approach them? If anything was clear it was that the professionals had no psychological sense of community with the community. It would have been surprising in the extreme if the situation had been different, because the process whereby one becomes a professional specialist has the effect of emphasizing differences rather than similarities between the professional and everybody else. When Rosenhan (who was one of the pseudopatients) seriously recommends that mental health professionals experience for themselves the impact of institutionalization, he is suggesting a vehicle whereby the professional's psychological sense of community can be enlarged. But that, we should not forget, is no substitute for a similar sense of communality with the larger community, and it is that sense which is crucial if a community center is to be truly of, rather than merely being in, a community.

A second consideration that should temper enthusiasm for community centers is a derivative of the first, and that is that they are organized in an administrative hierarchical way little different from what Rosenhan describes in the mental hospital, and there is little reason to expect that the adverse consequences will be discernibly less.

It is the third consideration which virtually guarantees that the potential of these centers will not be realized. It also exposes the degree of insensitivity of the professions to the needs of the community. I refer to the indisputable fact—long known within the professions and discussed and documented in the literature (Albee, 1954; Albee, 1968a and b; Matarazzo, 1971) that as long as mental health problems are defined in ways so as to require the service of professionals there is no solution. When defined in this way the discrepancy between the number of professionals and those deemed to need their service is scandalously large. *And yet these centers were set up because they were seen as being able to give more service to more people than ever before.* Never was there less basis for the promises of a program. I do not wish to suggest that there was any deceit; it would be a less serious problem if that were the case. What was involved was the complete (and I am afraid it was complete) inability of the professionals to redefine the problem so as not to require the services only, or even largely, of the traditionally trained professional.

To redefine the problem in this way would have required a very different stance in relation to the community. It would have meant taking a very different view of potential resources and how they could be located and utilized, and it would have meant that the center was not the responsibility of the professionals alone.[6] Indeed, to redefine the problem along these lines would have required that the professionals *refuse* to accept sole responsibility; they would, obviously, be part of program planning and service activities but now in the context of a serious community problem which required wide community participation and acceptance. What happened, instead, was that the professionals defined the problem in their terms and as their responsibility, rendering it insoluble and setting the stage for future community disillusionment.

But, some could argue, what does the community know about serious psychological disturbance? How can people be given responsibility when they have no familiarity with the complexities of etiology and treatment? Who is the community? How do you justify shared responsibility when it can mean a lowering of the quality of service? Besides, aren't these new centers so new and such an obvious improvement over the mental hospital that we should refrain from being overly critical? Will they not evolve over time into being truly community centers? One way of beginning to answer these questions is to distinguish sharply between matters which are community issues and those which are ordinarily considered professional, in the sense that they deal with the nature of service. Whenever there is a gross discrepancy between community needs and an available service, it is a matter of community policy, not professional policy, how the available service should be distributed and what alternative steps should be taken to meet com-

---

[6] A concrete example of the consequences of this stance is given in Chapter Nine.

munity needs. To put the case in clearest form, if people considered professionally rendered psychotherapy 100 percent effective but knew that it would be made available only to a very few of those who needed it (either by definition or demand), it would be obvious we would then be dealing with a problem that belonged to the community and not to the professionals. How limited resources were to be distributed, how alternative approaches could be developed, what degree of compromise between alternatives and outcomes the community could accept—these would be issues for the larger community to confront and decide. These are not issues for the professionals to decide, and to the extent that they are taken over by the professionals as being within their perogatives it virtually guarantees that there will always be inequities in the distribution of services. There is one consequence to what I am suggesting: the process whereby a community accepts responsibility—which is another way of saying that it becomes more informed and sophisticated about the ins and outs of the issues—tends to increase the number of service alternatives which are possible and which the community is willing to support. It is a process whereby community change occurs through redefinition of its problems and solutions. And, needless to say, it is a process which can serve to strengthen and enlarge people's psychological sense of community. It is not (as we shall see in later chapters) a process without serious problems and pitfalls, and it is not one which assumes that a community has a kind of folk wisdom insuring an appropriate match between problems and solutions. It is, at the very least, a process which puts the responsibility where it belongs.

Another consideration tempering enthusiasm about community mental health centers is more empirical than the first. Although there can be no doubt that these centers see more people, there is also no doubt that this has been largely accomplished by the use of drugs, together with a quality and quantity of service which, in the state of Connecticut for example, has increased the *re*-admission rate to state hospitals by over four hundred percent. There are fewer patients in the state hospitals, their stay is shorter, but their number of stays has increased. The community mental health center virtually guarantees the continued existence of the state hospital even though its initial rationale was opposed to that of the state hospital! It could hardly have been otherwise because these centers were conceived within the same traditions of professional practice and theory—the same nomenclature, administrative hierarchical structure, professional preciousness, and professional responsibility—that are the basis for the state hospitals.

It is more than an act of faith on my part to say that these new centers represent an improvement over the state hospitals. They have prevented the institutionalization of some troubled people, they try to be helpful to segments of the urban population that never have received any service, and because of their geographical location the barriers between the center and the surrounding community are more permeable than was ever the case with the mental hospital. And in some instances they have tried (usually because they were forced to by events) to seek community representation in their activities and their decision-making process. In the sweep of history, it may turn out that these community centers will be seen as other than a ritualistic break with a professional-institutional tradition which had long been ineffective and harmful. But it may also turn out to be the case that they will be seen as instances of new developments subverted by suffocating traditions and parochial values. What if it turns out—what if it is *now* the case—that the kinds of studies done by Rosenhan in the traditional institution will not differ markedly in their findings from studies adapted to and carried out in these new centers? Have we not learned that because a type of institution exists it does not mean that it should exist or that there is a congruence between its intended purposes and actual outcomes? And have we not learned that segregation, particularly when it involves "atypical" people feared or not understood by the community, has the self-fulfilling effect of "proving" that they need to be segregated? And have we not learned that whatever the virtues of professionalism and specialization may be, they are accompanied by serious defects not the least of which are an insensitivity to community needs, a confusion between professional and community perspectives, and the inability to confront the necessity of some overarching values about community living— values which if confronted can alter the definition and solution of what are, in the final analysis, community problems?

As an overarching value by which to judge any community

effort, the psychological sense of community is neither panacea nor
program: agreement on values in no way insures that there will be
agreement on what action is consistent with the values. Neither in
logic nor in reality does a particular value give rise to one and only
one course of action, and the inability to recognize this—to confront
the fact that there is always a universe of alternatives—is one of
the causes of ineffective action. The special class, the residential
institution, the community mental health centers—in the rhetoric
justifying their existence it is unmistakably clear that one of their
major functions is to create those conditions which would restore
in people a sense of and a desire for community. To put it in
another way: they seek to integrate the individual in the community
in mutually productive ways. It was not my purpose in this chapter
to demonstrate that the residential institution and the special class
do not realize their goals. (In the case of the former it needs no
further documentation, and in the case of the latter it needs only
to be noted that there is no research evidence that it meets its goals.)
My purpose was two-fold: to illustrate how one looks at these
settings if one takes seriously the psychological sense of community
as a basic value, so that, for example, one is forced to look not only
at what happens to those being served but also to the servers. The
second purpose was to suggest that the way in which professionals
think of community responsibility and of community needs dilutes
rather than strengthens the psychological sense of community of
the professionals themselves, of those they seek to help, and of those
in the wider community.

   But why make the psychological sense of community the
overarching value? Is it not revealing that in the hundreds of times
I have discussed these issues (with individuals in classes, and with
diverse community groups) nobody has ever questioned the
supremacy of that value? They questioned many other things I said
but not that. Indeed, when I discussed the psychological sense of
community I could always count on an outpouring of feelings about
loneliness, alienation, impotence in regard to social forces, the
desire to belong, and to be mutually dependent. If, therefore, I
maintain that the psychological sense of community is the overarching value by which to judge community programs, it is because

the felt lack of that sense is so pervasive and it is contributing to so much human misery.

I repeat, that I do not mean that if we take seriously the need for a sense of community, we are on the road to the elimination of human misery or to a state of blissful togetherness. What I do mean is that we should take it seriously now knowing full well that the process of appropriate actions will itself create problems and new issues: that we create new problems as we solve old ones. As sages have long pointed out: the more you know the more you need to know. The more old problems we begin to understand and to solve the more will we be faced by new problems.

VIII

A Total Intervention in a Total Institution

In this chapter I shall describe a research effort illustrative of some of the major themes of previous chapters. It is an effort distinctive in several ways in that its goals were to change an entire institution (not just a part of it); to do this through the development of a token economy; to take the concept of community responsibility seriously; and to do all of this in the service of establishing a psychological sense of community among a large number of people who had little of such a sense. The project, three and a half years old, is still ongoing and has become more comprehensive as a result of a legislated merger between this and a second total institution. Of necessity my description will be far from comprehensive in terms of what was done and with what consequences. My primary purpose is to present enough description to convey what this particular institution was like, and the rationale governing and the obstacles confronting the intervention. If the emerging picture looks like a hell transformed into a heaven, it will represent an unwitting distortion on my part. By any set of criteria this institution has changed dramatically, but the change was not accomplished without errors of omission and commission, and no claim is made by the project staff that their rationale was crystal clear from the outset or that it was always technically implemented in the best possible way. When the reader examines the full account, I am confident that he will be more impressed by what was accomplished than by how far this degree of accomplishment fell short of some ideal state.[1]

The Connecticut School for Boys

The Connecticut School for Boys (CSB) is a state institution for juvenile offenders sixteen years of age or younger. Located on a main street within the limits of a small city (Meriden), the CSB is one of the oldest of its kind in this country. It is an "open" institution consisting of a number of large residential cottages and other buildings. Physically and architecturally it does not fit the usual stereotype of a "reform school." It can house upwards of two hundred boys, although in recent years it has not been near this (crowded) maximum. It is the only such institution in the state and, consequently, the bulk of the boys come from the largest centers of population, that is, from Hartford, New Haven, Bridge-

---

[1] I participated in this project's earliest phases and I have always been an interested observer of its subsequent course. The way I describe in this chapter the project's significance would not be the same as that by Dr. N. Dickon Reppucci, the project leader. That is to say, I give the psychological sense of community a more central explanatory role than he does, although the difference is not so very great. This project is being written up for publication in book form. It has been reported in several preliminary descriptions containing description and results (Dean, C. W., 1971; Dean, C. W., and Reppucci, N. D., in press; Reppucci, N. D., 1973; Reppucci, N. D., Saunders, J. T., and Wilkinson, L., 1971; Saunders, J. T., Reppucci, N. D., and Wilkinson, L., 1971; Wilkinson, L. and Reppucci, N. D., 1973; Wilkinson, L., Saunders, J. T., and Reppucci, N. D., 1971).

port, Waterbury. For decades the CSB enjoyed a national reputation as progressive and successful. Within Meriden and around the
state the CSB was favorably viewed. This status was primarily the
achievement of the long leadership of one Superintendent who
retired in 1960.[2] It was not long after his retirement that the CSB
had all the most negative characteristics of residential institutions,
and that its reputation disintegrated.

It is fruitless to expect that words can adequately convey
what the CSB was in 1970. Hardly a day went by when the newspapers did not report some kind of misfortune at the school. And I
do not only mean the local newspapers. Connecticut is a small state,
and what is big news in one part of the state stands a good chance
of coverage in newspapers in other parts. The happenings at the
CSB were big news: mass runaways, deaths, employee strikes and
picketing, charges of staff cruelty, stationing of State Police on the
grounds—these were some of the happenings reported in the news
columns and about which countless editorials were written. Political
leaders in Meriden were clamoring that the CSB should be closed
and moved elsewhere, preferably to another planet.

All of this establishes the fact that the CSB was a scandalous
mess but, not surprisingly, it does not illuminate how it came to be,
or what should have been done. To some, the cause was a breakdown in law and order, to others it was poor leadership. The
professional-clinical staff criticized the residential staff who criticized
the teachers in the school buildings who inveighed against the administration who fought the three labor unions and the rest of the
world. The fact is that anyone with a modicum of institutional

    [2] An intriguing question is how come the CSB was as favorably
viewed as it was by the local community in comparison to how it was viewed
when Reppucci and his colleagues entered the scene? Terry Saunders began
to look into the question by interviewing former employees, the Superintendent who was still alive and active, and by reading institutional records
and archives as well as newspapers of that period. It is running ahead of our
story to note that there were some striking similarities between what the
CSB was in that period and what it later again became, particularly in terms
of community responsibility and of the significance of its psychological sense
of community. If the Superintendent was revered by the community and the
school's employees and residents, it was not because of what *he* was but
rather what he helped *them* experience.

experience could have pinpointed areas of conflict without setting foot in the CSB. Here are only a few of them:

(1) The professional-clinical staff (psychiatrists, psychologists, social workers) will view everyone else as either unsophisticated, or well meaning but blundering, or uninterested in their work, or wittingly or unwittingly sadistic, or undependable, or just plain stupid, or impossible to teach. The severity of the judgment will vary, of course, but what will not vary is the basic judgment that the problem inheres in the fact that professional knowledge and wisdom are inadequately understood and implemented by non-clinicians.

(2) The professional-clinical staff will be perceived, particularly by aides, attendants, or cottage personnel, as remote, pompous people who spend their time dispensing instructions and wisdom, almost totally unaware of (and perhaps uninterested in) what is involved in being with and managing clients on a minute-to-minute basis over a period of hours. As one aide (a student of mine working in the summer in a state hospital) said: "It is unbelievable. They *can't* know what's going on because they are only here on flying visits. Do you know that I have been on the ward for three weeks and not one of the professionals has ever asked me my name!"

(3) In residential institutions for young people the teachers in the school building are perceived with envy and criticism, envy because they work "short" hours and then can leave the grounds, and criticism because the teachers either do not "really" know the children, or what they teach them is worthless. Teachers are seen as having the easiest jobs: short hours, summer vacations, good salaries (in comparison to cottage staff), and little real responsibility. When a child acts up in school the teacher can send him back to his cottage. When he acts up in the cottage the personnel there have no place to send him, they must cope with him.

(4) The Superintendent is seen as one who plays favorites, makes policy on the basis of ignorance, has no feeling for what is really going on and, besides, does not want to know what is going on. He could do more than he is doing, he could know more than he knows, if only he did not surround himself with stupid schemers who were feathering their own nests, and, one will be told, if only access to his ears was less a function of one's education and status.

(5) Within each one of the institution's personnel empires there are predictable conflicts, for example, between different shifts in the residential quarters (day vs. night shifts particularly), among the different professional-clinical personnel for status and power.

I repeat: these are some of the predictable features of the residential institution and the CSB had them all, exacerbated and exposed to public view. It is understandable if the reader with no institutional experience has difficulty understanding the similarities among these institutions. Many, indeed most, people with institutional experience either have difficulty arriving at an explanation or come up with one that indicts personalities and personnel selection or the failure to communicate—treating these as causes rather than as what they are, consequences.

Events and public pressure required that new leadership be brought into the CSB. Dr. Charles Dean, a sociologist with a good deal of research and administrative experience in the field of corrections, was appointed superintendent. He had worked closely on several projects with Dr. Reppucci and his colleagues. One of the conditions Dr. Dean stipulated for assuming the new role was that he have the services of Dr. Reppucci and his team. Within a few months it was explicit that one of the goals of the intervention was to establish a token economy throughout the institution, that is, a clear set of tasks, rules, and criteria by means of which boys could earn tokens or points which they could use to "purchase" things, privileges and ultimately release. The details of the token economy were not pre-packaged but were based on what the boys and staff considered fair values for performed tasks and how these tasks and values could over time lead to return to the community.[3]

---

[3] There was, of course, an existing economy at the CSB. More correctly, there were two economies: the official and unofficial. The official one was contained in many booklets describing in great detail what a boy was expected to do (the criteria he had to meet) from the day of his arrival to the day of departure. On paper, at least, it was quite clear how a boy could earn privileges, visits, and release. But that was on paper and it bore little relationship to reality, i.e., the unofficial economy. For example, if a boy was sixteen and a "trouble maker" he stood a very good chance for release. Even if he was a good deal less than sixteen, he stood a good chance to be released—a relationship of which most boys and staff were quite aware. It was not unusual for a boy who had broken every rule in the book to be told that if he could be "good" for a week or so, he would be released. And, needless

But I am ahead of the story, because in the beginning weeks of the new regime there was hardly any talk about a token economy. A great deal had to be clarified and done before talk about a token economy made sense.

The Beginning Weeks

From the outset several short and long term objectives were formulated that determined the nature and pacing of the intervention in its earliest phase:

(1) The thoughts, feelings, and advice of all employees had to be obtained in a way and with consequences that would maximize their participation and responsibility for new programming. This did not mean that it would be an employees' program, but rather that there would be forums by means of which their ideas could be voiced, discussed, compared to competing ideas, and viable compromises sought. These could not be forums to sample public opinion but to discuss opinion as it relates to decisions that would have to be made. To the extent that these forums were empty rituals or a form of window dressing or unrelated to proposed action, to that extent they would reinforce the belief that having trust in the leadership and being committed to innovation were the hallmark of stupid employees who had not learned that the more things change the more they remain the same. To stir up a wave of hope and then dash it on the rocks of deceit may win a battle but it will lose a war.

(2) The same principles would be applicable to the boys. Here too the objective was not simply to adapt a program to their desires but rather to seek their aid in formulating a program that they could support because it was to them clear, fair, reasonable, and feasible. Their initial support for a new program might be temporarily secured because they had a hand in its development, but unless the criteria were consistently employed and the agreed upon rewards available and promptly granted—unless there was

---

to say, the boys were quite adept in finding out how the staff varied in "softness" and "blindness." So there was, as there is everywhere, an economy. The token economy instituted by Dr. Reppucci was distinctive in several respects: its development *with* the boys and staff, the degree of monitoring of its functioning by the intervention team, and the consequences of the economy for staff selection and responsibility.

little or no discrepancy between the official and unofficial "economy"—the initial support would dissolve and the cynicisms of the black market would prevail.

(3) The role of an employee in a program would not be determined by education, professional label, or job title, but either by what he had demonstrated he could do well or appeared to have the potential for doing well. This objective would run headlong into civil service regulations, union policy, professional preciousness and imperialism, and the rigid boundaries of departmental empires. It would, however, strike a very responsive chord in many employees desiring to test themselves in new ways, to experience new and challonging (and anxiety arousing) roles heretofore unavailable to them because of vocational caste and class. This objective would make for certain kinds of conflicts and it would require of the superintendent a large degree of courage, finagling, and persistence if this objective were to be even partially met (which was all that was expected, given the nature of the real world). To the extent that this objective was achieved it would dilute the insidious consequences of the traditional organizational structure in which allegience to one of its subsystems takes precedence over that to the institution itself.

(4) The responsibility for rehabilitating its residents could not be assumed by the CSB. That is to say, as long as the CSB presented itself to the public as if it alone could rehabilitate the boys sent to it, it would continue in practice to be a dismal failure. The CSB should refuse to assume sole responsibility but should redefine its role as one which coordinates the rehabilitative efforts of the community from which a boy comes, the CSB, and the local community of Meriden. This redefinition of responsibility would not easily be accepted either by Meriden or the boy's own community but the difficulty of the task bespeaks its basic importance. Indeed, for almost all the boys the CSB was a self-defeating placement precisely because their own communities had no sense of obligation to them, developed no programs alternative to the CSB, and was unprepared for their re-entry. *From the outset the intervention team regarded the death of the CSB as one of its ultimate objectives.* The concept of community responsibility rather than CSB responsibility had to be in the forefront of efforts at public education.

This also meant that two other things had to take place: anyone could visit any part of the CSB at any time, and employees had to look at community activity as part of their job.

Although Reppucci did not formulate the problem in just these terms, these objectives rested on the value of an ever-enlarging psychological sense of community. Initially, the major effort was directed against the traditional type of institutional organization and thinking that accentuated differences rather than communalities among people, such as, departmentalism, professionalism, and credentialism. But this was not an end in itself in the sense that the CSB would become an oasis of happiness and togetherness to be protected against a psychologically arid surround. Quite the contrary, the psychological sense of community that would be developed among those at the CSB would, from the very beginning, have as its goal geographical referents far beyond the school. Metaphorically speaking, the refusal of the CSB to be alone with its problems was not a sign of inadequacy or even a plea for help, but a recognition of the need for mutuality. And, paradoxically, it was hoped that this mutuality would lead to the demise of the CSB because the communities that had used it would have a new sense of responsibility that reflected its members' new psychological sense of community. Granted, this was a far-off goal, but if one were ever to reach it one must take a first step that reflected the goal, a first step that was already the hallmark of change.

Shortly after Dr. Dean and the intervention team had started work, each employee (and every newspaper and radio and T.V. station in the region) received the following letter:

July 22, 1970

TO: All Staff
FROM: Charles W. Dean, Superintendent

I have been Superintendent for somewhat more than a month. When I agreed to take this position, I knew the following:

1. The situation was scandalously messy.
2. No one disagreed with point No. 1.
3. I had and would have the full support of Commis-

sioner Mucci, Deputy Commissioner Brown, and Director of Institutions, Mr. Maloney.

4. I had a lot to learn in a very short period of time before acting decisively. I knew that in the first month I would be forced to make decisions I would rather not make, that some of these decisions I would regret, others I would feel far better about. In other words, the first month would be very difficult and indeed it has been.

I have learned a lot about the Connecticut School for Boys, not as much as I would like or need to know, but enough to justify beginning a process of *drastic* reorganization which over time will create a more favorable climate for the boys and the staff.

What have I learned? I am going to list some of the major problems and, as I shall make clear below, these are the problems I shall ask you to think about and to come up with suggested solutions.

1. The amount of conflict, anger, and undercutting that exists between departments is without parallel in my experience.

2. For most people, their primary allegiance is to *their* department and not to an overall program for the boys. Each department has a piece of the action which it considers more important than anything anybody else is doing. The major result is that boys are caught in the middle and there is no coordinated program. As anyone with institutional experience would tell you, and as I am sure you know, the boys are fully aware of the infighting.

3. Most people spend a good deal of time blaming someone else or some other department for the situation we are in.

4. A lot of employees are unhappy in part because they do not feel that what they are doing is worthwhile. In other words, when your job is just a job and you regard it as no different than a factory job, you simply do not put out your best. What bothers me is that we are not only doing very little for the boys but we are doing even less to make employees feel that what they are doing is worthwhile. Employees will not change for the same reasons the boys will not change, *we have not provided them with the incentive to change.*

5. This place seems to be set up so as to see how boring

and unstimulating one can make it for the boys. This place, particularly evenings and weekends, is like a tomb. If you cleared out all our boys and put here instead a group of bright, well-adjusted boys, I have no doubt with our present program that their level of boredom would soon provoke them to the same kind of behavior we see in *our* boys. Boys are bored and edgy and so are our employees.

6. The Connecticut School for Boys is isolated, in the most self-defeating ways, from the rest of the world. We want this community (and others) open to us and this means we will have to be open to it and them. *We* don't own the Connecticut School for Boys. It is a public facility from which we have no right to wall the community off, except if we are doing, as has been the case, a lousy job.

I have developed a number of ideas about what might be done. None of them is simple or magical. There is no such thing as instant cure. My ideas would effect everyone and it is precisely because they will have such effects that I am recommending the following:

1. I do *not*, at this time, wish to impose my ideas on the staff and employees. What I need to know is how *you* would deal with the problems I listed. I am not asking for gripes and complaints but *concrete* ideas about how we should change things so that we are serving the boys better than we now are. I am not asking for vague generalities about cooperation and communication. What I need are concrete steps which will get us out of the mess we are in.

2. I am going to set up groups whose task it will be to discuss the problems I listed and come up with a plan of action. Those groups (about ten in a group) will meet twice weekly for 2 or 3 weeks.

3. I am asking Seymour Sarason, Dick Reppucci, Sonny Cytrynbaum, and Brian Sarata to act as leaders for the groups. They are from the Yale Psycho-Educational Clinic and I can assure you of two things: they know institutions, and they are independent thinkers. Their job will be to keep you on the task of deciding what *you* think, recommend, and would get behind.

4. I have also invited Deputy Commissioner Brown and Director of Institutions Maloney to participate in these groups. They will not be there to tell you what to think. *Anything*

they say will represent their personal opinions and should not be taken as official policy. Policy for the Connecticut School for Boys is primarily my responsibility and I will discharge it. Mr. Brown and Mr. Maloney know this and I am delighted that they agreed to participate as individuals.

5. These groups should conduct their discussion as if any change is possible. *They are not to be bound by any existing departmental structure or practice or even policy.* The Connecticut School for Boys will not change by nice words, pussy-footing, or token changes. The situation demands a lot of change.

I hope you take this responsibility seriously. I know that a number of you have good ideas but they have not been "put on the table" for public discussion. This is your opportunity to do justice to *your* ideas. From this point on, we move forward and the more these groups face issues squarely, the more will the Connecticut School for Boys reflect what your consciences know needs to be done. We are here to serve boys, not ourselves.

Although the deputy commissioner and the director of institutions did not end up participating, attendance and participation (by 60 percent of all employees) in these group meetings were surprisingly high, despite the fact that they were mostly conducted over a hot, steamy summer. In each group every negative characteristic of the residential institution was brought up and discussed. If any themes were persistently dominant, they were inconsistency and insincerity at and among all levels of employment, the failure to communicate, and the fear of hoping. This fear was poignantly experienced by almost all of the participants, a kind of approach-avoidance conflict that was as understandable and justified as it was strong. In two of the groups the concept of the token economy was spontaneously brought up, in one instance by an employee who had visited a federal institution organized on such a basis, and in the other by someone who was struggling with the problem of how boys could be assured that they would be treated fairly and earn their release without resorting to outrageous behavior (that is, a kind of blackmail). One could say that in each group the discussion was pregnant with the concept of the token economy, given the fact that so much of the discussion was about the existing inconsistent economy.

Each group wrote a report on its discussions and recommendations. A new group was then formed consisting of two representatives from each of the initial groups. The task of the new group was to discuss each of the reports and write a single one containing a plan of action which would be supportable by most of the employees. The final report suggested a structural reorganization to increase communication and the development of a comprehensive token economy in two cottages as a first experimental step to total change. As soon as consultant and staff manpower were available, more cottages would be converted to the newly evolving system and all staff throughout the institution would be kept informed of the progress being made.

The Threat of the Token Economy

With few exceptions, the more education an employee had and the greater his job, the less he participated in any group discussion, and the more he viewed the token economy idea as gimmicky and beside the point. This did not mean that those who volunteered to participate in the development of the token economy did so without qualms and ambivalence. (Because of the experimental nature of the program at first, the staff of the first two cottages were volunteers from the regular staff, and there was nothing else that distinguished them from the remaining staff.) By and large those who volunteered were at the bottom of the pecking order or unhappy in their work and future prospects. Fortunately, there were enough volunteers so that each of the "counseling teams," responsible for all aspects of management of a cottage, contained at least one representative from existing departments. It was understood by the volunteers that they were taking on new responsibilities, they would receive training in the principles and administration of the token economy, and for some time to come they would be putting in more time than ever before at no extra compensation or change in civil service position. And as it turned out, each of these first two counseling teams put in a great deal of time renovating and painting their cottages, attending training sessions, and pretesting various recording schedules.

The token economy was far more than a system of earnings and exchanges, precisely because it was tied to the concept of "local control" (each counseling team responsible for its cottage); to the expectation that everyone on the counseling team was governed by and had a similar role in implementing an agreed upon system; to the participation of the boys in counseling meetings and the formulation of their own individualized program and goals; to the explicitly stated "rule" that leadership and roles would never be decided on the basis of job title or educational level; and to the rule that all decisions would be made by majority vote. It is obvious that the token economy at the CSB rested on a series of conclusions about what makes the parts of a residential institution become armed against each other and all of them armed against the outside world. In this regard it should be noted that parole officers, who really had had little to do with the internal workings of the schools, were made part of the counseling teams. The planning for a boy's release began on his first day in the school and, it was thought, unless the parole officer knew the boy and the program—unless the parole officer felt *he* belonged to the program—the officer could not effectively help the boy bridge the gulf between school and community. Counseling team meetings were public.

Although the new program was antithetical to the traditions of departmentalism, professional imperialism, and credentialism, it was not strongly opposed in the beginning. For one thing, the CSB had been such a scandalous mess that it would have been foolish for an individual or group to try to stop the new program. For another thing, there was a history at the CSB of "experimental" cottages which had failed, so why not wait out this new wrinkle? Why take seriously the plan that in several months two more cottages would be changed, and several months later still another two, until the entire institution was on the same plan?

It took longer than expected but all of the CSB was transformed to the new program, and this was accomplished primarily because those who manned the first two cottages had demonstrated that not only could they survive but that the boys and employees were discernibly more satisfied and productive than they had ever been before. And on the way to this transformation the archaic academic school building was closed and educational programs put into the cottages; an employee senate was organized; a constitution was written spelling out the rights and obligations of employees, counseling teams, and boys; aid and support from the local community were obtained in numerous ways; a program for parents at the school and in their own communities was developed; and a public education program was begun to get across the point that the CSB had no good reason to exist and that there were alternatives which communities could and should explore.

If the realistic threat which the intervention posed did not produce the expected uproar and controversy, it was also true that the low expectations the employees had about getting moral and material support from the Meriden community were proved wrong. It seemed inconceivable to some employees that there were people in the local community sincerely desirous of being helpful to the boys, willing to give time and materials, even willing to have some boys visit their homes or to provide them with work experiences they had earned in the token economy. Within the CSB employees had felt alone and uncertain about who was friend or foe; they saw the CSB as surrounded by an unfriendly, uncomprehending, and unyieldingly hostile community; and they saw the future as a continuation of the past or present, except for the real possibility that the community would succeed in having the CSB moved elsewhere—and according to the overworked rumor mill, the sites to which the school would be moved would mean the loss of many jobs. In light of this it is little wonder that the first two counseling teams could not see themselves as adequate to approaching the community, and it fell primarily to the intervention team to pave the way, that is, to demonstrate that here were individuals and groups wishing to enlarge the sense of community *even with* those living and working at the CSB.

As I indicated at the beginning of this chapter, it is not my purpose (indeed it is not possible) to describe in detail what was done over a period of three and one-half years and with what results: changes in recidivism rate, employee absenteeism, job satisfaction, social climate, and so on. My aim is to spell out a rationale for an intervention that sought to delineate some of the major sources of institutional conflict and deterioration. It was never assumed that this could happen by focusing only on the CSB, as if one could transform the institution without transforming its relationships to local and more distant communities. It was never assumed that it was the CSB that had *the* responsibility for rehabilitating its residents, as if the problems of the boys inhered in them and by working its magic the institution could then return the boys to their communities. It was never assumed that one could "change" boys without a concomitant change in the ideas and actions of staff. It was not an intervention that took a part of the institution, isolated it, changed it in some ways, and expected that it would positively affect the rest of the institution through some process of social osmosis. It was not an intervention that began by looking at organizational charts, changing them, and expecting that the end result would be greater efficiency and happiness. It was an intervention that was based on the knowledge that however "efficient" the division of labor might appear on paper, it divided people, emphasized their differences rather than communalities, their isolation rather than their need for mutuality, and, let us not forget, diluted the efficacy of efforts to help those by whom the existence of the institution was justified.

The Weight of Tradition

The major fear of the intervention team was that in the process of making the CSB a saner community for boys and employees, and more productively and mutually related to the communities from which its residents came, that people would be unresponsive or insensitive to the message that CSB did not have to exist at all. In Connecticut this was less a message than an established fact because Goldenberg (1971) had demonstrated in New Haven in the Residential Youth Center that precisely the kind of population that the CSB was sent could be "rehabilitated" or "saved" in their own community if the sense of community and community responsibility could be engendered in certain of its individuals and groups. Undoubtedly, there have been other such demonstrations. Within the past year Massachusetts has literally terminated the use of its institutional equivalents to the CSB, an action possible only because it became state policy to do so. How the new Massachusetts program fares is less important for our purposes than the fact that it was done, and that it has been demonstrated elsewhere that there are viable alternatives to the self-defeating residential institution. If the Massachusetts program fails, it will not be because its basic rationale is faulty but rather that it will have done it in ways that dilute rather than strengthen an already weak sense of community responsibility. Good ideas and impeccable values are no guarantee that the actions to which they lead will be appropriate (Sarason, 1971, 1972).

From the standpoint of the intervention team, it appears that they may well become a victim of "success," as success would be defined by most people. Within the apparatus of state government there is relief that the CSB is not the frequent occupier it was of the front page of newspapers, and there is pride that the institution has become a positive force in the lives of boys and employees. It has become a kind of conversation piece and showcase. In fact, at the time this is being written the CSB is being phased out and merged with the nearby institution for delinquent girls, in the hope that what was done at the CSB can be continued in a more natural social setting for the boys and girls, and that the combined institution will be smaller than either of the separate institutions was three years ago. However, if there is any doubt that the segregated institution is seen as a necessity by state policy makers, it is dispelled when one learns that this new move will soon have as a "resource" a brand new multimillion dollar maximum security and diagnostic center building. If the new building was only a useless affair, one might sigh and express regret at the use of one's taxes. But it is not only useless, it is another harmful reinforcement of the public's conception that the segregated setting needs to exist as a protection for the public. Needless to say, this takes place over the objections of the intervention team who can take consolation only in the knowledge that the total number of young people incarcerated is much less than previously, and those that are participating in a rehabilitation program are not "killing time." Moreover, the relevant state officials agree with them that the segregated institution is less than useless, but they then go on to maintain that communities are not ready to mount alternative programs for all youth. These developments were seen as possibilities by the intervention team when it began its work.

There is a fundamental question here. How does one justify a terribly complicated, long-term intervention when there is a good chance that one of its consequences will be to strengthen the existence of institutions which one considers on balance to be unnecessary and harmful?[4] There are those who would say the answer is obvious: by strengthening practices and ways of thinking which over time are inimical to one's most important values (one's judgments of how lives should be lived and society should function), even

---

[4] I am aware that there is a very small group of dangerous youngsters who are not only extremely difficult to cope with in an institutional setting but in any other as well. At the CSB there are about fifteen such youngsters, a few of whom have already committed more than one murder. A special setting is obviously required for them but let us realize that these special settings will inevitably become dumping grounds for some who do not require such placement. From past experience it is clear that an institution built for a particular type of problem becomes in short order, because of the prepotent tendency to segregate problems, a place to which individuals are sent for whom that institution is inappropriate or harmful. In recognizing that there is a small core of individuals who may require a special setting, we should not overlook the possibility that the means we adopt to be "helpful" brutalize everyone. The following item about the Patuxent Institution for Defective Delinquents in Jessups, Maryland, appeared in *The Washington Daily News,* April 27, 1972: "Patuxent opened in 1955 to provide intensive psychiatric aid to rehabilitate men legally sane, but habitual lawbreakers. Prisoners may be held there until the staff or a court finds them 'cured' of 'defective delinquent' or criminal tendencies—which may be never—regardless of how short a jail term an inmate may have received originally as a sentence. However, a panel of two Maryland Judges in November (1971) stated that the maximum security prison subjected inmates to such brutal and harsh treatment as a part of its 'therapy' that it amounted to cruel and unusual punishment. . . . Judges Miller and Watts issued an 18-page ruling to stop inmate abuses and set up administrative regulations for the prison. . . . Patuxent has steadfastly resisted the court's order, refusing to make any but minor changes within the prison and fighting court-ordered changes by appealing parts of the two-judge ruling. . . . Records obtained by *The Washington Daily News* revealed that Patuxent, after 16 years and at a cost of more than $40 million dollars has pronounced 'cured' only 97 inmates. . . . of the 2,297 prisoners sent to Patuxent from 1955 to 1971. . . . Inmates testified that 'negative reinforcement therapy' for breaking rules consisted of sometimes being placed strapped to a board by their ankles, wrists, neck and chest and left to lie in their own excrement for days on end in a cell devoid of light or any other human sound but their own."

though in the process one may be helpful to individuals by relieving their misery to some extent, one is allying one's self to a "sick" system, that is, helping to perpetuate what one believes to be wrong. Note that the question and the answer are not concerned with individuals but rather with institutions and related networks of institutions, with the rationale for their existence, with support of a state apparatus, and with tradition which justifies removal of young people from their communities at the same time that it further limits the opportunities whereby community responsibility is strengthened and people can experience a psychological sense of community.

In the case of the intervention at the CSB there were several reasons for proceeding. The first, and perhaps the most important, was that the issue was confronted. It was not simply a matter of proceeding unaware of the possibility that one would fail in the main goal of demonstrating that the institution did not have to exist. There was a chance that the goal could be achieved—not a great one, to be sure, but the chance existed. The intervention team had, so to speak, a "subversive" goal from the beginning: the second justification had less to do with segregated institutions or juvenile delinquency than with the general question of how one goes about changing any complicated social setting devoted to human service, such as a school. In the modal attempt at change the most frequent strategies have been either to effect change all at once or to restrict the change to a part of the social setting, with the vague hope that somehow or other it would appropriately effect the rest of the setting—in most of the latter instances the effort has been in the form of a "demonstration." Neither strategy has been distinguished by success (Sarason, 1971). Given this interest in the theory and tactics of generalizing change, together with administrative support, the CSB was for Reppucci an opportunity not to be passed over. The third justification inhered in the consequences of the goal to destroy the insulation of the CSB from the local community and other communities, because in the process of doing so one would learn a great deal about how to stimulate community responsibility, and locate and develop community resources and talent, as well as about what the problems would be when employees began to adopt roles in the community. In short, much could be learned and reported that could be very valuable to anyone interested in community organization and change.

But there was another very important justification which was in the picture although it was far from decisive, and which complicates the resolution of the fundamental issues we are discussing. The CSB was a totally scandalous mess, the lives of several hundred people (boys and employees) were being very adversely affected, brutality and conflict abounded, and although it was difficult to conceive how matters could get worse, it was not impossible. When asked to help, how does one justify a quick negative answer based on the principle that such institutions are inherently harmful and self-defeating and one will have no part of patching them up? My use of the word "quick" is in no way to suggest that the answer should be in the affirmative but rather to emphasize that one should experience the dilemma. That is to say, one's obligations to other people who need one's help cannot be lightly set aside because of some other value or principle one cherishes. In situations like these one always has more than one value which is appropriate, making it difficult to decide which value should be decisive in the particular circumstance.

The process of deciding about an intervention involves far more than clarity about or choices among values, because neither clarity nor choice leads one directly to the universe of alternatives for action one might consider. The frequency with which interventions are made is truly cause for wonder—it is as if clarity and choice of values as well as their relationship to action were simple affairs. Whatever criticisms may be directed at the intervention at the CSB, it was not guilty of this kind of thoughtlessness, undoubtedly because of earlier experiences which the intervention team had in institutional change.

I must remind the reader that I did not present the CSB intervention because of its scope, or as an exemplar of the virtues of a token economy, or as confirmation of the view that juvenile delinquents can be rehabilitated, or as a demonstration of the view that our "humane institutions" do not have to be, as they usually are, centers of man's inhumanity to man. Certainly these are not unimportant matters, but if they were the only issues the study addressed, I would find its significance for understanding human behavior in our society to be quite limited. *The fact that an intervention is ambitious in scope is not inherently "good." A token economy approach may be an effective technology to increase clarity of communication and to be a spur to consistent behavior, but if like so much of technology it is mindlessly employed in the service of the goals of unthinking tradition and of the unreflectively accepted values of conformity, we end up with another demonstration of how technical sophistication becomes an obstacle to intellectual and moral clarity.[5] The capacity to do something extraordinarily well tends to obscure the question of whether it should be done at all. Similarly, if the study had aimed to demonstrate that our institutions can be more humane than they are (more accurately, less inhumane than they are) it would have been another obstacle to asking if the institution has to exist at all.*

What lends distinction to this study, powers each of its aims and puts them into relationship with each other, is the bedrock belief that the existence and characteristics of the institution are the consequences of the absence or attenuation in our society of the psychological sense of community. Why it is absent or attenuated is not at issue here: the reasons are diverse, complex, and rooted in our culture, traditions, and social history. The fact is that members of our communities experience little or no sense of community and, therefore, when confronted with problems of deviancy, remove it in one way or another from their midst, always justifying the practice so as to make a virtue out of a necessity. When periodically the community is made to recognize that the practice is not working, that in fact it often worsens the very problems it is meant to solve, the inevitable result is a resolve to do better what it is already doing. To set about handling the problem differently requires, at the very least, an explication and examination of the values underlying the existing practice—the "shoulds and oughts," usually unverbalized, which govern social relationships and obligations. It was this type of re-examination which informed all aspects

---

[5] An example of how mindless fascination with technology can lead to disaster is given by Biklen (1973) in his unusually detailed account of an attempt to install a token economy in two "back wards" of a mental hospital.

of the CSB study. It led to the realization that the very existence
of the institution was symptomatic of a more general problem, and
underlined the absolute centrality of the goal of creating an awareness that the fate of the boys, the staff, and the communities were
inextricably related, and that unless these groups could come to
experience a sense of communality and mutuality—a changed sense
of responsibility and obligation—they would remain apart from and
in conflict with each other. Such a re-examination did not permit
justification of the study in terms of what happened to the staff and
community groups. When the achievement of a psychological sense
of community is the overarching criterion by which an intervention
wishes to be judged, it makes no sense to look at what happens to
only one of the many groups related to the problem, if only because
by its very nature this criterion seeks the same things for all. Indeed,
it requires it of all because it speaks to a central need of which
most people are poignantly aware: to be and feel needed in a
mutually supportive network of relationships.

No one would deny that the psychological sense of community is an important human need the absence or weakness of
which can have debilitating consequences. But are there not other
important needs which when unsatisfied also have grave consequences? Of course. Is it not dangerous, if not foolish, to suggest
an overarching criterion which emphasizes a single need? It is
dangerous but not foolish, and at this particular time in our society
one must risk the dangers. The phrase "at this particular time in
our society" implies both the danger in and the justification for
emphasizing one particular need. One risks the danger that a
distorted or narrow time perspective will contribute to a confusion
between symptom and cause and lead us to see discontinuities and
overlook continuities, but there is a difference between an economical and an oversimplified explanation—an economical explanation
suggests that a choice has been made among alternatives. The
justification inheres in the possibility that there are times in a
society when a myriad of social phenomena indicate that a particular human need is so seriously frustrated, with consequences
sufficiently widespread and ominous, as to force us to give it special
emphasis. We are living in such times. The young and the old;
residents of any geographical area; the more and the less educated;

the political left, right, and center; the professional and the non-professional; the rich and the poor—within each of these groupings sizeable numbers of people feel alone, unwanted, and unneeded. They may spend a large part of their time in densely populated settings, interacting with other people in a transient or sustained way, and yet be plagued by feelings of aloneness and the stabbing knowledge that physical proximity and psychological closeness can be amazingly unrelated. They may be involved in all kinds of "giving and taking" activities and relationships, but always aware that the boundaries and the permeability of their private world are unaltered. They may be by personal *knowledge* in roles that are by definition necessary and even crucial, and yet this personal knowledge mystifyingly has little or no positive effect to bolster the fragile *feeling* that one is needed for what one is as a person. And these dysphoric feelings, related to family, work, and local community, are increasingly exacerbated by the perception that there are forces in the nation and the world that make one feel as autonomous and safe as an atom in a nuclear accelerator. The point is not whether these feelings are "objectively" justified, or to what extent they are justified, but that increasingly people feel they are justified, and that they are important to change the situation in which they experience the anxiety of perceived personal isolation.

IX

Budgets
and
Beds

In this chapter we shall look at the residential institution in terms of a deceptively simple question: what are its financial costs and what do they reveal about its purpose? Initially, at least, we shall not be concerned with human values, psychology, feelings, attitudes, or social consequences. Quite the contrary, we start with dollars and cents considerations because economic feasibility is always one of the major justifications for these institutions. They are never built or their maintenance justified unless their humane objectives are economically "practical"—at least that is what people say. And they truly believe what they say. They may feel differently after the institution is built, but even then, as we shall show, their knowledge of the economics of the situation is both superficial and misleading, and in ways which guarantee that existing social policy will never be confronted with the necessity to consider alternatives. If there is any "moral" to be drawn from the data we shall present, it is not that we get what we pay for, but rather that we do not know what we are paying or getting, or, worse yet, the more we pay the less we will get.

This study was undertaken for several reasons.[1] First, experience taught us that the kinds of philosophical and social psychological arguments presented in the previous chapters were mildly convincing to a few people and unmoving to others. A concept like "psychological sense of community" sounds virtuous to all people; the horrors of our institutions offend all, and everyone wants to right wrongs, but it is impossible for most people to conclude from these ideas and conditions that the very existence of these institutions is or may be symptomatic of a more general problem in community living. This is surprising because the very nature of our position requires that people see themselves differently in relation to those we segregate. That is to say, in part the problem exists because people feel unrelated to it, and asking or persuading them to become related to it is only as successful as attempts of religious believers to convert unbelievers and vice versa: it is successful, but only occasionally. The second reason for the study was the belief that if it could be shown from a purely economic standpoint that the cost of these institutions was far greater than the conventional budget indicated, that there were alternative solutions which would be less costly (again in purely economic terms), and that in "human" terms the alternatives were incomparably better, perhaps more people would be persuaded to consider and support alternatives. The third reason was that we wished better to understand how a single institution is embedded in a larger system so that it is

---

[1] The data reported in this chapter are taken from a study entitled *The Institutional Phenomenon: a Socioeconomic Inquiry,* by Robert McLellan (1973). This was a very comprehensive economic analysis which looked into various aspects of a residential institution. I am indebted to McLellan for permission to use some of his data and to reproduce some of his charts.

in the interests of that system to insure the institution's existence regardless of its effectiveness or necessity.

So, if in the first part of this chapter I undertake an economic analysis of an institution embedded in and proudly viewed by the community, it is not because I am intrigued by numbers or view precision of findings as a desirable end in itself. We hear much these days of cost-benefit analyses and why we should feel obligated to determine to what degree the money we spend has the intended social or educational or psychological consequences. Predictably, these analyses are far more sophisticated technically than philosophically; they reflect ingenious and comprehensive statistical-analytic methodologies not matched by or based on a critique and clarification of the values without which the particular service or institution cannot be justified. As a result, these analyses usually blithely assume that the central question is to determine how the service or institution can do what it does better: How it can be more effective with more people (at the same or lesser amounts of money)? Whether the service or institution should even exist, or how adapting a new scale of values presents an expanded universe of alternatives for action, or how the existing scale of values is in conflict with other values—these questions rarely inform the thrust and consequences of cost-benefit analyses.

The Regional Center

A number of years ago the State of Connecticut adopted the policy that it would never again build a large residential institution for mentally retarded individuals; this policy was adopted fifteen years after it had built, in 1941, the second such institution. That institution, the Southbury Training School, was for some time an international showcase because of its novel and striking architectural features, country setting, commitment to being an educational rather than a custodial setting, and its objective of returning its residents as quickly as possible to the community (Sarason, Grossman, and Zitnay, 1972). The educational emphasis was a response to the fact that Southbury was built to take care of the waiting list of the other and much older training school. Needless to say, things did not work out as they were supposed to, and it was not long before Southbury had its own waiting list and had settled into familiar institutional traditions.

However, some far-seeing individuals at Southbury realized the self-defeating nature of the large institution which is placed, as this one was, in the middle of nowhere. It was obvious to them that as pressure would grow to build a third institution there would also develop a strong resistance based on purely economic considerations. (In 1941 it cost nine million dollars to build Southbury, and to build a comparable one within the past decade would cost fifty or more millions.) Instead, it was proposed and accepted that the state be divided into small regions, each one of which would have a regional center strategically located near population centers. Each would have very few beds, and its major thrust would be to avoid institutionalization by developing day programs for non-resident children, supporting and strengthening existing community programs, and providing various home services. A major selling point was that by building a community orientation into the regional center concept, vast economies could be effected. And what skeptic could be unmoved by the threat of having to spend millions upon millions to build another Southbury?

Four assumptions were crucial to the hoped-for success of the regional center concept:

(1) An institution was necessary because there were individuals who would require full-time care. It would be a very small institution in terms of beds, and would remain so; but an institution it had to be.

(2) The need to build an institution and to plan programs for its full-time residents would not interfere with the development of programs and services for scores of nonresidents. Indeed, one of the consequences of the community thrust would be to reduce the pressure for beds.

(3) It would be possible for the regional center to educate and stimulate community forces to assume responsibility for their retarded citizens—that is, to come to see that responsibility had to be shared, that it was not only the state's responsibility. This goal, of course, could be realized only through the regional center's community thrust.

(4) All of the above would demonstrate that the regional center concept was economically superior to past practices.

The particular regional center we studied consists of four buildings. The main building houses the administrative, clinical, and business offices as well as two twenty-bed residential units, five day-school program areas, a work activity center, a dining room and kitchen, an all-purpose room, and a basement storage area and maintenance room. Besides two other buildings which serve as thirty-bed residential units, there is a wood frame house on the grounds which is presently used for additional office and programming space.

Of particular import to this study is the fact that there are four physically separated residential units, each of which is responsible for individuals functioning at a level relatively distinct from the residents of the other units.

We chose this regional center because we could expect maximum cooperation from its administrators and staff. In addition, at the time we began the study, the state of Connecticut was requesting human service agencies to engage in a cost accounting analysis, similar to the one used experimentally in this study, in preparation for the possible adoption of the Planning-Programming-Budgeting System (PPBS) and to qualify for federal reimbursement. The federal government had the legislative mandate to reimburse state and local governments for some of the costs of their programs. To determine the allowable costs, Connecticut was required to use a cost accounting scheme based on guidelines distributed by the Department of Health, Education, and Welfare. Essentially, the scheme was designed to insure that federally assisted programs bear their fair share of the costs recognized by the principles outlined in the guidelines. Although the scheme to be implemented was not as rigorous as was necessary to reveal some of the more interesting costs not presently included in the agency budget, the time was clearly ripe for maximal cooperation in developing and applying a more detailed analysis.

The Traditional Budget

In determining annual agency costs, two factors are considered: the General Operating Fund and the Bond Fund. The General Operating Fund encompasses the bulk of the everyday expenditures necessary for maintaining the agency and its programs.

It covers the costs of all personal services (regular salaries, over-time, and other salary expenses, such as shift differential, longevity, and standby pay) and other expenses, such as transportation, food, and laundry. The other major consideration of agency costs, the Bond Fund, accounts for all expenses of capital improvements—for example, a new hot water system or expansion of a parking lot. This fund is not a part of the annual operating budget even though it is recognized as an annual cost consideration.

There are two other factors recognized in the business management of the agency but not reported in the annual budget. They are not considered as contributing to the total annual agency costs and are never used in computing per capita costs. One such factor, the Welfare Fund, accounts for all private donations to the agency. The other funding factor, the Activity Fund, used for the recreational activities of staff and clients (for example, Christmas decorations or parties) is derived from the commissions and proceeds from vending machines, art sales, and workshop activities. Neither of these factors represent expenditures near the magnitude of the General and Bond Funds.

Presently, operating costs are allocated from the General Fund to functional categories representative of the six departments of the agency: administration, food services, general services, patient care, education and training, and social services.

It is the responsibility of the state comptroller to report to the Commissioner of Finance and control the annual per capita costs of residents of humane institutions. These costs are computed by dividing the total operating costs of the agency by the average resident population. In the case of the New Haven Regional Center then, if the total costs of the agency in a given year were one million dollars and the average resident population were one hundred, then the annual per capita cost would be ten thousand dollars. Several facts are worthy of emphasis: (1) Total costs include the operating costs for all provided services (less care of those outside) of which residential service is but one. (2) The computation of total costs is derived from expenditures made only from the General Fund. (3) The average resident population for the year, calculated on the basis of daily average, does not include clients of any of the nonresident services.

That there is room for improvement of the existing system of analysis becomes clear when the effects of some of its specific characteristics are studied. The major inadequacies and their effects on the determination of agency and per capita costs are presented in Table 2.

It is apparent that the current system of accounting, typical of that used for all institutions of all kinds in Connecticut and elsewhere, obscures factors relevant not only to the short-term management of existing programs, but also to the formulation of future social policy. For example, there is no way of determining what a particular program costs or finding the cost differences among different residential units. Similarly, and this will become even more obvious in the next section, the traditional budget unjustifiably ignores cost factors which if included could be critical to evaluating present policy and alternatives to it.

An Alternative Accounting System

Table 3 lists the cost factors and the method of determination in the alternative accounting system. The cost accounting procedure used to analyze real costs is a method developed by Sorensen and Phipps (1971) under NIMH sponsorship in 1971. The system, derived from a recently created American Hospital Association model, was devised for community mental health centers but is readily adaptable to regional centers for the retarded.

Initially, the procedure requires the definition of all agency functions in terms of cost centers. There are two types of cost centers: support, and final producing. A support center—for example, business administration—exists solely to service final producing centers. A final producing center—for example, a residential unit—provides services directly to clients.

To further clarify the distinction between support and final centers, it is helpful to observe that no final center provides services to another center; it receives services from other support centers but offers services only to its own clients. On the other hand, a support center provides services for other centers and also receives the services of other support centers. For example, social services is defined as a support center even though it offers direct services

Table 2.

EFFECTS OF SYSTEM CHARACTERISTICS ON DETERMINATION
OF AGENCY AND PER CAPITA COSTS

Characteristic	*Qualitative Effect*
(1)	(1)
Per capita computation is: total agency costs/average residential population.	Since the total agency costs include the costs of all nonresidential programs, the per capita cost is overestimated.
(2)	(2)
Severe restriction on number of costs factors considered in determining total agency costs. *Example:* initial capital costs not considered.	Underestimation of total agency costs. Underestimation of costs of departments (e.g., care of patients). Underestimation of costs of departmental programs (e.g., residential services). Underestimation of per capita costs (since the per capita cost computation is total agency costs/average residential population).
(3)	(3)
Use of present gross departmental analysis does not distinguish between support and direct service functions. A support department (e.g., administration) exists solely to serve direct service departments. A direct service department (e.g., residential services) provides direct services to clients.	Clouds economic as well as management interdependencies of departments.
(4)	(4)
Does not include costs of support services in costs of direct services.	Characteristics (3) and (4) disallow possibilities of accurate determination of costs of direct services. Determination of direct service costs, including per capita cost, underestimated.

Table 2. cont.

Characteristic	*Qualitative Effect*
(5)	(5)
Does not distinguish between residential units in allocation of costs or in per capita computation. Costs are allocated in a lump sum to the residential program in the department of patient care. This sum is not reallocated among the residential units.	A simple average per capita cost is obtained. Neglects possible differences in costs of operating units.
(6)	(6)
Utilizes average resident population in per capita computation without reference to the total number of residents served.	The economic effects of servicing a large number of clients through the mechanism of short-term admissions are neglected, A unit working at its full capacity of 20 beds may in fact serve 21 clients. A bed may be used by one client for 4 days and by another for 3 days of a week.
(7)	(7)
Future budget appropriations from state government prepared, in part, on basis of average resident population.	Agency reinforced for operating at maximum bed capacity. Because there is no reference to the total number of clients served, there is no reward for serving 21 rather than 20 clients in a unit of 20 beds.
(8)	(8)
Annual agency budget is organized so as to stress inputs (e.g., purchasing, hiring) of departments without reference to the programs associated with them. *Example:* General Services costs reflects purchasing of equipment for residential services but these costs are not directly linked to these services.	Difficult to compare costs of existing programs with alternative means of attaining same end.

Table 3.

Cost Considerations of the New Approach

Cost Factors	Method of Determination

I. *General Fund*
(State considerations in annual agency operating budget)

Regular Salaries

Overtime

Other Salary Costs

Other Expenses

All of these factors are presently considered in the annual state budget. They were determined with the traditional methods.

II. *Additional Cost Considerations*

Other State Costs. Telephone bills and agency insurance premiums paid by the comptroller's office.

(1) Telephone bills first sent to NHRC before forwarding to comptroller. Costs were recorded (2) State Board of Insurance sends copy of premium payments to NHRC.

Fringe Benefits. State employee's share of Social Security, medical insurance, life insurance, and retirement contributions paid by the state.

Payroll reviewed and appropriate percentages, derived from guidelines set up by the state comptroller, were applied to each salary to compute benefits.

Federal Funds. Federal grants which subsidize the operation of such federal programs as behavior modification and personnel employment under the Emergency Employment Act (including fringe benefits for personnel so employed).

Federal funds are entered in ledger like state cost factors. The costs can thus be determined using the same techniques as used for the state cost factors.

Private Funds. Private donations (Welfare Fund) plus commissions and proceeds from vending machines, art gallery sales, workshop activities (Activity Fund).

A separate ledger exists for both the Welfare and Activity Funds. Costs can be determined from these ledgers in the same way as the ledger which is used to account for the General Fund.

Table 3. cont.

Cost Factors	Method of Determination
Indirect Costs. Costs to other state agencies of providing services to NHRC, e.g., cost of: Department of Health to administer NHRC, comptroller's office to administer accounts of NHRC expenditures, etc.	Indirect cost rate computed by the state, in accordance with federal guidelines, applied to all general and federal funds. The rate applied was 9.74 percent of all original allocations. Briefly, this rate was computed using the Short Method outlined by the DHEW guidelines. The rate is expressed as a percentage resulting from the ratio of the allowable (under the guidelines) indirect costs of State support departments (A) to the allowable expenditures of the direct service agencies for all other purposes (B). The computation then is $A \div B = 9.74$ percent.
Plant Depreciation. Depreciation of original and additional capital costs of plant.	Assuming complete depreciation in 40 years, total capital depreciation for the quarter was computed.
Equipment Depreciation. Reflects loss in value of all NHRC equipment for the quarter.	All equipment depreciated, assuming complete depreciation in 10 years.
Tax Assessment. Reflects tax assessment of plant and property (presently New Haven is reimbursed by the state only for the land taxes).	Plant and property value (real value) multiplied by the assessment rate to arrive at the assessed value. The assessed value was multiplied by the mill rate to determine tax assessment.

to clients, because it offers services to other cost centers, such as the day school or the several residential units.

In Sorensen and Phipp's method, matrix algebra is used to solve simultaneous equations to allocate costs between support and final centers. With this method, the cost of a support center's services can be reallocated according to the extent to which another center uses the particular support services. Note that initially some costs of support services may be reallocated to other support services. This intermediary reallocation is logical because support centers provide each other with services; Food Services, for example, feeds administrators. Ultimately, all of the costs of each support center are reallocated, by what is called the step-down method, to the appropriate final center. In order to employ this method, it was necessary to determine the percentage of support services devoted to each final center. The percentages were then used in matrix form to perform the manipulations essential to the calculation of the reallocations.

To illustrate the reallocation method a simple example borrowed from *Cost Finding and Rate-Setting for Hospitals* (American Hospital Association, 1968) is presented. Let us assume that there are four support cost centers, labeled 1, 2, 3, and 4, and four final cost centers, labeled A, B, C, and D. Let us also assume that the support centers render services as illustrated in Tables 4 and 5. In other words, center 1 renders 10 percent of its total service to center 2, 15 percent to center 3, and so on. The original allocations of the support centers will be reallocated according to the percent of services rendered.

At this point it is important to emphasize that our decision about how to calculate "indirect costs" results in a considerable

Table 4.

SAMPLE PERCENTAGE ANALYSIS OF SERVICES

Cost Center	Support Center				Original Allocation
	Center 1	Center 2	Center 3	Center 4	
Center 1	–	20	–	10	$160,000
Center 2	10	–	10	–	120,000
Center 3	15	20	–	20	70,000
Center 4	25	–	20	–	100,000
Center A	10	15	40	70	240,000
Center B	20	15	20	–	150,000
Center C	10	15	–	–	60,000
Center D	10	15	10	–	50,000
Totals	100%	100%	100%	100%	$950,000

Table 5.
Cost Finding by the Step-Down Method

Cost Center	Original Allocation	Support Centers				Total
		Center 1	Center 2	Center 3	Center 4	
Center 1	$160,000	**160,000**				
Center 2	120,000	16,000	**136,000**			
Center 3	70,000	24,000	34,000	**128,000**		
Center 4	100,000	40,000		28,444	**168,444**	
Center A	240,000	16,000	25,500	56,890	168,444	506,834
Center B	150,000	32,000	25,500	28,444		235,944
Center C	60,000	16,000	25,500			101,500
Center D	50,000	16,000	25,500	14,222		105,722
Totals	$950,000					$950,000

underestimation of actual costs. Specifically, the indirect cost rate was calculated by the state for the purposes of federal reimbursement. As a result, the rate (9.74 percent) is an indicator only of costs allowable under guidelines published by the Department of Health, Education, and Welfare. Therefore, a number of costs (for example, state plant, equipment, and offices) are excluded from consideration. In addition, the calculation of the rate assumed that all activities of state agencies benefit to approximately the same degree from the state functions which generate the indirect costs. This is obviously not the case. In fact, if anything has changed in state government over recent decades, it is the amount of time devoted to the problems of its residential institutions.

For example, during the quarter for which we obtained the data for our study the administrative and legislative parts of the state government were spending a lot of time dealing with "exposés" of the deplorable conditions in some of the institutions for the retarded. It would be a huge undertaking, but we have no doubt that if one cost-accounted how much of administrative and legislative activities were devoted to the problems of state institutions, the indirect cost factor would be markedly above that allowable by the federal government and used in this study. Similarly, we have not put a cost on volunteer time, which is enormous. Without volunteer contributions of time, as well as money, this regional center could not exist as it is today; it is likely that it could not exist at all. We feel justified in asserting that the actual costs we obtained are an underestimate of the true picture. Indeed, they may be a sizeable underestimate.

Determination of Percentages

The key to the reallocation procedure is a determination of the percentage of service provided by a given support center. Two methods of determination, by questionnaire and by using available statistics, were employed. A questionnaire was designed which requested support service administrators to estimate the number of hours in an average week they devoted to each cost center. The questionnaire was administered in conjunction with a short interview to clarify any possible misunderstandings. Using the results of these questionnaires, estimates were computed of the percentage of support personnel service time devoted to each final center. Questionnaires were administered only to the heads of support service departments. It was assumed that secretaries, clerks, and others devoted service time in the same proportions as their superiors.

To evaluate the breakdown of the service time of the maintenance personnel, a questionnaire of simpler design was employed. Every day for 52 days, from January 8 to February 29, forms were collected which indicated in which cost centers each maintenance man was spending his time. The compilation of these figures allowed percentage breakdowns of maintenance service.

Statistical records made possible the analysis of other support services. For example, the reallocation of food costs was based on the number of meals served to each cost center. This number was derived from the number of clients and/or staff members of each cost center. If meals were served only to centers X and Y and X consisted of one person and Y consisted of three people, then 25 percent of the expense of food would be reallocated to X and 75 percent to Y.

The use of questionnaire data raises, of course, the question of their validity. In point of fact, allocations determined from questionnaire data represented a small part of total allocations. For example, data from seven of the twelve *support* centers were not based on questionnaire data, and they accounted for more than fifty percent of the total costs of support centers. Only the data from two *cost* centers (Administration and Speech and Hearing) came solely from questionnaire responses. Ideally, one would want to check on the questionnaire data by direct observation, but we did not have the resources to do this. This would have required a tremendous amount of time, personnel, and funds, which would have been hard to justify in light of the fact that questionnaire data were not predominant in the total analysis. We have no basis for assuming that the questionnaire data we obtained reflected any systematic bias on the part of the respondents.

Major Findings

The discrepancy between residential costs computed by the old and the new accounting methods is 39 percent, showing that the traditional budget obviously underestimates the real costs of the regional center. The hope that a network of regional centers would cost significantly less than building and maintaining the large congregate institutions of the past is not likely to be realized. But, it could be argued, even if it turns out to be as expensive, is not the regional center a more humane setting? Is it not true that it is providing day-care services for many nonresidents who otherwise might require a residential program? And from the standpoint of employees, is it not less dehumanizing or brutalizing to work in a regional center rather than in a large institution which, as countless exposés have described, adversely affects everyone's humanity? *These and other questions which can be asked in defense of the regional center assume that one needs an institution, that there are no alternative ways of rendering care and service unless one has, at the least, a small institution.* Later we shall examine this assumption, bearing in mind for the present that in terms of sheer economics the regional center is no rousing improvement over past practices. But now let us turn to another finding that will permit a partial answer to the questions raised above.

In the old accounting system it is not possible to differentiate accurately between the costs of residential and nonresidential programs and services. The nonresidential programs, of course, represent the "community thrust" which was to have two consequences: to increase the chances for residents to be returned to the community, and to prevent the institutionalization of nonresidents. In light of these goals it is important, indeed crucial, to know how much money is being allocated to the implementation of nonresidential programs and facilities. One would be justified in expecting that community programs, services, and facilities would be supported on a level equal to that of the residential components, if not at a higher level.

But the lesson from the past is unambiguous: to the extent that resources are put primarily into "beds," more beds become needed; the harder it is to place individuals back into the community; the institution grows larger; employee morale plummets, employee turnover skyrockets, and on and on until the scandalous conditions are exposed, money is spent to make things look better or to hire more people to give better custodial care, the public breathes a sigh of relief, and the more things change the more they remain the same. Those who developed the regional center concept and program were determined to break into this vicious circle; they had been riding around the circle for a long time. They understood full well that unless the community took more responsibility for its mentally retarded individuals, devised different ways whereby they could be maintained in and by the community, and stopped looking to the state institution as the major vehicle for dealing with the problem, the regional center program would fall far short of its mark.

The fact is that we found that on a per capita basis the amount of money spent to maintain the residential program was almost four times the amount devoted to day care and community services for nonresidents. In other words, there was precious little going to the "community thrust." This means that the number of nonresidents that can be accepted into programs at the center is limited, and that the kinds of work and social living programs in the community (*not* at the regional center) which could maximize the chances that the nonresident could live productively and happily in the community are very limited, indeed virtually nonexistent. Furthermore, the inability to develop work and social living programs in the natural community for the nonresidents has adverse affects on the fate of the more than half of the residents, who are capable of living and working in the community. The bulk of these residents are at the regional center not because they require an institution but because appropriate working and living programs in the community have not yet been developed for them, and their stay in residence will be prolonged as long as these community programs are not available. It is more likely that when they are returned to the community it will not necessarily be in a setting appropriate to their needs (a group home, for example), but in one that happens to be available (such as a foster home), however questionable such placements may be in the individual case. These consequences for residents and nonresidents are predictable on the basis of the discrepancy between levels of financial support for residential and community programs. One does not have to know the particular institution to make these predictions; one only has to know the size of the discrepancy in support, and the larger the discrepancy the sadder the situation.

What about the employees of this regional center? How well do they understand what has happened and is happening? The fact is that many of them, particularly those working with the non-residents, are demoralized, relatively unmotivated, and looking for employment elsewhere. And similar feelings are expressed by employees dealing with those residents who are capable of living and working in the community. In short, the employees see little or no payoff for their efforts either to prevent institutionalization or to shorten the stay of those who live there. How can even a moderate level of job satisfaction be maintained when the goals of one's efforts are rarely achieved and there is no reason to hope that the future will be any different? How can we look forward to to-morrow with any degree of eagerness, let alone with creativity, when it will be as frustrating and unchanging as today? Is it any wonder that they feel that no one "out there" really cares? Can one blame them for being cynical about the discrepancy between stated aims and actual practice? Is an ever-increasing employee turnover rate and absenteeism really difficult to understand? This is not a pretty picture, and no one wanted it to look this way. Then how did it happen? Why does it happen with such lawful regularity? The following "story" about this regional center suggests an answer.

While the regional center was being built there was no staff to speak of—only the newly appointed superintendent and his secretary. However, the superintendent had informally picked some of his key staff members, and for the year before the regional center opened they met fairly regularly for planning purposes. These meetings were held at the Yale Psycho-Educational Clinic, with which the regional center was to have a close working tie. I was director of the clinic and had long been working in the field of mental retardation. The conceptual basis for the tie between the clinic and the regional center was that both were committed to the idea that mental retardation was a community responsibility. To the extent that the regional center was seen as the major source of programs, services, and funding, and to the extent that community talent and resources (latent and actual) were not developed and organized to man and maintain a wide variety of programs and services, the regional center would be regarded as a failure. The population to be served was a very heterogeneous one in terms of level and needs, and this required a greater variety of services and settings than one agency could possibly provide.

The suggestion was made that we approach the problem by dealing first with the emergency waiting list: those individuals for whom institutionalization was considered essential, not tomorrow or today but yesterday. There was no institution yet and there would not be one for at least a year. What help could we be to the individuals (and their families) on this emergency waiting list? What resources in the community could we bring to bear to be helpful? From the time we began to work with the individuals on the waiting list only the superintendent was paid by the state; everyone else volunteered time. We secured the help of clergymen, students, community agency personnel, the visiting nurse association, school personnel, and an assortment of interested citizens, physicians, and so forth. The persons we sought out for help depended on the nature of the problem, where the individual lived, and the agencies that had had contact with the case. We viewed ourselves as "talent scouts" and as prodders of social agencies to assume meaningful responsibility for individuals who because of the label "mentally retarded" were not considered appropriate for these agencies, even though their services were very much needed by the retarded individual and his family. It was no secret that many social agencies had little or nothing to do with mental retardation either because they felt they had no expertise in this field or because they did not regard it as interesting or fruitful—this latter opinion being the cause for their lack of knowledge. This was as true for public agencies (local and state) as for private agencies.

We quickly found that individuals on the emergency waiting list were there not because they required institutional care but because a variety of community services and programs (such as group homes, homemaker services, parent education and counseling, baby-sitting help, marital counseling) were not available or, if available, were unknown to the family. Some of these families were requesting institutionalization because they had been told that it was the best course of action, and not because they personally desired it. There was not a single case, regardless of severity, for which an alternative to institutionalization was not possible if community resources, actual and potential, could be utilized. *This*

*does not mean that these alternatives would or could solve all prob-
lems in the individual case.* But neither could institutionalization,
as we so well know. What struck us forcefully was that these
alternatives would *create* fewer major social problems than institutionalization would (or has). Indeed, in the process of developing
some of these alternatives we found many people in the community grateful for the opportunity to be helpful, to be part of
something that brought new knowledge and challenge into their
lives.[2] Whatever we were able to do in conjunction with these people was in large measure due to a feeling of community we com-
municated to and instilled in them. We needed them, even though
they had no special knowledge or skills. We were prepared to help
them help us. In some quarters this was not viewed with approba-
tion because we were using "untrained" people, which could be
harmful—a suffocating professional view that justifies doing
nothing.

It needs to be emphasized that in approaching the families
on the emergency waiting list we did not have beds to offer, and
since it would have been ridiculous to predict when the new regional center building would be ready for occupancy, we could not
say when their retarded child could be admitted. What we could
offer them was our willingness to be helpful now. In short, whatever we could do was not presented as a substitute for what they
had been told was the best course of action—institutionalization.
As a consequence, the families cooperated with us.

These were exciting months for everyone. *They were also
disturbing because we began to see that we did not need the regional center.* If the millions that were going into buildings were
made available to us we could develop scores of programs and
settings in *and* by the community, and in ways that would bring
new meaning into the lives of many people. Our disturbance
deepened the closer we came to the opening date because we found

[2] The productive and gratifying ways in which "ordinary" citizens
can be used to serve and protect dependent individuals have best been conceptualized and described by Wolfensberger (Wolfensberger, 1969; Wolfensberger, 1973; Wolfensberger and Zauha, 1973). His work deserves the most
careful attention not only because of his illuminating historical-conceptual
analyses but also because he successfully launched a multifaceted "citizens
advocacy" program for the state of Nebraska.

ourselves forced to think about institutional programs, modes of
staffing, recruitment, and the host of other issues and problems that
are consequences of opening a new and complicated institution. At
the last meeting held at Yale Psycho-Educational Clinic, someone
said: "The regional center has seen its best days." It was a comment that mirrored accurately the vague dysphoric feeling of
everyone at the meeting.

No one doubted that from that point on the community
thrust would take second place to what went on within the walls
of the regional center. We were going to struggle against this, but
as time went on it was apparent that we would not be successful.
The enabling legislation, the nature of budget allocations, the pre-
occupation with filling beds and determining their per capita costs,
state-dictated staffing patterns, job descriptions—an examination
of these and other factors made it all too clear that the major
justification for the regional center was to provide beds. Put in
another way, the regional center was embedded in a state legisla-
tive-judicial-administrative apparatus and tradition that was geared
to build and maintain institutions. (The same, of course, is true
for the mental hospitals and youth correctional settings.) If through
some miracle the state was prevented from building more institutions, and was required to phase out existing ones, only then could
one grasp how much of state government existed because of institutions. Is it any wonder that the suggestion that institutions are not
necessary, that they defeat the purposes for which they were built,
that they dilute the sense of community responsibility, and that
they produce all the evil consequences of segregation are not
looked upon kindly by the state apparatus?

This account of the prehistory of the regional center should
restrain us from placing all the blame on the state government, or
viewing it as a grand conspiracy against new ideas, because state
policy is primarily a reflection of four interrelated factors: long-
standing professional opinions about the necessity of institutions,
the weakening of the sense of community responsibility, the strength
of our society's tendency to segregate atypical people, and the
presumed economic advantages of institutions over alternatives.
*It was not until we began to deal with the emergency waiting list
that we began to see how ingrained in us was the belief that an*

institution was necessary. If it took us years and a special set of circumstances before we could see this point, we ought to be sympathetic to those who have had no basis for questioning the necessity of institutions.

And let us not forget that one of the most important determinants of public policy has been the opinions of the professional community. To criticize state policy is to criticize professional knowledge and values. No one has done this with more compelling data and observations than Blatt (1970a, 1970b, 1973). In instance after instance, he demonstrates how the evils of the institutions are in part a consequence of professional knowledge, practices, and values. Wittingly and unwittingly, directly and indirectly, they help perpetuate policies which compel a Burton Blatt (or an Erving Goffman, or a David Rosenhan, or a Thomas Szasz, or a Dorothea Dix) to expose the bankruptcy of these policies. These policies have not worked and are not working—these are sad facts which are hard to dispute.

But can they work? This question has always been answered in the affirmative, mostly on the basis of hope. Make the institutions smaller, build them in more accessible places, relate them more to the community, take advantage of the most advanced theories and practices of organization and management, develop pre-service and in-service training programs, and, of course, allocate sufficient sums to make all of this possible. If this package can be put together, we have been told, our institutions will cease to be self-defeating and dehumanizing. They can work, indeed they have to work, we say, as if strength of resolve is the chief ingredient.

It is significant, therefore, that in his most recent publication, Blatt (1973), who heretofore had written extensively and concretely about how institutions can be made more humane, comes to the conclusion that institutions are not necessary, that their very existence betrays the consequences of the dilution of the psychological sense of community and the sense of community responsibility. Blatt maintains, and rightly so, that there is not a single institutionalized, retarded individual who cannot be accommodated in a more humane fashion within the community. We do not need, he says, the formal, complex, highly professionalized institution.

These are not words from an armchair philosopher commenting on human injustice, ignorant of the most intimate workings of institutions. Blatt knows and has described institutions in intimate detail, always assuming that they could become what they were intended to be: settings in which the best in man could flower in the effort to help those who could not or did not know how to help themselves. For a time he had responsibility for administering and changing an entire state program, a task he was asked to undertake after public disclosures of the scandalously inhumane conditions in the state's institutions. When someone like Blatt completely rejects a conclusion he had previously advocated, his views must be given serious attention, all the more so because he encourages others to give voice to their nagging doubts about the necessity of these institutions.

Vail (1966, 1973) is another who tried valiantly to humanize institutions, only to conclude that the task is impossible and that the root problem has been the failure to question the assumption that these institutions are necessary. As a psychiatrist, for a number of years he headed a state mental health program. Courageously he exposed the horrors of institutional existence, indicting professionals and their fields, community apathy, and unthinking tradition. In his last (and posthumous) book he describes in great detail the truly heroic efforts he initiated to make the residential institutions more hospitable to the needs of residents and caretakers, and more meaningfully related to and embedded in community life. As one reads it, one gets the picture of a selfless, driven, sensitive, young man painfully aware of a constant gulf between what needed to be done, on the one hand, and what was being done, on the other. As I read his accounts I was struck by two things: his desire to make institutions "humane," and his inability or unwillingness to confront the possibility that his efforts were doomed, even though that possibility shows between the lines of every page he wrote. Why, I kept asking myself, doesn't Vail "see" the obvious? Why can't he at least play with the idea that he is trying to cure the incurable? Is it that his position in the staff apparatus effectively prevents him from questioning the very basis of the activities of his far-flung department? And so when I finished reading this posthumous work it was with respect for what Dr. Vail had attempted and accomplished, and with disappointment that he had remained a prisoner of tradition. But then I read his Preface, which of course was written last, and there he says in the clearest terms that he has finally concluded that the residential institution is a community disaster incapable of being maintained in a humane way. They are unnecessary, Vail says, and there are viable community alternatives.

It is not, I think, fortuitous that social activists like Blatt, Vail, and Reppucci have concluded that the traditional residential institution has historically had the effect of helping to destroy the psychological sense of community. In recent years an increasing number of university people have tried their hands at humanizing the segregated residential institution, and it should have been expected that some of them would at least give voice to a question heretofore ignored (or considered nonsensical): are these institutions really necessary?

McLellan's (1973) study strongly suggests that any state program which has embedded in it the concept of the institution, a program that "belongs" to the state, is an economic disaster. Judged by the degree to which is achieves its purposes, it is as economically wasteful as one could imagine. Judged by the degree to which it poisons the lives of those in relation to it, the segregated institution is a social cancer that in subtle but potent ways undermines the health of our communities. Countless remedies have been proposed and tried, but like so many forms of bodily cancer which temporarily disappear or are arrested, this underlying disease asserts itself in virulent form. Unfortunately, these institutions do not die or fade away. The institution and the community are linked together in a symbiotic relationship, but one which tends to destroy the purposes of both.

If the institution cannot be justified on an economic basis, if indeed it is true that the more we spend the less we will get, then what are the alternatives? *The question is in a form that obscures the fact that the alternatives one can come up with depend on the values one holds as to how people should be in relationship to each other.* Put in another way, what is the nature of our society? What problems in community living does it engender? What are the unmet needs of its citizens? And how can we think about helping retarded individuals (or those in mental hospitals) so that these needs and problems, *our* needs and problems, may in some measure be met and solved? Can we *give* at the same time we *get?* Can we on the community level continue to think about mental retardation (or so-called mental illness) apart from all other community problems, with the same negative consequences that individuals experience in feeling apart from each other? Can we think about the problem as an instance of segregation, and, knowing as we do what segregation does to individual and community living and structure, can we begin to undo these consequences?

The question about alternatives is not initially about procedural or technical or professional matters, but rather about the values by which we will be guided as members of a community— not as members physically, but rather belonging psychologically to a community. It is inordinately difficult to think in these new ways because we are such unwitting prisoners of contrary values and categories of thought ingrained in us by our culture. It takes unusual and compelling experiences to challenge our accustomed ways of thinking, and even then we struggle against giving up the old ways. To see the emperor as naked is hard; to say that he is naked is even harder. Fortunately, when we are compelled to see and deal with "reality" in new ways, the question of alternatives ceases to be as thorny as our old ways of thinking suggested. Indeed, we then understand that one of the consequences of acquiring a culture is that it drastically constricts the alternatives in thinking and action which we are able to conceive. The difficulties in freeing oneself from accustomed but unexamined ways of thinking, and the liberating consequences of doing so, are illustrated in the following account:

On four occasions I had the opportunity to ask the following question of a group of individuals who either had or would have responsibility for creating an institution for mentally retarded children: "What if you were given the responsibility to develop residential facilities with the restrictions that they could not be on 'institutional land,' no one of them could house more than 12 individuals, and no new buildings could be erected?" The following, in chronological order, were the major reactions of the different groups.

(1) Initially the groups responded with consternation, puzzlement, and curiosity. For some members of each of the groups, the question seemed to produce a blank mind, but for others it seemed as if the question quickly brought to the surface all their dissatisfactions with the usual mode of residential care and stimulated consideration of alternatives.

(2) In the early stages of discussion, the chief stumbling block was the restriction that "no new buildings could be erected." I should say that throughout the discussions I adopted a relatively nondirective approach and tried only to answer directly questions which would clarify the meaning of the initial question. For example, when asked if one could remodel existing structures, I indicated that this was, of course, permissible. When I was asked if there was any restriction as to where these houses or small buildings could be bought and rented, I said there were no such restrictions. The point deserving emphasis is that many individuals struggled for some time until they realized that there was no one way to act and think but rather that there was a potentially large universe of alternatives for action from which they could choose. In addition, as some individuals came to see, there was no necessity to choose only one alternative, i.e., one could and should proceed in different ways at the same time.

(3) Midway in the meeting the behavior of the members began to change in rather dramatic ways. Whereas before most were hesitant, deliberate, and cautious in their remarks, they now seemed to respond as if they were engaged in an exciting intellectual game in which one possibility led to thinking about other possibilities, and what at first seemed to be unrelated were then seen as crucially related. Faced with the task of creating settings they truly began to think and talk creatively.

(4) In two of the groups—and for reasons I cannot wholly account for—a plan for residential care evolved which brought together the renovation of substandard housing, training programs for nonprofessional personnel, volunteer services, and neighborhood involvement and responsibility. In short, these two groups were no longer dealing with mental retardation in its narrow aspects but in the context of some of the most crucial aspects of what has been termed the urban crisis.

One of the more experienced superintendents pointed out to his group that in the plan they had discussed "we are meeting more social problems, and providing more meaningful service to children and their families, at far less money than we are now spending." It was indeed remarkable how intellectually fertile the discussions in these two groups were. For example, one of the group members made the point that if these small housing units were strategically placed around our high schools they could be used by the schools in at least three ways: for educating youngsters about mental retardation, for purposes of training child-care workers, and for enlisting volunteers for recreational and other purposes. Another group member, in the context of a discussion about food preparation in these small units, maintained that if neighborhood participation and responsibility were taken seriously, food preparation and feeding could be handled on a volunteer basis, besides which the food would probably taste better. In my opinion, the creative thinking and planning that went on in these two groups were, in part, a consequence of a process which permitted the members to think not only in terms of the retarded child but in the context of pressing urban problems which ordinarily are not viewed in relation to the field of mental retardation [Sarason, Grossman, and Zitnay, 1972].

To become aware of alternatives requires that we transcend the limitations our culture has imposed on our thinking, and in the process we inevitably perceive a clash of values. When we become aware of a cultural change, and ordinarily it is long after the change process was started, it is obvious that the dynamic that is powering the process was a change in some basic values. To a far greater extent than ever before, the values justifying the existence of the residential institution are being questioned. What has been missing in the past is clarity about a new value (or values) which would illuminate the inadequacy of the old values at the same time that it gives direction to truly radically new actions. There is some evidence, by no means impressive or general, that the new emerging value concerns the psychological sense of community. This is not surprising, because the hungering for that sense has become so general and insistent in our society. I do not believe in the inevitability of progress, when progress is defined not in terms of knowledge, technology, and a production ethic but in terms of man's relationship to man. This belief, however, is no excuse for irresponsible hopelessness, or inaction, or retreat into something one knows to be ultimately self-defeating: personal isolation. If one does not try to act in accord with one's basic values, one becomes a willing victim to self-hatred. A poet (I think it was James Rorty, ages ago in *Partisan Review*) wrote: "Life takes its final meaning in chosen death." As usual, it is the poet who pithily reminds us of the basic question: by what values do we wish to live and die? Apart from or with others? A community psychology that does not choose to begin with these questions will have a very feeble, unproductive, and short life.

X

Social Action as a Vehicle for Learning

In this chapter I return to the issues surrounding action for the purpose of effecting community change. I touched upon these issues in earlier parts of this book devoted to the social-historical context of the sixties out of which community psychology emerged; they were briefly discussed or alluded to in subsequent chapters, particularly in relation to the work of Blatt, Reppucci, and Vail. This "neglect" was quite intentional because I considered the goals for community change—the values which justify action and provide direction for education—to be the prior question about which clarity was essential. As Cowen (1973) has so clearly demonstrated in his review of the community psychology literature, one can easily be overwhelmed by the heterogeneity of efforts to effect

244

community change, and it is next to impossible to discern any communality in underlying conceptions about what a community is or should be. Heterogeneity in action is in itself not a bad thing if it reflects different ways of illuminating or testing some agreed upon, underlying conceptions, values, and generalizations. But when this heterogeneity, overall, is conceptually characterless, and someone like Cowen is ready to throw in the towel in his fight for meaning and direction, it underlines the priority which needs to be given to some overarching goal or goals.

In discussing the role and problems of action I shall limit myself to the confines of the university setting. I do not justify this restriction on the basis that the university contains most of the people who are engaged in efforts to promote community change, because that is patently not the case. Nor do I justify it by the claim that the most important efforts, practical or theoretical, have come from university people. The most innovative and comprehensive efforts at community change have been described and critically analyzed by Marris and Rein (1969) in *Dilemmas of Social Reform*. These efforts, whose prehistory includes events and legislation of the fifties, represent "the most imaginative and ambitious attempt to manipulate deliberate social change in the years 1960–1964."

These projects were promoted, and largely financed, by the Ford Foundation and the Juvenile Delinquency and Youth Offences Control Act of 1961: absorbed into the poverty programme, and diffused as a national strategy, they are now known as community action projects—local agencies, drawing on federal funds, which concert the resources of a community in a democratic, coherent attack upon the handicaps of the poor. But though, from the first, this movement of reform was concerned with poverty, it arose less from protest or moral indignation at injustice, than from a sense of breakdown in the institutions which should be diffusing opportunities to all. The reformers in the Ford Foundation, in the President's Committee on Juvenile Delinquency, and the executives of the projects they funded were intellectuals, for whom poverty was more a problem in social engineering, than a cause. They attacked it by expert knowledge and political

manoeuvre, as technicians to whom the guidance of social
change was a career [p. 1].

Although some of the ideas which powered these programs came
from university people, it should be noted that their leadership,
institutional structure, and base were unrelated to university settings; in fact, they arose from and were embedded in the community. Marris and Rein, two university persons, have provided us
with a creative critique of the relationship between the goals, tactics,
and results of these community action programs, and no one with
an interest in the disjunctions that can arise between ideas and
social action can afford to ignore their book. The point I wish to
emphasize, however, is that people like Marris and Rein did not
initiate or administer these kinds of programs, and as they and
Moynihan (1969) suggest, one of the major sources of trouble in
these programs was an acceptance of academic theories of dubious
validity. Moynihan is crystal clear in his assertion that one of the
root causes of the failure of some aspects of these programs was
that they were based on theorizing by social scientists who at best
had an unrealistic and oversimplified knowledge of social reality,
and at worst were simply ignorant of how things are and get done.
Moynihan is so pessimistic about the contributions of social scientists to the formulation of policy and the development of action
programs that he recommends restricting their role to evaluation of
what others do. As I point out later, this not only bypasses the
problem of the relation of theory and practice but also maximizes
the chances that the evaluation will be misleading, if not irrelevant.
The Marris and Rein evaluation is a clear exception, but my
reading of Moynihan suggests that he would not regard the Marris
and Rein effort as evaluation because it does not have the trappings of "hard data" and statistical analysis. Moynihan's criticisms
of the academic community are familiar, and it was not until the
turbulent sixties that a significant number of university people
acknowledged that the criticisms were not without some merit. The
relationship between social science theory and social action could no
longer be easily bypassed.

A viable community psychology must draw upon all the
social sciences if it purports to try to understand what a com-

munity is, and how it changes. Social action is, in my view, one way of deepening our understanding. It is a way, however, which has been viewed as inimical to the research traditions of the university in general and of the social sciences in particular. Precisely because of this view, community psychology, so related to the social sciences, has been unable to do justice to its conceptual and social promise. It is necessary, therefore, that we reexamine the traditional view in the university about permissible and impermissible means of acquiring valid knowledge and generalizations. What is at stake is not the university or the social sciences but the acquisition of knowledge which validly reflects the social realities at the same time that it provides direction to efforts to alter those realities.

The Definition and the Purposes of Social Action

I begin with some long-standing attitudes toward the role of social action in graduate education in the social sciences. These attitudes, of course, are those of the faculty, and not surprisingly they tend to become the attitudes of the graduate student. From time to time turmoil in the larger society gets reflected in the university, and when it does the role of social action by university people is elevated and three major positions emerge: one, it is an obligation of the university to help remedy social injustice; two, it is a subversion of the basic purposes of the university to direct its energies toward solving practical problems; and three, a position reflecting different stances ranging from indifference to "this too shall pass." Anyone who has been in the university in the past decade knows what I am talking about. At the moment it appears that those who predicted that "this too shall pass" were most accurate. Compared to what it was two or three years ago, the university is a paradise for those who staunchly defended the position that its major purpose was to contribute to knowledge, that is, to knowledge illuminating the nature of man and society.

By social action as a vehicle for learning and contributing to knowledge, I refer to any instance in which an academic person takes on a socially responsible role—in government, politics, business, schools, or poverty agencies—which will allow him to experience the "natural" functioning of that particular aspect of society.

The role must be an operational one with responsibility and some decision making powers. He becomes an insider. He is not a consultant with the luxury of giving advice without responsibility for implementation. He is at bat. He is not sitting in the stands passively observing the game and passing judgment on the players. He is in the game and he is a player. Finally, he assumes the new role not only to learn but to change and move things. He is there to "win," and winning is defined in terms of ideas and theories about the game that he or others developed prior to assuming the new role. He assumes the new role to test the adequacy of ideas and theories, to see how they fit with social realities. His motivations have both an intellectually selfish and a selfless quality. The period of time he spends in this role will vary, but there is no doubt in his mind that at the end of the period he must discharge the obligation to determine and communicate the general significance of his experience. Part of winning is in contributing to new and general knowledge about man and society.

Machiavelli founded political science by writing about his social-political-military experiences. He was a scholar before he was a social activist, but his social activist roles gave him the basis for making provocative conceptualizations which are still quite relevant today. Proshansky (1972) has recently said rather eloquently some of the things I take up in this chapter. In regard to the role of social action in graduate education his plea is identical to mine.

> Clearly, direct involvement—whether for educational purposes or otherwise—in community problems is fraught with all of the sociopolitical difficulties with which we are familiar. But again I must say that it is the only way to provide a viable basis for new and meaningful research roles for our students. In the late 1940s, Kurt Lewin first postulated the notion of "action research," that is, research done in an actual problem context and which would be socially useful as well as theoretically meaningful. Given the recent recommendations by the National Science Foundation, the Social Science Research Council, and other groups of the need for problem-oriented social issue research, it is evident that Lewin was far ahead of his time. But to achieve Lewin's objective,

we will need doctoral programs organized in terms of an inter-disciplinary problem orientation, in which there is a close and continuing set of interrelationships between the community or problem setting and the students and faculty that make up these programs.

In the last year, two very high-level community ad-ministrators of public agencies have said almost the same thing to me. Each indicated his strong belief in the value of be-havioral science research in the actual context of the problems they dealt with. But each was quite wary about moving ahead in this respect because of what he had experienced in the past. Let me paraphrase what one of them said: Too often you people come in not as problem-oriented researchers but aca-demic purists more interested in searching and testing what is important for your theory than for the problem itself. But what really gripes me is that there is no long-term commit-ment. You come in, do your research, and then go back to the university and that's it. I am not asking for the solution to practical problems or what you call "quick and dirty re-search." I want a long-term commitment, because this is use-ful for us and scientifically important for you. Give us the word, and we will make you permanent members of the team. You can't come in, have your fun, and then leave—and expect us to welcome you back, particularly after you have left a mess [pp. 211–212].

Two Arguments Against Social Action

If we try to understand why the university tradition is inim-ical to social action as a vehicle for contributing to knowledge, we must distinguish between two arguments: the one which points to the value of contributions stemming from basic scholarship and research carried out without regard for their practical and social consequences; and the one which asserts that involvement in society for the purpose of changing it is both dangerous and corrupting and had best be left to others—in other words, that social action, however desirable and inevitable it may be, cannot be carried out with the dispassion, objectivity, and controls that are the hallmark of traditional scholarship and research. These two arguments are not logically related in the sense that agreement or disagreement with one determines one's position in regard to the other. The failure to keep these arguments separate has had the effect of obscuring issues and raising murky questions, an effect which I shall attempt to show has effectively diluted the possibility that the social sciences can open themselves to new and basic knowledge.

In regard to the first argument, there is no need to document the conclusion that much has been learned and illuminated by social scientists about man and society. One can generate quite a controversy trying to get agreement about what these basic contributions and illuminations have been, but I assume that for some of them there would be fair agreement even among those social scientists who disagree widely on other issues. To argue that little or nothing of a basic sort has come out of the social sciences in the university makes no sense to me, and in any case I have not heard this argument even from the most vociferous critics of American social science. The fact that some fundamental contributions have emerged from university social science tends, of course, to strengthen the attitude that research and scholarship unconcerned with application and social action are the only kind of geese that lay golden eggs. (This is a metaphor used by Samuel Fernberger after World War II to make the point that bringing clinical psychology into academic departments of psychology would lower the production of golden eggs.) It neither denies nor amends this argument to point out that most social scientists think that most social science research and scholarship are trivial affairs, at best, and stupefying stupidities at worst. Irrelevant is the adjective I most frequently encounter. In his Preface to the 1935 *Handbook on Social Psychology,* published in the middle of the Great Depression, Murchison says:

> The social sciences at the present moment stand naked and feeble in the midst of the political uncertainty of the world. The physical sciences seem so brilliant, so clothed with power by contrast. Either something has gone all wrong in the evolution of the social sciences, or their great day in court has not yet arrived. It is with something akin to despair that one contemplates the piddling, trivial, superficial, damnably unimportant topics that some social scientists investigate with

agony and sweat. And at the end of all these centuries, no one knows what is wrong with the world or what is likely to happen to the world.

And Nisbet in his Preface to the 1970 edition of *The Quest for Community* states:

> More than anything else it is the massive transformation of the American social scene since the Second World War that has focused attention upon the relative poverty of resources in the social sciences. Vast industrial relocations, redevelopments of central cities, city and regional planning, community organization, serious efforts on the part of civic agencies to prevent, rather than merely punish, crime, the innumerable social and psychological problems involved in the administering of both governmental and private social security systems—all of these and other problems have led to an almost desperate turning to social scientists for help.
>
> Of a sudden, a good deal of so-called social science was proved empty or irrelevant despite the public pretense to the contrary of some academic intellectuals. It became evident that more reliable knowledge—slim though it was— frequently lay in the experiences of social workers, businessmen, architects, city-managers, and politicians than in whole volumes of the social science journals. Several generations of social thought based upon determinism had produced very little of value to society. The familiar prescriptions of governmental ownership or management, by which liberals had for decades salved their social consciences, began to turn sour in the mouth when it became apparent that the real problem often was not *whether* the government shall render aid, but *how*.

And most recently Gouldner (1970), in his massive indictment of a good part of American social science, carries the argument to the present day. And then there is C. Wright Mills. And no one said or described it better than Veblen. For those who prefer the poignant and tragic, I would recommend Ernest Becker's (1971) moving account of Albion Small, one of the fathers of modern sociology. I think it is a fair assessment of the contributions stemming from the traditional stance—which defends "basic" scholarship and research

that is unconcerned with practical problems and social action—
to say that it has produced a few nuggets of gold and a mountain
of trivia.

Now let us turn to the argument that social action or immersion in practical problems is, for the university social scientist,
a dangerous, corrupting business because it involves pressures and
goals that subvert objectivity, adherence to the rules of evidence,
and the attainment of generalizations or "laws" that make sense of
the world of appearances. Like the first argument, this one has some
truth to it. We need only look at the biographies which politicians
and statesmen write to agree that in the real social world truth is a
frequent victim of self-interest. And each of us can probably point
to an academic colleague who either assumed some sort of public
position or focused his interests on solving a practical problem and
then subsequently seemed unable to relate what he did in any clear
way to a larger picture. That is to say, he did not contribute to
basic knowledge, however successful or helpful he otherwise was.
(That is a better outcome than one in which the individual becomes
such a partisan, such a blind advocate of policy and ideology, that
one holds suspect anything he reports.) But this argument, like the
first one, has its notable exceptions. Some of the nuggets of gold
that the social sciences treasure were not mined in academia but
rather by people very much involved in the affairs of their day.
For those who need their memories refreshed on this score I recommend Schlesinger's (1971) *The Historian as Participant,* in which
the author in no way denies the validity of the second argument at
the same time that he convincingly demonstrates its limits.

At this point we can conclude that both arguments have
very limited validity. Then why in the university is there such a
strong and unreasoned tradition against social action as a possible
way of learning and contributing to general knowledge of man and
society? Schlesinger provides part of the answer, and although he
is talking about the historian, what he says, in my opinion, is no less
true of all the social sciences:

> In the later nineteenth century, however, a new ques-
> tion arose, I think for the first time—the question whether
> participation in public events might not disqualify the partici-

pant from writing about these events as a historian; whether, indeed, experience in the public world might not be incompatible with the ideal of historical objectivity. Such questions were a direct consequence of the professionalization of history. Historians were now increasingly segregated in universities, enshrined in academic chairs, surrounded by apprentices; and the crystallization of this distinct and specific status brought with it a tendency to reject, first, historians who participated in the events they described and, soon, historians who participated in anything beyond the profession of history. Indeed, it may have been unconsciously felt that eyewitness history, by involving the historical profession in on-going conflicts, might raise threats to the hardwon new status. As Sir Walter Raleigh, one of the few historians to suffer the ultimate criticism of the executioner's axe, had warned two and a half centuries before, "Whosoever, in writing a modern history, shall follow truth too near the heels, it may haply strike out his teeth." . . .

Professionalization meant rigorous training in the techniques of the craft; it meant specialization; it meant bureaucratization; it meant a stern insistence on critical methods as the guarantee of objectivity; it meant a deep pride in the independence and autonomy of the historical guild and an ardent conviction that the new professional techniques were winning history unprecedented new successes. "The historians of former times," wrote Acton, "unapproachable for us in knowledge and in talent, cannot be our limit. We have the power to be more rigidly impersonal, disinterested, and just than they."

Such severe standards created the image of the historian as a monastic scholar, austerely removed from the passing emotions and conflicts of his own day. From this viewpoint, participation in the public world meant the giving of hostages —to parties, to institutions, to ideologies. In retrospect, it seemed that Macaulay was too deeply a Whig, Bancroft too deeply a Jacksonian, Henry Adams too deeply an Adams. The view arose that not only participant-historians but even historians who wrote about contemporaneous events were too deeply compromised to fulfill the pure historical vocation [pp. 341–342].

I have no doubt that when the final history of the human race is written, high on the list of diseases contributing to its downfall will be professionalization, which whatever its origins in social virtue, dialectically gave rise to its own destruction.

Professionalization within the university rests on what I call the myth of contamination by society: the non-university world is organized in ways and for purposes, and populated by kinds of people, that are personally corrupting, truth-killing, and crassly materialistic. That is only one part of the myth. The other is that what is true of society is not true of the university. If you go into society you get diseased. If you stay in the university, you will be healthy. What would transform the myth into a description of reality would be the recognition that the university must reflect the larger society, and staying in or venturing out of the university both possess the potential for true learning and profound corruption.

By venturing into the everyday world two ways of getting new knowledge become available to the social scientist. The first way is particularly important to those who develop theories, mini or maxi, to explain something about man and society, because the assumption is usually made that either what needs explanation "out there" is adequately described or that the description is incomplete or incorrect and the theory serves to tell one the true state of affairs "out there." For example, over the years there has been a lot of theorizing by every brand of social scientist about what schools are like, and the amount of theorizing increased as the schools became objects of national concern and controversy. In one way or another these conceptual efforts were addressed to how schools should be changed, the assumption being that what schools *are* was pretty well known. That assumption was crucial, of course, because if what was considered valid knowledge about schools was in error, then efforts to change the schools would likely misfire. And does anyone doubt that they misfired? The reasons they failed and will probably continue to fail are complex, but there is no doubt in my mind that a major factor is sheer ignorance about what schools are. Ignorance is bad enough, but when in addition the available "knowledge" is based on unexamined prejudices and incompleteness that produces caricature, the outcome is not in doubt.

I devoted a recent book, *The Culture of the School and the*

Problem of Change (1971) to these issues and I have space only to describe briefly some of its major points. First, those who developed theories about what schools are and how they should change obviously had no first-hand sustained experience in schools; this applies to those who developed the new math, the new biology, the "new" community-school relationship. Second, those agents of change *within* the school (usually using the concepts of the Christian Diors of academia) tended to be equally ignorant about the culture of the school—a good example of how being in or out of the university need not make for a profound difference.[1] Third, the theoretical literature is remarkably devoid of meaningful descriptions of how schools work or change. We have a plethora of anecdotes and case histories, but these almost invariably tell us more about the phenomenology of the change agent than about schools. Fourth, the failure of efforts at change rarely has the effect of changing theories, but frequently results in further criticism of the schools by "blaming" the stupidity or recalcitrance of teachers and administrators. Fifth, when one looks carefully at instances of change it becomes apparent that the theories on which they are based never justify the particular time perspective that is employed.

What permits me to make these points about change agents in the university and in the schools? That is a long story (Sarason, Levine, and others, 1966), but it all began with the decision that in our desire to understand the culture of the school we would establish an intensive helping relationship to schools, a relationship that would require us to be *in* them on a sustained basis for the purpose of being helpful *there*.[2] We were not going to be participant ob-

---

[1] Our lack of knowledge about the actual functioning of schools is by no means peculiar to these parts of the educational scene. For example, in a four-paragraph comment on university governance (*Saturday Review,* January 1970) Logan Wilson states: "I don't know of a single empirical study of a campus that delineates just how decisions are made. In many institutions it is a kind of shell game, and I suspect that this is a source of frustration to many students who make recommendations and then are mystified about what happens to them." This simple, clear, and justified statement should give pause to those who believe that the different efforts to change the university in one way or another are really directed to the way things are.

[2] At an earlier point I gave consideration to a more traditional methodology: questionnaires, interviews, observations. When I realized that much of what we know about personality has come from efforts to change

servers, passive consultants, or so-called crisis interveners. Each
of us at the Yale Psycho-Educational Clinic spent a good deal of
time in a school.[3] We learned a lot. We learned about the extent
of our ignorance about what schools are, and about the unexamined
assumptions with which we approached them. Once the unlearning
process was well under way, we could begin to understand schools
from the standpoints of the different groups within them. We were
able to observe numerous attempts to introduce change in the
schools and why in each instance failure was guaranteed because
there was an amazing ignorance of "the way things are." And we
learned to be intellectually alone because when we read the social
science literature on schools there was pitifully little (there were a
few nuggets) that we could use or that squared with our experiences. Candor requires that I report that we became increasingly
hostile to colleagues in universities who in the turbulent sixties
became "relevant" by becoming interested in the schools, willing
to contribute their "hard science" expertise in a kind of noblesse
oblige manner. Their motivations were as clear as their ignorance
was profound. They were going to share their "basic" conceptions
and rigorous methodology. They were going to determine the true
state of affairs, and many of them had nothing to determine because they already knew what the score was!

In his book *Maximum Feasible Misunderstanding* (1969),
Moynihan describes some of the unfortunate things that happen
when academic social scientists are brought into the "public sector"
to provide the basic understanding on the basis of which successful
practical programs can be mounted. Fortunately, Moynihan's wit
and literary style help the reader stay with his account of the ineptness of the social scientist: well-woven theories that bear the
stamp of creative thinking and unexamined partisanship and social
values, ignorance of how federal bureaucracy works and its ties
with legislative power and politics, and the inability to foresee the

---

it, I decided that it would be productive to work in schools in the same
way. It is not that one approach is good and the other bad. They give you
different pictures because you are experiencing the setting in different ways.

    [3] The Yale Psycho-Educational Clinic no longer exists as an orga-
nized entity. The explanation for its demise is given in my book, *The Creation
of Settings and Future Societies* (1972) and is part of the background
context from which this chapter emerges.

practical consequences of recommendations. In fact, Moynihan's disillusionment with the social scientist is so great that he recommends that his role be restricted to evaluating programs, not suggesting or implementing them. Moynihan seems to be saying that by keeping the social scientist in his academic cage he will do less practical harm and conceivably might even do some good.

This recommendation is unfortunately superficial, if not thoughtless. How can you evaluate social action programs if you do not comprehend the social contexts of their origins as well as the contexts of their implementation? How do you evaluate positive or negative results when you have no secure basis for knowing whether the study was appropriate in the first place, whether the study was directed to the right questions and would be carried out in ways that would not be self-defeating? How can you talk about the significance of consequences if you are not deeply knowledgeable about antecedents, and how can you be knowledgeable if you have no first-hand experience with the relevant social contexts? Is the social scientist someone to be given data to determine if they are statistically significant? Is the social scientist to be the servant of the public officials who determine what needs to be done, do it, and then ask the social scientist to find out if it was worthwhile? *And on what basis does Moynihan assume that the non-university agent of change does not daily commit the same errors of ineptness of which he accuses the social scientist?* It is strange that Moynihan does not ask and pursue the question why the academic social scientist is so inept when he ventures forth into the social world, especially since I assume Moynihan knows that, his recommendation notwithstanding, social scientists are going to be drawn into public affairs. (A less charitable way of putting it is that they will be seduced by their own view of their expertise, as well as by public agencies who have come to believe what the university has in recent decades told them to believe: that "basic" research pays off, like in physics with the atomic bomb!)

Social Action and the Consequences of World War II

Thus far I have been discussing the social scientist as he pursues social action for the purpose of applying basic theory to the

solution of the problems of society. There is a second way, far less
ambitious and more unplanned or fortuitous, which can be illustrated by World War II experiences. It first has to be noted that in
World War II almost everyone in the university willingly and
eagerly sought to be helpful. No one was saying that the rest of
society should fight the war while the university should continue its
pursuit of basic knowledge. Academic people in or out of the armed
services concentrated on practical problems with which they frequently had no background or previous interest. They were not
seeking basic knowledge or developing new theoretical systems. The
problems were immediate, pressing, and in need of some practical
solutions. Overcoming visual problems of pilots, instilling certain
attitudes in soldiers, managing mental breakdowns near the field of
battle, learning how to form groups and maintain morale, teaching
of heretofore neglected foreign languages, increasing industrial
efficiency and output, developing effective propaganda, training
people for espionage, predicting reactions to stress, improving
decision-making and planning processes—this is a very small sample
of the problems academic people were dealing with. World War II
had personal and professional consequences for university people,
personal in the sense that for many it simply expanded their
knowledge of the larger society and its problems, and professional in
the sense that it changed the substantive nature of many fields. It
is hard to overestimate how much World War II changed the
direction of basic research and theory because it was an unpredictable consequence of dealing with some practical or applied problems. Garner (1972) has recently discussed and illustrated this
process in regard to experimental psychology. Let me quote one
instance from Garner:

> The topic of space perception is almost synonymous
> with the name of James Gibson these days, so when I want to
> talk about concepts and research in space perception, I can-
> not do so without talking about James Gibson's research. He
> was well established as an authority on perception before
> World War II, but his experiences during that war, working
> on some applied problems, changed the nature and direction
> of his theorizing considerably. Specifically, his experiences led
> him to his "Ground Theory" of space perception as described

in his book, "The Perception of the Visual World" published in 1950.

As Gibson describes the experience in that book, he and some other psychologists were trying to understand how aircraft pilots estimate the distance to the ground when they are landing an airplane. He found that the traditional cues for depth perception, listed without fail in every introductory textbook on psychology, simply failed to explain the perception of depth at the distances required in flying and landing an airplane. He furthermore found that experiments had to be done in the field to get at the process, that laboratory experiments changed the nature of the process too much. So into the field he went.

It was from these experiments that Gibson came to the conclusion that the prerequisite for the perception of space is the perception of a continuous background surface; thus the "Ground Theory" which evolved from this work.

The important point for my thesis today is that Gibson's whole way of thinking about the problem of space perception changed when he was faced with the problem of understanding how pilots in a real-life situation actually land their airplanes without too many crashes. His theoretical notions were changed by his contact with people with problems. He did not develop these important ideas by a continuous relation to his previous work. Rather, his research and thinking, according to his own report, took a decided turn for the better as a result of this experience [pp. 8–9].

Garner could have used his own illustrious career as an example.

It is unfortunate that it was as a consequence of a world war that theory and research in practically every university discipline changed markedly and the pace of new knowledge accelerated. The lesson, of course, is not that we should have more wars but that concern with practical problems can lead to new and fundamental knowledge. But this lesson was not drawn, so that in 1972 Garner is compelled to say: "The quality of basic research is improved by communication between the basic research scientist and the people who have problems to solve. Thus for scientists to engage in goal-oriented research, research aimed at solving problems known to exist, is both to perform a service to society and to improve the quality of the basic research itself. . . . If the scientist will talk to people with real problems, and just as important, if those people will talk to those of us who are scientists, then both those who acquire knowledge and those who apply it will benefit. The relation is truly symbiotic."

I should remind the reader that the thrust of my discussion has not been to deny the validity of the tradition that holds that research and theorizing untrammeled by practical considerations or the need to solve immediate social problems can contribute new general knowledge about man and society. I have argued against the exclusivity of this tradition and its historically unwarranted assumption that dealing with the practical problems of people and society is dangerous and unproductive. I hope that it has also been clear that I have not advocated that the academic social scientist should become involved in practical matters as an end in itself but rather as a means of testing his comprehension of social realities or for the deliberate purpose of experiencing a new role in its actual fullness.

I must turn again to personal experience. One of the several major reasons I started and directed the Yale Psycho-Educational Clinic was to test myself in the role of leader. It was an inchoate kind of motivation but in some dim way I felt I had to do it if I was to understand better why new settings fail, and rather quickly so. I was painfully aware of the self-defeating character of most organizations, new and old, but I was vaguely uncomfortable in the knowledge that my understanding was from an outsider's perspective. And, frankly, the literature I read on leadership and organizations was far more effective than seconal as a sleep producer. I also found what was for me a fantastic omission in this literature: There was practically nothing on how to create a new setting, even though new settings were being created at an ever-accelerating rate. The more I dug into the literature the clearer it became that what we know is based on chronologically mature, malfunctioning organizations. So in my curiosity about myself as a leader I was led to the problem of the creation of settings, which I defined as two or more people coming together in new and sustained relationships to attain stated objectives. As best I could, it is all described in my book *The Creation of Settings and Future*

Societies (1972). I experienced leadership and the creation of settings in their fullness. I would like to believe that what I learned and reported are fundamental and a contribution to general knowledge. What I believe is ultimately of no significance unless others agree that what came out of ten years of planning and working—ten years of continuous, day-by-day, month-by-month responsibility, influencing and being influenced, experiencing anxiety, joy, and controversy—is of general import. If my recent book was a biography of a particular clinic in a particular university in a particular city, I should not be surprised if it met with disinterest. What may be interesting to *me,* or what was the most self-transforming experience of *my* life, is important to me personally, but unless I can relate the particulars of my experiences to more general contents and issues I am not fulfilling my role as a member of a university faculty. *The more pertinent point here is that as a member of a university faculty I had an obligation to pursue knowledge even if that meant "messing" in a sustained way with the realities of modern society.* But, as I pointed out before, that sense of obligation is not shared by many people in the university, who have successfully innoculated themselves against a contaminating society.

How the Tradition Is Maintained

I have described a set of beliefs inimical to the idea that immersion in practical problems, that taking some form of social action aimed at changing something or creating something new, is a productive way of contributing new and general knowledge of a fundamental sort. Having said something about the rhetoric of this tradition, I would like briefly to comment on how the tradition is maintained. If we have any desire to change or add to this tradition, we should know how it works.

Each year I read scores of letters from colleges and universities seeking to employ young faculty members. The letters are monotonously alike. What they seek is a young person who is "rigorous in approach," "interested in a career in research," and "shows promise of being a productive contributor to the literature." Not surprising, in recent years many centers ask for someone with

"community interests." Of course he should also be a good teacher
and a responsible departmental citizen. I list these sought-after
characteristics in the order that they are usually given in the letters.

So what is wrong? For a partial answer let us turn to how
graduate students are chosen. Faculty members select graduate
students on precisely the same grounds that they choose new
faculty members. If there is any basis for inferring that the pro-
spective student is a social activist or "do-gooder"—that he or she
wants to be in and change the world—the chances for admission
fall almost to zero. If the application does not contain statements
that the student is interested in the world of ideas, rigorous research,
and theory—if he remains general and vague and has not already
developed interests in a specific and restricted area familiar in the
literature—the odds against admission drop. If he presents evidence
that he was already an undergraduate researcher, and his recom-
menders attest to his devotion to basic research, the odds for him
or her increase sharply. Faculties choose new faculty members and
graduate students in terms of how the candidates fit the dominant
academic tradition, and it is a process intended to screen out
"deviants." It is a process deliberately carried out to reduce the
risk of choosing people who may not fit in with the dominant
tradition.

In the past decade two new factors have altered either the
"success" of the selection process or the population from which
students are selected. The first of these factors is that undergraduates
have become very knowledgeable about how to write an application
to graduate school. That is to say, many of them have social activist
inclinations and goals but they know that to express them is to
invite a kiss of death. They know that they can learn much in
graduate school but they also know that they do not accept the
exclusivity of the dominant academic tradition. Phenomenologically
they see themselves as needing knowledge and skills, and a union
card, which will permit them after graduate school to make their
mark in society, not in the university. These are the ones who seek
to beat the system. If they get into graduate school, their problems
begin. Rarely will they find a faculty member who meets their conception of a role model, that is, someone who is actively engaged in
trying to do something about some aspect of a social problem. Even

more rarely will they find a faculty member who is engaged in social action not only for the purpose of doing good but also with the purpose of learning and conceptualizing; and for this kind of graduate student a role model of this sort is crucial, for otherwise he will get lost in particulars. So what is he to do? The more appropriate question is, What is he required to do? He is required to go through a program which, instructive and stimulating though it may be, does not get to the center of his interests. No less than the factory worker the student feels alone and alienated: a significant part of him or her is untouched or unused in work. Some students succumb to the system, with what personal consequences, short-term or long-term, I cannot say. Some "make trouble." Some drop out.

The other factor affecting the selection process has to do with those who do *not* apply because they reject the values and substance of graduate education as they see them. For the majority of these nonapplicants, the decision is a wise one in the sense that they are social activists dedicated to ideologies which are tantamount to a way of life in which the demands of untrammelled intellectual pursuits have little place. These kinds of ideology can be no less confining than the dominant academic one. But there are other nonapplicants I have known who had the appropriate mixture of social activism and the capacity to conceptualize, think critically, and generalize from their activism. Their rejection of further education is a tragic waste of human resources. What life has in store for them I find distasteful to contemplate. I hope I am wrong. I have no doubt that among them are some of the finest minds I have known.

It is clear, I hope, that I am not recommending that students be chosen because of their social activist interests. Aside from maintaining that such interests should not be a disqualification, I maintain that certain intellectual or conceptual talents have to be present—not fully formed but of a quality which can benefit from intellectual confrontation. It does not bother me if such a student comes to me in possession of the "truth," or with the self-assurance that is always based on oversimplification; or with the attitude that youth has a grasp of the social realities that age only weakens; or with a view of past human efforts (of social and intellectual history in general) that at best borders on tolerance and at worst reflects sheer ignorance; or with that biblical prophetic stance that says the world must be saved and he will do it. These things do not bother me if I feel I can "fight" with that student in such a way that both of us will want to continue the battle. What am I there for if not to engage in intellectual battle with the student, to provide "out there" experiences that will help clarify and perhaps resolve the differences that divide us, to help him experience the continuity between theory and action, to aid him to see that self-change is a prerequisite to social change, and that being able to take distance from oneself is no less important a skill than taking distance from whatever it is one wants to change? I have learned the least from students with whom I have not had to do battle. I in no way subscribe to the notion that a university faculty should be sensitive to the needs and interests of students in order to satisfy them. I must be sensitive to their needs and interests in order to see what the battle is going to be like: where we differ and to what extent, whether we can agree on a constitution that permits, indeed encourages, peaceful struggle, and whether he or she is willing to share experiences with me in the social world so that we have a degree of communality from which to view our presumed differences.

The Present and Future Picture

The attitudes of the university toward social action as a vehicle of learning and contributing to general knowledge have not changed very much in recent years. At the present moment universities are experiencing a financial crisis, and it would appear that new programs which do not fit in with traditional attitudes toward scholarship and research will be weakened or eliminated. Indeed, I have heard some academics argue that the current financial plight is in part the result of a misdirected expansion of frilly, social-action-type programs which drained precious resources away from what they consider the most intellectually substantial activities of the university. In any event, it is unrealistic to expect that graduate education in the social sciences will change quickly in the ways I have suggested. The dominant attitudes are too strongly held by too many academics, and this has been true for too long a time, to justify optimism for change.

And we must not forget that these attitudes reflect a tradition with some solid achievements. Those of us who feel that this tradition is narrow and confining, that it is robbing the social sciences of new experiences which are the lifeblood of new ideas, have no alternative but to fight the self-defeating exclusivity of the tradition. But it should not be fought in terms of superficial polarities—good-bad, virtuous-sinful, progressive-reactionary. I say this because it is conceivable that as time goes on, non-university-based vehicles will be created to avoid the obstacles of academic tradition, and there is a real danger that these new ventures will ignore what is best in that tradition—the search for continuity and generality in face of the fact that the search is beset with serious obstacles, not the least of which are in the searcher himself.

Immersion in social action or the affairs of the social world can be justified in a number of ways, but contributing to a general *knowledge* of man and society is not among its most frequent justifications. Such a contribution requires at least three characteristics: the action must be intended for the purposes of learning; it must require one's total involvement; and it must be intended that at some point the general sense one makes of the experience will be published for critical scrutiny. I would add one more "condition": the immersion must be limited in time, precisely to safeguard the requirement that one organize and present publically what one has learned.

There is a contradiction between the intent to learn and total involvement, and my critics point to this as a fatal flaw. How can you be true to the intent to learn at the same time you engage in a value-ridden, partisan action which creates pressures that deceive the self and defeat the search for truth? I borrow the principles of an answer from Freud, who, faced with the task of how to be sensitive to the conscious *and* the unconscious messages contained in verbal and motor communications, recommended the stance of "listening and not listening." That is to say, one adopts a set which maximizes the chances for becoming aware of multiple meanings. It is a control against focusing exclusive attention either on the other person or on one's own fleeting ideas and feelings. Freud's dictum "to listen and not listen" was no foolproof control, particularly in the therapeutic context, in which the desire to be a good healer and the sources of resistance in the patient to being healed can collude to unwittingly corrupt both. Freud was quite aware that partisan action, as analyst or patient, could distort the pursuit of truth, which is why he recommended that analysts be analyzed every five years. Freud, of course, is a beautiful example that one can engage in actions, very "practical" kinds of actions, and cull from them understanding and generalizations which enormously influence theory and practice in many academic fields. I would suggest that this was possible because his desire to learn was as strong as his desire to heal. (If Freud was not an outstanding therapist it was probably because he could not contain his intellectual curiosity, which is not always helpful to the conduct of therapy.)

The contradiction is a real one but it is no excuse for retreat. Our task is to learn whatever we can, to experience whatever we can, in the quest for general knowledge. We are models for our students. If we close off avenues of experience to ourselves, we also do so for our students. If we do not take risks, neither will our students. If we fear being contaminated by society, if we are afraid of testing our ideas about society by intervening in it, and if we are always detached observers of society and rarely if ever participants in it, we can only give our students ideas about society, not our experiences in it. We can tell our students how society ought to be, but not what it is like to try to change the way things are.

The social acion role as I have described it is not everybody's cup of tea. It is, however, a brew without which the social sciences will remain insipid and trivial. In their quest for scientific respectability the social sciences have erected "experimentation" and the "experimental attitude" as a supreme value. An essential feature of this attitude, so obvious that it rarely receives elaboration, is that if you want to understand how things work you have to *intervene*, you have to introduce something new into the accustomed order of things. The additional feature of manipulating variables, contrasting control and experimental conditions, is a consequence of the basic assumption that you must *intervene and change* things in some way. Social action is a form of intervention no less than changing the feeding schedules of rats is an intervention. Where it is possible to introduce controls one should do so, of course. But the fact that such controls may not be possible, or that they may fall short of the ideal mark, is an argument for caution in interpretation, and not an argument against intervention. One does the best one can and relies on the efforts and criticisms of others to do better the next time. *But that is also true for the most rigorous experimentalist.* In the final analysis the best control is in what others say and do in response to what one claims to have learned. Rigor is no guarantee of significance and importance. Calling something social action or fieldwork is no excuse for sloppiness. What we ask of everyone is that they do justice to themselves and to the problem, uninfluenced by fashion, unconstrained by narrow tradition, and unfearful of the new.

Most of this book has been about issues of value and substantive scope confronting the new field of community psychology. In this chapter I have taken the position that community psychology should be socially activist in the way I have defined social action. Over the years we have learned a good deal about communities, and most of our knowledge is descriptive in nature. Where our knowledge has been incomplete or misleading (or simply wrong) has been in the area of community dynamics—of how a community "works" and how it changes, how its parts have been interrelated over time, and how it is susceptible to different kinds of pressures and conflicts. The situation is analogous to that of the study of personality, where there has been a vast accumulation of descriptive knowledge. It was primarily the effort to help and change personality that deepened our understanding of personality organization and dynamics. Indeed, these efforts discovered variables that the descriptive data obscured. A community psychology that does not value the "help and change" methodology is certain to be a limited, if a not sterile, one.

XI

Some Cautions

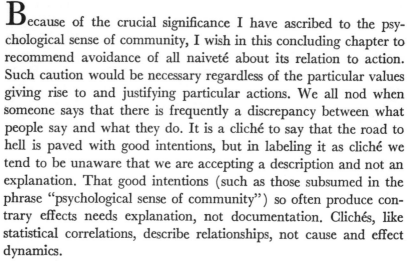

Because of the crucial significance I have ascribed to the psychological sense of community, I wish in this concluding chapter to recommend avoidance of all naiveté about its relation to action. Such caution would be necessary regardless of the particular values giving rise to and justifying particular actions. We all nod when someone says that there is frequently a discrepancy between what people say and what they do. It is a cliché to say that the road to hell is paved with good intentions, but in labeling it as cliché we tend to be unaware that we are accepting a description and not an explanation. That good intentions (such as those subsumed in the phrase "psychological sense of community") so often produce contrary effects needs explanation, not documentation. Clichés, like statistical correlations, describe relationships, not cause and effect dynamics.

Agreement on values is easier to reach than agreement about

the appropriateness of value-derived actions. This alone should caution one against the tendency, tempting and understandable, to assume that because the psychological sense of community is a value which should inform action, it is a value that ensures certain desired outcomes. The failure to resist this tempting oversimplification leads only to disillusionment. It brought much grief, for instance, to community psychologists and psychiatrists during the sixties, when they failed again and again to effect change in existing settings (such as schools) that were seen as contributing to community turmoil and were judged unable by themselves to change in desired ways. The effect of this oversimplification can also be illustrated quickly by looking at the myriad of new settings which were created to strengthen the community fabric. In some of these efforts the aim was not only to strengthen but to weave a new fabric out of new materials. As I have discussed elsewhere (Sarason, 1972), studying the creation of a new setting is tantamount to studying the more implicit aspects of a culture as they interact with and determine the response to change.

By a new setting I mean any instance in which two or more people come together in new and sustained relationships to attain stated objectives. Marriage, legal or otherwise, would be the smallest instance, and revolution for the purpose of creating a new society would be the largest. Marriage aside, the rate at which settings are created in our society has been very high. And it was probably never higher than during the sixties, when a veritable flood of federal, state, and local legislation spawned new and old types of settings, programs, or vehicles to combat poverty, racial conflict, educational inequality and inadequacy, juvenile delinquency, and so on. (Single pieces of legislation, like the one providing for Headstart, gave rise to several thousand discrete new settings.) However different these settings may have been in other respects, they shared one new and one old characteristic. The old one was so obvious that it was rarely stated: the new setting will be one in which the psychological sense of community will be experienced by those who are part of it. If queried, the creators of the new setting would say that unless its staff experienced the psychological sense of community, the quality of the service rendered by the setting would be adversely affected. The new characteristic was that the setting should be in, for, and by the community. Being in and for the community were not novel features, but the idea that the substance and form of the setting should reflect some degree of citizen-consumer participation was new. There was a third characteristic, again rarely stated because it seemed so obvious, and that was that the new setting would establish mutually productive relationships with other settings. That is to say, the new setting was not to be an organizational isolate but rather was to become part of a community of organizations, to feel that it was a part of a network of related and mutually supportive settings. In one way or another, then, those who were part of these new settings were to develop and experience a differentiated psychological sense of community having internal and broad external referents. Members of these settings were not to feel that they were a part only of their discrete setting. Their "sense" would have to have a broader base if their problem-torn communities were not to deteriorate further.

Why these new settings fell far short of their mark is an extraordinarily complex question, which I have dealt with in some measure in my book *The Creation of Settings and the Future Societies* (1972). I shall make no attempt here to summarize its contents, but instead shall very briefly state certain conclusions relevant to the present discussion. I must emphasize that these conclusions represent a small part of my overall analysis. Although I shall be rooting them out of this contextual analysis, they may give the reader some idea of the sources of failure, or why good intentions, like love, are not enough.

(1) Those who created the new settings eagerly looked forward to having a "happy family" whose members would willingly put forth their best in order to accomplish stated goals. There was little or no anticipation that verbal agreement on values and goals would inevitably be confronted with disagreement about the appropriateness of actions. This lack of anticipation was reflected in the absence of vehicles to handle disagreements. Furthermore, in the early stages of the new setting, forcefully expressed disagreements tended to be seen as threatening to the sense of unity; that is, the development of an internal sense of community was seen to require the dilution if not the inhibition of controversy. Far from strengthening the sense of community it began to produce cleavages,

cliquishness, and a heightened sense of individual separateness. As the setting would grow and become subdivided, an individual's allegiance came to be given far more to his piece of the action than to the setting's overarching goals.

(2) The primary basis on which the new setting wished to be judged was the degree of help it rendered to its clients. Absorption with this criterion, often to the exclusion of everything else, effectively diverted attention from what was happening internally to the psychological sense of community. Even though the creators of the setting may have originally understood that an internally weak psychological sense of community would adversely affect service to clients, they early on got so caught up in helping others they could no longer help themselves. The internal psychological sense of community became a victim of a production ethic.

(3) The tendency of the creators of a setting to possess it zealously, to regard it psychologically as their own, erected relatively impermeable barriers between it and community or consumer representatives, and between it and other community agencies. (The latter barrier was not erected only by the new setting, because the existing agencies had long been unable to develop and maintain a more than superficial sense of relationship among themselves.)

(4) In terms of the way in which these new settings defined the problems with which they were to deal, and the kinds and numbers of professional personnel they would require, it was inevitable that there would be a disillusioning discrepancy between services rendered and services needed. This discrepancy, stemming in part from the initial failure to view the problem as one that was a community and not an agency responsibility—requiring community decision-making about how resources could be used and developed—led, as time passed, to an increasing gulf between the setting and the community. To put it another way, the tendency to define and solve problems in terms of traditional concepts of professionalism worked, as it always has, against enhancing the psychological sense of community of all who were directly or indirectly affected by the setting.

The rhetoric accompanying the creation of these new settings explicitly asserted that, unlike traditional social agencies which had become insensitive if not irrelevant to community needs, they would be in, for, and by the community. No longer would the community be a "thing out there" for which a small group of people decides what needs to be done. The community had to be *involved,* and the word involved did not *then* refer to tokenism and empty ritual. It was more than rhetoric, because these settings were born in times of acute sensitivity to the fact that communities were paying the price of past insensitivity to certain problems and groups. The price was high, but not to pay it was to court disaster. Somehow the community experienced as a geopolitical entity had to begin to be experienced as a psychological community. It is not a simple thing to explain why this goal was only minimally achieved, but any attempt at a comprehensive explanation will have to deal with the question of why the overarching goal of enhancing the psychological sense of community lost its "overarchiness," and in so doing provided further data confirming the maxim that the more things change the more they tend to remain the same.

The psychological sense of community is a high-sounding phrase. To be against it is to appear to be for sin and against virtue. The eagerness with which we accept it as an unalloyed "good" testifies more to the strength of our need for it than to our understanding of the realities of social existence.[1] The psychological

---

[1] For example, it is obvious that the attainment within one subsegment of a community of a psychological sense of community may be associated with hostility toward other community groups. That is to say, each of many subgroups may have some psychological sense of community but at the expense of a larger sense of community. This was not unusual in the upsetting sixties, which is why so many people in the newly emerging community fields saw the absolute necessity of trying to build bridges over gulfs of destructive hostility that threatened the existence of all groups. And some of these individuals were soon caught up in some age-old dilemmas: what does one do when the understandable effort of a community group to maximize its psychological sense of community heightens the level of intergroup conflict in the community? At what point is a heightened psychological sense of community a threat to community functioning? By what criteria should we be guided in deciding when the maintenance of the larger community takes precedence, a question identical to that of when do the interests of a group take precedence over those of an individual? And in giving precedence to the larger community, how do we do it so as not to stir the waters of hate and injustice even more? In "real life" these are inescapable problems,

sense of community is a transient experience that is always preceded and sooner or later followed by some kind of conflict or tension between individual and group norms or interests, or between different groups. This tension is inevitable and in itself should not be regarded as either negative or avoidable.

The destructive situation is one in which individuality is completely overwhelmed or inhibited by the larger group, or one in which individuality is treasured to the point where there is no sense of community. Achieving a psychological sense of community almost always requires some sacrifice or accommodation on the part of the individual, as well as some capacity of the group to recognize, tolerate, and support the need for individuality. However, the very fact that I have used the word *community* in the phrase "psychological sense of community" indicates that when there is tension or conflict between the individual and the group (or between groups), the decisive consideration for action is the maintenance of the sense of community. In my book on the creation of settings I devote a separate chapter to Skinner's way of thinking about the design of new cultures. Although I find his conceptions wanting in very fundamental ways, I agree with him in one important respect relevant to the present discussion:

> One cannot understand Skinner unless one recognizes that he has posed and answered an age-old question: What should be the relationship between the individual and the larger society? Put in another way: Should the value of individual freedom take precedence over that of group survival? Skinner's unambiguous answer is that although it may once have been justified to consider the rights of the individual as supreme over all else, this should no longer be tolerated because it threatens the very existence of society. And for Skinner, as for so many other thoughtful people, the number one question on the world agenda is how to save society from self-destruction. Furthermore, he points out, it is difficult to look at human history and be very impressed by the number of people who have enjoyed individual liberty and freedom.

and if I present no easy solutions it is because my main purpose is to emphasize the importance of the psychological sense of community: its necessity and its dialectical nature.

On the contrary, most people have led miserable, unfulfilled, imprisoned lives. No, says Skinner, I have far less to defend than those who worship at the shrine of individualism. The individualist "has refused to be concerned for the survival of his culture and is not reinforced by the fact that the culture will long survive him. In the defense of his own freedom and dignity he has denied the contributions of the past and must therefore relinquish all claim upon the future" (Skinner 1971, p. 210). Fine, say his critics, but if Skinner's answer is *Walden Two,* then we have to decline to share his vision. Such a wholesale rejection misses some of Skinner's most cogent points, points that anyone interested in new settings should not overlook.

The most distinguishing features of Skinner's utopia are how willingly its citizens give priority to the needs of their society. Each of its citizens understands that however important his own needs and goals might be, and they are important in that society, they are secondary to those values and rules upon which the society rests and because of which it will survive. Phenomenologically no one experiences a conflict between individual and group values, and if such conflict should occur, it is resolved quickly in favor of the group values. Skinner's citizens are not selfless or automatons but rather individuals who have a crystal clear commitment to the survival of their community. And they are happy people. What Skinner describes is far from utopian because it is one of the most frequent characteristics of the earliest phases of the creation of a setting, namely, an unconflicted willingness to be part of a larger group, to give priority to its needs and survival and to give of one's self in various ways that an observer would call selfless. And they are happy people. In fact, they are for the rest of their lives likely to look back on this period nostalgically, full of memories of belongingness, joy in work, and the excitement of shared accomplishments. These memories do not contain elements of coercion or stagnation or cattlelike contentment; on the contrary, the memories are full of the sense of growth and challenge. It happened in their lives and not in a literary utopia. In earlier chapters I have tried to understand why this happens, why it is such a brief period in the life of the new setting, how it comes about that individual needs become dominant over group needs (and the level of unhappiness increases), and the setting loses its momentum and purpose. The point is that it is possible for the values of the group to be dominant over individual ones without loss of freedom and dignity. In fact, as I have tried to show, in a new setting the feeling that one has lost freedom and dignity appears after that early phase which is remembered, as so frequently it was actually experienced, with fondness.

If one cannot accept Skinner's assurances about the validity and completeness of his science of behavior or about our readiness to start the technological task of designing new cultures, one should not be blind to the fact that in raising the issue of the relation of the one to the many Skinner is asking the important question. And if one does not like his clear rejection of the primacy of the individual, one is not absolved from answering Skinner's argument that the primacy of the individual is not unrelated to the ills of modern society and threatens its very existence. Just within this century we have witnessed a level of human slaughter and abuse within and between societies that makes a mockery of the concept of progress. And if everyone who has rushed into print has not indicated how the world is going to hell, no one has verbalized that we are making a heaven on earth.

Skinner wants to go "beyond freedom and dignity." If the reader wants to go beyond Skinner's "science of behavior," he will find himself at the point where Skinner starts: the need to develop a psychological sense of community within which belongingness and growth are not incompatible.

There is an old saying in the literature of psychotherapy: You can't treat a patient who is not there. The point is that unless a relationship between patient and therapist has been secured, the patient may not be able to tolerate the therapist's interpretations, and will terminate the relationship. Securing the relationship often requires that the therapist alter his accustomed ways of proceeding in order to establish the basis which permits conflictful material to surface productively. Securing the relationship is initially the overarching goal. Analogously, unless the psychological sense of community is an overarching value having some strength among people in the particular instance, tension and conflict are likely to produce and intensify divisive acton. This, of course, was what was perceived to be happening in our communities in the sixties, and the fear was that unless these centrifugal tendencies were stopped by centripetal ones the future was worse than bleak. For a short time there was a willing acceptance of the value that the development of a sense of community had to take precedence over the accustomed needs and styles of individuals and groups. If this did not last long it was not because the value was demeaned, but rather that it had never had much strength and could not withstand conflict, controversy, and turmoil.

There is no formula for how to instill and maintain the psychological sense of community. Indeed, the thrust of this book has been that before we indulge our tendency to develop formulas and techniques (to become absorbed with technical-engineering issues) in our endeavor to effect change, we need to understand better how the nature of our culture produced the situation we wish to change. And when I say the "nature of our culture" I mean to emphasize that precisely because the situation reflects *our* culture, *we* (as individuals and as professionals) have been part of the problem: our ways of living, the theories we hold, and the actions we take unwittingly reflect both the weaknesses and strengths of our culture. The problem is not only "out there," it is in us as well. It is far easier to say this than it is to confront it and work through it. Culture does its job too well to make efforts at transcending it an easy affair.

The one thing we can be certain about is that in our society the absence or dilution of the psychological sense of community is a destructive force. In other societies the major problem may be hunger and sheer physical survival, and in our efforts to help these societies we seem to be steering them in ways that will ultimately produce what we find intolerable in our own society. It is not, I think, grasping at straws to see some hope in the different ways in which individuals and groups in our communities are beginning to insist that the quality of community life—be it in terms of ecology, architecture, transportation, or redevelopment—can no longer be determined solely by private actions and interests. More people have learned that you *can* "fight city hall," and that in fact you *must,* just as more occupants of city hall have learned that the community they serve is no longer the passive object it once was. I do not want to overrate these trends; we are still too close to them to be able to say what they portend. But when we view them in terms of past decades, there can be no doubt that they reflect the quest for community. Community psychology and community psychiatry have not led this quest, and as I have tried to show in this book, they may well have been unwitting obstacles to it. If, as academic disciplines, they made the mistake of transforming problems in ways that made dealing with them more compatible with their own pasts and traditions, and in so doing rendered themselves insensitive to the basic problem of social living, it should be no cause for surprise. We can learn a lot from failure if we are able to see how *we* contributed to it. If I end with the plea that we begin with ourselves and our fields, it is because I believe we will better understand the problems "out there" as we learn the old lesson: what characterizes us and our fields cannot be qualitatively different from what we see to be the problems of those "out there."

Bibliography

ALBEE, G. W. *Mental Health Manpower Trends.* New York: Basic Books, 1954.

ALBEE, G. W. "Models, Myths, and Manpower." *Mental Hygiene,* 1968a, *52,* 168–180.

ALBEE, G. W. "Conceptual Models and Manpower Requirements in Psychology." *American Psychologist,* 1968b, *23,* 317–320.

American Hospital Association. *Cost finding and Rate setting.* American Hospital Association, 1968.

ANDERSON, L. S., COOPER, S., HASSOL, L., KLEIN, D. C., ROSENBLUM, G., AND BENNETT, C. C. (Conference Chairman). *Community Psychology. A report of the Boston Conference on the education of psychologists for community mental health.* Department of Psychology, Boston University, and the South Shore Mental Health Center, Quincy, Mass., 1966.

BARKER, R. G. *Ecological Psychology.* Stanford: Stanford University Press, 1968.

BEACH, F. A. "The Snark was a Boojum." *American Psychologist, 5,* 1950, 115–124.

BECKER, C. L. *The Heavenly City of the Eighteenth Century Philosophers.* New Haven: Yale University Press, 1932.

BECKER, E. *The Lost Science of Man.* New York: Braziller, 1971.

BERNSTEIN, R. J. *Praxis and Action.* Philadelphia: University of Pennsylvania Press, 1971.

BIDDLE, W. W., AND BIDDLE, L. J. *The Community Development Process. The Rediscovery of Local Initiative.* New York: Holt, Rinehart, and Winston, 1965.

BIKLEN, D. (Ed.) *Human Report: I. Observations in Mental Health-Mental Retardation Facilities.* Syracuse, N.Y.: Division of Special Education and Rehabilitation, Syracuse University, 1970.

BIKLEN, D. *Patterns of Power. A Case Study of Behavior Modification on a "Back Ward" in a State Mental Hospital.* Ph.D. Thesis, Syracuse University, 1973.

BLATT, B., AND KAPLAN, F. *Christmas in Purgatory.* Boston: Allyn & Bacon, 1970a.

BLATT, B. *Exodus from Pandemonium.* Boston: Allyn & Bacon, 1970b.

BLATT, B. (Ed.) *Souls in Extremis.* Boston: Allyn & Bacon, 1973.

BROWN, J. F. *Psychology and the Social Order.* New York: McGraw-Hill, 1936.

BURGESS, E. W., AND BOGUE, D. J. *Urban Sociology.* Chicago: University of Chicago Press, 1967.

COSER, L. A. *Men of Ideas. A Sociologist's View.* New York: Free Press, 1970.

COWEN, E. L. "Social and Community Interventions." In *Annual Review of Psychology,* 1973.

COWEN, E. L., GARDNER, E. A., AND ZAX, M. *Emergent Approaches to Mental Health Problems.* New York: Appleton-Century-Crofts, 1967.

COWEN, E. L., AND ZAX, M. "The Mental Health Fields Today: Issues and Problems." In Cowen, Gardner, and Zax, Eds., *Emergent Approaches to Mental Health Problems.*

DANIELS, R. S. "Community Psychiatry—A New Profession, A Developing Subspecialty, or Effective Clinical Psychiatry." *Community Mental Health Journal,* 1966, 2:1.

DEAN, C. W. *From a Superintendent's Perspective.* Paper presented at the American Psychological Association, Washington, D.C., 1971.

DEAN, C. W., AND REPPUCCI, N. D. "Juvenile Correctional Institutions." In D. Glaser, Ed., *Handbook of Criminology*. New York: Rand-McNally (in press).

DOLLARD, J. *Criteria for the Life History. With Analyses of Six Notable Documents*. New Haven: Yale University Press, 1935.

DOLLARD, J., AND MILLER, N. E. *Personality and Psychotherapy; An Analysis in Terms of Learning, Thinking, and Culture*. New York: McGraw-Hill, 1950.

DUBERMAN, M. *The Uncompleted Past*. New York: Random House, 1969.

FARIS, R. E. L. *Chicago Sociology*. Chicago: University of Chicago Press, 1967.

FELLMAN, D. (Ed.) *The Supreme Court and Education*. New York: Teachers College, Columbia University, 1969.

FREEMAN, E. *Insights: Conversations With Theodor Reik*. Englewood Cliffs, N.J.: Prentice-Hall, 1971.

FROMM, E. *Marx's Concept of Man*. New York: Ungar, 1961.

GARNER, W. "The Acquisition and Application of Knowledge: A Symbiotic Relation." *American Psychologist* 1972, 27:10.

GAY, P. *The Enlightenment: An Interpretation; the Rise of Modern Paganism*. New York: Knopf, 1966.

GAY, P. *The Enlightenment: An Interpretation. Vol. II; the Science of Freedom*. New York: Knopf, 1969.

GOLANN, S. E., WURM, C., AND MAGOON, T. M. "Community Mental Health Content in the Graduate Programs in Departments of Psychology." *Journal of Clinical Psychology*, 1964, *20*, 518–522.

GOLDENBERG, I. I. *Build Me A Mountain. Youth, Poverty, and the Creation of New Settings*. Cambridge: M.I.T. Press, 1971.

GOULDNER, A. W. *The Coming Crisis of Western Sociology*. New York: Basic Books, 1970.

HASSLER, F. R. "Psychiatric Manpower and Community Mental Health: A Survey of Psychiatric Residents." *American Journal of Orthopsychiatry*, 1965, *35*, 695–706.

ISCOE, J., AND SPIELBERGER, C. (Eds.) *Community Psychology: Perspectives in Training and Research*. New York: Appleton-Century-Crofts, 1970.

ISCOE, J., AND SPIELBERGER, C. "The Emerging Field of Community Psychology." In Iscoe and Spielberger, Eds., *Community Psychology: Perspectives in Training and Research*.

JACOBS, J. *The Death and Life of Great American Cities*. New York: Vintage Books, 1961 (paperback).

Joint Commission on Mental Illness and Health. *Action for Mental Health*. New York: Basic Books, 1961.

KAPLAN, S. R. "Teaching of Community Psychiatry in Psychiatric Residency Training Programs." In T. Lidz and M. Edelson, Eds., *Training Tomorrow's Psychiatrist. The Crisis in Curriculum*. New Haven: Yale University Press, 1970.

LEVINE, M. "Some Postulates of Community Psychology Practice." In F. Kaplan and S. B. Sarason, Eds., *The Psycho-Educational Clinic: Papers and Research Studies*, 1969. (Available from S. B. Sarason, 70 Sachem St., New Haven, Conn.).

LEVINE, M., AND LEVINE, A. *Social History of Helping Services*. New York: Appleton-Century-Crofts, 1970.

LIDZ, T., AND EDELSON, M. *Training Tomorrow's Psychiatrist. The Crisis in Curriculum*. New Haven: Yale University Press, 1970.

LYND, R. S. *Knowledge for What? The Place of Social Science in American Culture*. Princeton, N.J.: Princeton University Press, 1939.

LYND, R. S., AND LYND, H. M. *Middletown. A Study in American Culture*. New York: Harcourt, Brace, 1929.

LYND, R. S., AND LYND, H. M. *Middletown in Transition; A Study of Cultural Conflicts*. New York: Harcourt Brace, 1937.

MC LELLAN, R. *The Institutional Phenomenon: A Socio-economic Inquiry*. Unpublished study. (On deposit in Yale University Library.) 1973.

MARRIS, P., AND REIN, M. *Dilemmas of Social Reform*. New York: Atherton Press, 1969.

MARROW, A. J. *The Practical Theorist. The Life and Work of Kurt Lewin*. New York: Basic Books, 1969.

MATARAZZO, J. D. "Some National Developments in the Utilization of Non-traditional Mental Health Manpower." *American Psychologist*, 1971, *26*:4, 363–365.

MAYHEW, K. C., AND EDWARDS, A. C. *The Dewey School*. New York: Atherton Press, 1966.

MEAD, G. H. *The Social Psychology of George Herbert Mead*, edited by A. Strauss. Chicago: University of Chicago Press, 1956 (Phoenix Books.)

MILLER, N. E., AND DOLLARD, J. *Social Learning and Imitation*. New Haven: Yale University Press, 1941.

MILLS, C. W. *The Sociological Imagination*. London: Oxford University Press, 1959.

MOYNIHAN, D. P. *Maximum Feasible Misunderstanding: Community Action in the War on Poverty.* New York: Free Press, 1969.

MUMFORD, L. *The Culture of Cities.* New York: Harcourt Brace Jovanovich, 1966. (Harvest paperback.)

MURCHISON, C. (Ed.) *A Handbook of Social Psychology.* Worcester, Mass.: Clark University Press, 1935.

MURRAY, H. A. (Ed.) *Explorations in Personality.* New York: Oxford University Press, 1938.

NISBET, R. *The Degradation of the Academic Dogma.* New York: Basic Books, 1971.

NISBET, R. *The Quest for Community* (rev. ed.). New York: Oxford University Press, 1970.

PLANT, J. S. *Personality and the Cultural Pattern.* New York: Octagon Books, 1966. (Originally published in 1937 by the Commonwealth Fund.)

Proceedings of the Second Colloquium on Personality Investigation. Baltimore: Johns Hopkins University Press, 1930. (First printed in *American Journal of Psychiatry, 9*, March 1930).

PROSHANSKY, H. M. "For What Are We Training our Graduate Students?" *American Psychologist,* 1972, 27:3, 205–212.

RAUSH, H. L. *The Halfway House Movement. A Search for Sanity.* New York: Appleton-Century-Crofts, 1968.

REPPUCCI, N. D., SAUNDERS, J. T., AND WILKINSON, L. "The Pre-history, Port of Entry, and the Mandate for Change." Paper presented at American Psychological Association, Washington, D.C., 1971.

REPPUCCI, N. D. "The social psychology of institutional change: general principles for intervention." *American Journal of Community Psychology,* 1, 1973.

ROSENHAN, D. L. "On Being Sane in Insane Places." *Science,* 1973, *17a,* 250–258.

ROSZAK, T. *The Making of a Counter Culture.* New York: Doubleday, 1969.

ROTHMAN, D. J. *The Discovery of the Asylum.* Boston: Little, Brown, 1971.

RYAN, W. *Blaming the Victim.* New York: Pantheon, 1971.

SARASON, S. B. *The Creation of Settings and the Future Societies.* San Francisco: Jossey-Bass, 1972.

SARASON, S. B. *The Culture of the School and the Problem of Change.* Boston: Allyn and Bacon, 1971.

SARASON, S. B., GROSSMAN, F. K., AND ZITNAY, G. *The Creation of a Community Setting.* Syracuse: Syracuse University Press, 1972.

SARASON, S. B., LEVINE, M., GOLDENBERG, I. I., CHERLIN, D. L., AND
    BENNETT, E. M. *Psychology in Community Settings: Clinical,
    Educational, Vocational, Social Aspects.* New York: Wiley,
    1966.

SAUNDERS, J. T., REPPUCCI, N. D., AND WILKINSON, L. *Toward the
    Development of a Rehabilitation Program.* Paper presented at
    the American Psychological Association, Washington, D.C.,
    1971.

SCHLESINGER, A. M. "The Historian as Participant." *Daedalus,* Spring
    1971, *100, 339–358.*

SKINNER, B. F. *Walden Two.* New York: Macmillan, 1962 (paper-
    back).

SKINNER, B. F. *Beyond Freedom and Dignity.* New York: Knopf, 1971.

SMITH, M. B., AND HOBBS, N. "The Community and the Community
    Mental Health Center." *American Psychologist,* 1966, *21,* 499–
    509.

SORENSON, J. E., AND PHIPPS, D. W. *Cost-finding and Rate-setting for
    Community Mental Health Centers.* Lansing, Mich.: Associa-
    tion of Mental Health Administrators, 1971.

STRAUSS, A. Introduction to *The Social Psychology of George Herbert
    Mead.* Chicago: University of Chicago Press, 1959. (Phoenix
    paperback.)

SZASZ, T. A. *The Myth of Mental Illness.* New York: Hoeber-Harper,
    1961.

SZASZ, T. S. *Law, Liberty, and Psychiatry: An Inquiry Into the Social
    Uses of Mental Health Practices.* New York: Macmillan, 1963.

SZASZ, T. S. *The Manufacture of Madness.* New York: Harper & Row,
    1970.

VAIL, DAVID, J. *The Attack on Dehumanization.* Posthumous manu-
    script, 1973.

VAIL, DAVID J. *Dehumanization and the Institutional Career.* Spring-
    field, Ill.: Charles C. Thomas, 1966.

VEBLEN, T. *The Higher Learning in America.* New York: Hill & Wang,
    1957 (paperback).

WILKINSON, L., SAUNDERS, J. T., AND REPPUCCI, N. D. *The Development
    of a Behavioral System for an Established Institution: A Pre-
    liminary Statement.* Paper presented at the 5th Annual Meet-
    ing of the Association for the Advancement of Behavioral
    Therapies, Washington, D.C., 1971.

WILKINSON, L., AND REPPUCCI, N. D. "Perceptions of social climate
    among participants in token economy and non-token economy

cottages in a juvenile correctional institution." *American Journal of Community Psychology, 1,* 1973, 36–43.

WILSON, L. "Other Voices, Other Views." *Saturday Review,* January 10, 1970.

WOLFENSBERGER, W. "The Origin and Nature of our Institutional Models." In R. Kugel and W. Wolfensberger, Eds., *Changing Patterns in Residential Services for the Mentally Retarded.* Washington, D.C.: President's Committee on Mental Retardation, 1969.

WOLFENSBERGER, W. "Citizen Advocacy for the Handicapped, Impaired, and Disadvantaged." In W. Wolfensberger and H. Zauha, Eds., *Citizen Advocacy and Protective Services for the Impaired and Handicapped.* Toronto: National Institute on Mental Retardation, 1973.

WOLFENSBERGER, W., AND ZAUHA, H. (Eds.) *Citizen Advocacy and Protective Services for the Impaired and Handicapped.* Toronto: National Institute on Mental Retardation, 1973.

Index